THE ECONOMICS OF CRISIS

For LeRoy J. Taylor

With the respect one student
of history owes another

E T Janeway

ELIOT JANEWAY

The Economics of

Crisis: WAR, POLITICS,

AND THE DOLLAR

WEYBRIGHT AND TALLEY : NEW YORK

Published in the United States by
WEYBRIGHT AND TALLEY, INC.
3 East 54th Street,
New York, New York 10022.

Published simultaneously in Canada by
Clarke, Irwin & Company Limited, Toronto and Vancouver.

Library of Congress Catalog Card No. 68–12133

PRINTED IN THE UNITED STATES OF AMERICA

First Printing, January 1968
Second Printing, February 1968
Third Printing, March 1968
Fourth Printing, April 1968
Fifth Printing, May 1968

PREFACE

SOME TWENTY YEARS ago, Allan Nevins, then the editor of the *Yale Chronicles of America*, asked me to write the history of how America mobilized her economy to win World War II. Under the wise guidance of David Potter, now Professor of American History at Stanford, but then the editor of the *Yale Review* and incumbent of the Coe Chair at Yale, I undertook to review and summarize the material I had gathered during my wartime coverage for *Time, Life* and *Fortune* of the experimental new economics as a by-product of mobilization, and of the equally new, but necessarily more personal, politics of crisis as a by-product of the economics of mobilization.

The Struggle for Survival had been projected in 1947 as a chronicle of the past. When it appeared in 1951, America was once more at war, and the political crisis over Korea and how to get out of it was building toward the climactic importance it took on in the 1952 Presidential campaign. At the practical level, economic mobilization for a new, if limited, war was raising old questions of management and forcing structural changes in the economy. With the economy on a war footing for the second time within a decade, the Administration began to project a plan to build a permanent base for war production into the economy.

The Truman Administration's commitment to a form of permanent mobilization, while realistic, came as a surprise to the public, and it provoked an intellectual counterrevolution. Twenty years earlier, the Soviet establishment had rejected Trotsky's theory of permanent revolution. Now Soviet power had grown and stabilized itself as a primary factor in a divided world. In response, America embarked on an experiment in permanent preparedness.

The confrontation between two systems of power is a familiar one in the history of the world. The current version has been described in ideological terms worthy of wars of religion. It has also been downgraded into a merely temporary clash between economic centers developing from different origins toward similar patterns of management and control. Overwhelming innovations in weaponry have added confusion to the already confusing situation in which the American economy has been charged with the task traditionally undertaken by a military machine, while the Soviet military machine has become an arsenal as if it were geared to a high-powered production apparatus. Nevertheless, the fundamental problems behind these changes remain rooted in the same structural imbalance between the industrial countries, developed and developing at an accelerated pace, and those left out and increasingly left behind— victims of power in its new economic form and puppets of power in its old military form.

The struggle in Vietnam is a classic example of this tragic, schizophrenic split. The politics worked out and the actions undertaken there have led step by step, with irrefutable logic, to an impasse. Foreshadowed in Korea, the dilemma has come to full growth in Vietnam. Reduced to its simplest terms, it asks America to consider the uses of power and the consequences of those uses. It forces this nation, which for nearly two centuries has blundered blithely through history, profiting by crisis and surmounting calamity by instinct, luck and momentum, to begin at last to think for the future. Where Providence once protected America, policy is now needed.

This book attempts to study the economic and financial

effects of past crises. It considers the functioning of the economy and the processes of finance in terms of the operations of politics —and vice versa. It considers war and wars as the solvent in which economics, finance and politics are dissolved, and out of which new forms, responses and institutions grow. America has lived with crisis for a long time, but we are just beginning to become aware of its presence as a continuing factor shadowing our lives and modifying the institutions of the past. We are overdue for a perspective on our economic history which can help to secure our political future; overdue for an economic rationale designed to bring the politics of crisis under control and to finance the prodigious cost it thrusts upon us.

In undertaking what can only be a preliminary and necessarily general study of this enormous, indeed monstrous, problem, I am indebted to many hands and many helpers. My first thanks go to Victor Weybright, whose enthusiasm for the project both hastened and heartened me. Next, I owe gratitude to the three colleagues who comprise my family. To my wife, Elizabeth Janeway, I am indebted for the clarity of judgment which insisted on the obligation of the economist to the political animal who reads to explain whether war still pays—and if it does not, as it no longer does, to explain the how, the why and the when of the change. I am also indebted to her for the application of her distinctive literary gifts to drafts badly in need of them.

To my elder son, Michael C. Janeway, an editor of *The Atlantic Monthly*, I am indebted for the application of his wide historical knowledge and his wise political judgment to the confluence of politics and economics, of history and responsibility. To his younger brother, William Hall Janeway, I am indebted for the expertise which his own professional researches at Cambridge University into the political economy of crisis of 1931–33 brought to the completion of the final manuscript. My three family helpers, separately and together, have forced me to retreat from many irrelevancies and have led me to advance upon many relevancies. When all three reacted with approval to a point, I have felt relevance coming within reach.

My indebtedness extends to the intimate and loyal friends

who compose my professional family. Without the virtuoso dedication of Mrs. Grace Martin, the editor of the Janeway Publishing and Research Corporation, this book could not have been started and would not have been finished. Tireless in her war on ambiguity, tenacious in her resistance to solecism, perfectionist in her mastery of the professional disciplines of editorial production, I am indebted to her for her cheerful acceptance of the challenge to win the battle of this book.

To our research associate, Mrs. Carol Kaechele, I am indebted for the swift and sure command of source material which translated queries, recollections and intuitions into documentation—also for the laborious job of indexing and of preparing the bibliography. The New York Society Library expedited our task as only a great professional library can. I am also indebted to the Boston Athenaeum for the permission to borrow its rare copy of Simon Newcomb's seminal critique of Civil War finance.

Mrs. Margaret Duhrssen, my friend and helper of 30 years, Miss Jacqueline Mullikin, and Miss Margaret Everett, daughter of my lifelong friend, President John Everett of the New School for Social Research, have labored beyond the call of duty at the arduous task of typing and proofreading. My secretary, Mrs. Gwenn Black, and Mr. Salvatore Provenzale, my long-time business associate, have taken over many burdens put on them by my concentration on this book. Finally, I am indebted to Professor David Potter and to Mr. Paul Cohen, now a partner in the investment firm of Stein, Roe & Farnham and, during the Korean War, the troubleshooting economic assistant to the Defense Production Administration, for helpful insights and guidance. Not last, I must thank my friend Mr. E. John Rosenwald for the imaginative act of generosity which turned his house at East Hampton, Long Island, into the retreat where this book was finished.

CONTENTS

1: ANGELL'S VISION

THE ERA of alternating periods of war and peace is over. A new
era of war-in-peace is unfolding instead. Gone with the formal
distinction between emergency and normalcy is the historic
pattern which has described the evolution of the American economy: the cyclical fluctuation from wartime governmental direction of the economy to peacetime laissez-faire. After World War
II was won, and after the fight to win the peace disintegrated
into the Cold War, America found herself caught between two
historic revolutions—one domestic and economic, the other international and political.

In 1946, the memory of wartime governmental management of the economy was still fresh in everyone's mind; and the
economic revolution that started with Keynes's theories and
Roosevelt's experiments had turned Washington's responsibility
for full employment and prosperity from an emergency takeover
into a peacetime commitment. Four years later, in 1950, the
preliminary to Vietnam, fought out in Korea, announced a global
revolution in political relationships. Since then, America has
been drawn into an uncontrollable vortex of chronic military
crisis unreachable by the traditional methods of foreign policy
and uncontainable even by the new weaponry.

In the past, America has relied on war to rev up the engines of prosperity; but now, thanks to the revolution in economic arrangements, she need no longer do so. Because of the revolution in political relationships, however, America is involved in a permanent crisis which she cannot control. She is no longer free to remain disengaged from crises that break out anywhere in the world; when they do, she is drawn into them from the word "go" as directly as their local belligerents. No doubt America is neither qualified nor welcome to serve as the world's policeman, but she seems unlikely to divest herself of her role as its most ubiquitous innocent bystander.

Historically, war has been the direct and immediate cause of America's cycles of economic expansion. But America's latter-day involvement in the world's permanent floating crisis of war-in-peace has been costing her immeasurable opportunities that have been brought within ready reach by the routine techniques of peacetime economic management. Here is the central irony of America's modern position. Here, too, is a bewildering but momentous reversal of the role of war in American economic life: where formerly it spelled prosperity, it now spells trouble.

The roots of America's present crisis run far back in her history and cross many intellectual and national boundaries. At the center of the modern crisis is the relationship of politics and economics. Any political operation has distinctive economic sources and impacts, even though they lie beyond the field of vision of the politician. And any economic hypothesis activates corresponding political operations, though the economic theorists may not be concerned with them. The pragmatics of history fuse politics and economics into political economy. In the American context, wars were the crises—for long, the only ones—which required that the political authorities assume responsibility for economic performance. Once these crises had been surmounted, the dynamic impact of America's wars went far to free her political authorities from having to take responsibility for peacetime economic performance. Only during the Great Depression did the economy become a peacetime government responsibility (although even then the Roosevelt Administration remained metaphorically within the guidelines laid down by history when it justified its intervention in the economy by announcing that it had moved forward on Hoover's promise to make war on the Depression).

The pattern has been consistent. Eight times, from the Declaration of Independence through June 25, 1950, America found herself at war. Always, her wars seemed to relate to problems which had resisted solution by ordinary peacetime political or economic methods. Each time, the sanction of war invited the government to bring new techniques into play and to deal with problems previously held to be beyond the scope of political authority. These techniques won the war at hand and, incidentally, solved the problem at hand as well. The economic aftermath of each war was growth, which freed the government to relinquish its responsibilities for directing the economy—until the next crisis. Thus, any study in the political economy of today's chronic crisis must take careful note of the war crises in America's past which both generated growth and linked American politics to economics.

Does war pay? American idealism has declared that it does not. But American idealism has found itself at odds not only with the Marxist assertion that war pays somebody, if only the "merchants of death," but also with American experience. America's wars seem to have paid not only somebody, but usually almost everybody. Yet perhaps it is time to ask the question again, and to ask it not in moral or idealistic terms, but in terms of economic calculus and political calculation.

If we assume that America's wars have paid in the past, we must then ask whether the economic structure, which these wars have stimulated and impelled America to build, has grown past the stage where it needs such further stimulus or can profit from it—or, indeed, can pay for it. War has a history, like everything else. Its scope, its nature and its effects change as much as its methods do. It is time to interrogate history with an open mind, to ask not only whether modern war pays, but to ask how and why some wars may have paid in the past; to ask what legacies they have left us; and to ask what we can learn from them that can help us to comprehend the crisis of war-in-peace that we face today.

THE EUROPEAN IMPERIALISM which reached its climax in the ferment that preceded World War I expressed itself in compelling terms and won widespread intellectual support. By contrast, the modern American commitment to worldwide engagement on a scale far beyond that even of Great Britain at the height of her Victorian pretensions is, to a striking extent, the result of drift and entrapment. Before the nineteenth century's rationalizers of imperialism came on the scene, it was said of Britain's first empire —the one she largely lost in the American Revolution—that she had won it "in a fit of absence of mind." The phrase admirably characterizes the process by which America woke to find herself committed to hold the frontiers of the world wherever they might be threatened.

But even the rationalized imperialism of the late nineteenth century was not immune from intellectual assault. The criticism directed against it provides a framework within which to gauge the nature and impact of America's neo-imperialist role in the latter part of the twentieth century.

In 1909, a prophetic voice was raised in England. It called for an audit—not of war itself, but of that expansive force which had already brought on so many wars: imperialism. "Does imperialism pay?" asked Norman Angell in his book *The Great Illusion*. It was an arresting question at the time, and it came as a challenge to the establishment and to the ruling orthodoxy.

Norman Angell was a journalist. He had no place in the inbred and then still stratified world of the British intellectual aristocracy. His past was varied. As a young man he had adventured as a farm hand, a cowboy, a prospector and a newspaper reporter in the American West—credentials which scarcely earned him a passport to the Bloomsbury, the Mayfair or the Whitehall of that era. Even his journalistic standing was far from prestigious. He had been a staff writer for that rambunctious press lord, Northcliffe, the ring-leader of "the jingoes," and Northcliffe had entrusted him with the founding and editing of the Paris edition of the *Daily Mail*. The *Mail*, Northcliffe had declared in his original manifesto, would stand for "the power, the supremacy and the greatness of the British Empire." And he added, "Those who launched this journal had one definite aim in view . . . to be the articulate voice of British progress and domination. . . . We know that the advance of the Union Jack means protection for weaker races, justice for the oppressed, liberty for the down-trodden." It was against this super-Hearstian background that Angell filed his dissent.

His argument was straightforward. The British Empire, he declared, although then at the zenith of its power, prestige and prosperity, could no longer afford its colonies. In the world of 1910, colonies had become status symbols for the developed countries, exactly as steel mills, national airlines and American military assistance have become prized status symbols for under-developed countries today. Any country which aspired to a place in the sun was thought to need colonies as show pieces. Accordingly, the various competing empires were hell-bent on accumulating colonies like so much wampum, as if imperialism still opened the same road to riches that it had in the days of Pizarro.

No doubt the imperialist theories that came into vogue after the rise of capitalism were holdovers from the plundering in which the medieval and Renaissance forays into overseas exploration found expression. The primitive beginnings of imperialism were really nothing but adventures in looting—most conspicuously, of precious metals and treasure. It was a precapitalist, imperialist variant of what Marx was later to term "primitive accumulation" in the context of the capital–labor relationship. But this primitive extractive imperialism, personified by the conquistadors and the piratical British merchant adventurers, was entirely different from the subsequent evolution of colonial attitudes and relationships as efforts on the part of developed countries to institutionalize social stability in undeveloped countries— efforts which were uniformly frustrated and frustrating. The purpose of the earlier waves of exploratory imperialism had been to conquer, to pillage and to bring home treasure. But, by the time of Angell's attack on the system, the growth of industry and the expansion of trade had developed a structured relationship of colony to power calculated to bring progress to the colony and prosperity to the power.

Germany's victory in the Franco–Prussian War offered Angell a rich and ripe target for his thesis, and he made the most of it. "However clearly the wastefulness of war and the impossibility of effecting by its means any permanent economic or social advantage for the conqueror may be shown," he wrote, "the fact that Germany was able to exact an indemnity of two hundred millions sterling from France at the close of the war of 1870–71 is taken as conclusive evidence that a nation can 'make money by war.' " But, as Angell went on to explain with historical realism and prophetic clarity, "The decade from 1870–1880 was for France a great recuperative period, although for several other nations in Europe it was one of great depression, notably, after the 'boom' of 1872, for Germany. No less an authority than Bismarck himself testifies to the double fact. We know that Bismarck was astonished and dismayed," Angell continued, "by seeing the regeneration of France after the war taking place more rapidly and more completely than the regeneration of Germany. Indeed, this weighed so heavily upon his mind, that in introducing his Protectionist Bill in 1879 he declared that Germany was 'slowly bleeding to death,' and that if the present process were continued she would find herself ruined."

Angell, of course, soon came under fire from his former associates at the Northcliffe press as a renegade from the imperial cause. His reply to the Northcliffe press's jingoistic attack on his critique of war and the imperialist spoils of war as a paying proposition has an ominously familiar ring: "We are examining," he said of the war of 1870, "what is from the money point of view the most successful war ever recorded in history, and if the general proposition that such a war is financially profitable were sound, and if the results of the war were anything like as brilliant as they are represented, money should be cheaper and more plentiful in Germany than in France, and credit, public and private, should be sounder. Well, it is the exact reverse which is the case. As a net result of the whole thing Germany was, ten years after the war, a good deal worse off, financially, than her vanquished rival, and was at that date trying, as she is trying to-day, to borrow money from her victim [exactly, it is relevant to note, as America did after she had financed the reconstruction of Europe during the 1950's in her role as the protector of Europe]. Within twenty months of the payment of the last indemnity, the bank rate was higher in Berlin than in Paris, and we know that Bismarck's later life was clouded by the spectacle of what he regarded as an absurd miracle: the vanquished recovering more quickly than the victor. We have the testimony of his own speeches to this fact, and to the fact that France weathered the financial storms of 1878–9 a great deal better than did Germany. And to-day, when Germany is compelled to pay nearly 4 per cent. for money, France can secure it for 3. . . . We are not for the moment considering anything but the money view . . . and by any test that you care to apply, France, the vanquished, is better off than Germany, the victor. The French people are as a whole more prosperous, more comfortable, more economically secure, with greater reserve of savings and all the moral and social advantages that go therewith, than are the Germans. . . . There is something wrong with a financial operation that gives these results."

Despite—or perhaps because of—the derision of the jingo press, Angell's book won and held intellectual influence. One reason it did is that Angell warned the newborn German Empire to stay out of the competition to acquire and subsidize colonies as urgently as he warned the established British Empire to break the habit. His warning to Germany was as popular as his warning to Britain was controversial. Angell's exposé of imperialism charged that the game was not worth the candle. His argument applied equally to adventures in empire-building and to the quest for continental domination. Balancing the theoretical rewards of imperialism against both the costs of acquiring colonies by force of arms and the uneconomic practices necessary to impose the dictat of victory, Angell's thesis argued that imperialistic war is a "can't win" proposition: the winners wind up choking on the spoils of war while the losers are reduced to ruins.

Nevertheless, by Angell's time, imperialism had become so fashionable that it had also come to seem profitable. It seemed so profitable that Angell's contemporary, Lenin, was inspired to conjure up one of his conspiracy theories. The supposed profits of imperialism, he speculated, were earmarked as a special dividend for the purpose of corrupting the new labor aristocracy. Lenin, with his dogmatic insistence on simplifying reality down to the level of slogans, saw in imperialism nothing but a compulsive power drive by the upper strata of the capitalist countries. But the truth was more complicated.

The social impetus for imperialism reflected the emergence of two phenomena distinctive to the late nineteenth century— one commercial, the other political. In America as well as in Britain, the popular penny press built its mass circulation by bragging about old imperialist adventures and by boasting of new exploits in the making. At the same time, in both countries, dynamic political types developed a distinctive technique of appealing directly to the masses independently of the established hierarchy of command. The audience which responded to the popular radical imperialism of Theodore Roosevelt in America and Joseph Chamberlain in Britain was the market to which Hearst and Northcliffe sold their papers.

J. A. Hobson, the most distinguished of Britain's pre-Keynesian economic heretics, recognized in his *Imperialism* the idealistic rationale for capitalism's expansive push even as he deplored its practical consequences. Hobson's downgrading of the motivation for and the benefits from imperialism commanded great influence if only because Lenin, in his own *Imperialism,* cribbed from Hobson's critique while ignoring Hobson's judgments. Hobson described what Chamberlain advertised: namely, imperialism as a search for markets to raise the living standard of Britain's workers, who were also Britain's new—and literate— electorate. Hobson himself advocated the redistribution of domestic income as the best solution to the built-in problem of underconsumption. In practical terms, however, mass opinion and the exploitation of mass opinion provided a more compelling rationale for imperialism than any accepted economic theory and all economic practice combined: the alliance of jingo journalism and political demagoguery explained imperialism better than either Lenin's simplistic devil theory or Hobson's more sophisticated hypothesis. Politically, imperialism provided a more familiar and alluring appeal to the masses than the harsh new Communist ideology even while, economically, it provoked Angell's reasoned and farsighted dissent.

Two rival strains of thought, each exerting major historical influence, stem from Angell's argument against imperialism. On the Communist side of the argument, the Lenin–Stalin position seized on Angell's thesis, developing from it the official Kremlin syllogism that capitalism breeds imperialism, imperialism breeds war, and war breeds Communist revolution. Thus, the Communists claim, capitalism's evolution into the stage of imperialism carried with it a passport to self-destruction which, thanks to the historical process, the imperialist powers had no choice but to use. On the capitalist side of the argument, John Maynard Keynes, the most persuasive and creative improvisor of practical alternatives to Communist theory from World War I through World War II, carried Angell's crusade forward in his jeremiad against the Versailles peace treaty and the economic structure pyramided on top of it.

Keynes's *The Economic Consequences of the Peace* enjoyed a *succès de scandale* in 1919. With a skepticism as devastating as Angell's, Keynes discussed the aspects of the Versailles treaty which made it no more than a tollgate set up for collecting the spoils of war, and he predicted its collapse. He showed that if the victors in the war had not entered it with imperialistic intent, they had left it with nothing less. They had made an imperialistic peace, which in time, he predicted, would bring economic catastrophe to victor and vanquished alike. His argument was that reparations required loans to finance them, and that debts contracted to pay reparations were sure to end in repudiation and credit collapse. But collapse would not come until the economic process of the war-spoils system had run its course—until the vanquished had turned the tables on the victors and begun to dominate the postwar economic competition. For Germany's

only source of the earnings needed to pay reparations and war
debts would be via export penetration of her conquerors' markets.

Keynes used coal—in those days still an export staple for
both Germany and England—as a particularly telling illustration
of the dilemma which the Versailles system created for its architects. The Allies counted on receiving reparations (which, indeed, they started to collect) by appropriating coal which Germany had counted on selling. How could a debt-burdened Germany, Keynes asked, deprived of earnings, meet its obligations?
And was not Germany's financial distress certain to set off a
progression of repudiation which would bring down the international debt structure? Contrariwise, he argued, if the Allies expected to collect on war claims and on postwar loans, they
would have to open their doors to German exports, even though
Versailles had committed them to rampant nationalism. Thus,
Keynes's attack on the economics of the reparations structure
also opened to question the economic supportability of traditional drives for national security, based, as they had largely
come to be, on government arms budgets.

Keynes's own language is incisive: "The provisions relating
to coal and iron are more important in respect of their ultimate
consequences on Germany's internal industrial economy than for
the money value immediately involved. The German Empire has
been built more truly on coal and iron than on blood and iron.
The skilled exploitation of the great coalfields of the Ruhr,
Upper Silesia, and the Saar, alone made possible the development of the steel, chemical, and electrical industries which established her as the first industrial nation of continental Europe.
One-third of Germany's population lives in towns of more than
20,000 inhabitants, an industrial concentration which is only
possible on a foundation of coal and iron. In striking, therefore, at her coal supply, the French politicians were not mistaking their target. . . . Germany cannot export coal in the near
future . . . if she is to continue as an industrial nation. . . . If the
distribution of the European coal supplies is to be a scramble in
which France is satisfied first, Italy next, and every one else takes
their chance, the industrial future of Europe is black and the
prospects of revolution very good."

But the Keynes of 1919, impressive though his credentials to the intellectual establishment were, was still a mere, if conspicuous, dissenter. The unbearable inequities and the unworkable strains for which Keynes had predicted an unhappy ending did indeed lead straight from World War I to the Great Depression and thence to World War II; so that Europe learned the hard way the lesson he had tried to teach years before. When finally, in 1931 and 1932, the Versailles system was collapsing into the convulsions that foreshadowed its end, Europe's victors vied with her vanquished in the race to repudiate debt. As the victors defaulted on their war debts to America, America responded by withholding advances of new money to Germany which she, in turn, had been using to service her obligations to the victors. Thus, the victors ended by eliminating the vanquished as sources of collectible tribute.

By September, 1931, the British financial crisis had forced the devaluation of sterling, which effectively closed the shrinking British market to imports and subsidized the dumping of British exports. The French, though still top dog in Europe, were sufficiently hurt and frightened to impose a retaliatory surtax on British goods. But the collapse of sterling brought the remnants of the German economy down with it. A shattering blow struck the vital German coal market. John W. Wheeler-Bennett sums it up in his book, *The Wreck of Reparations*: "British coal was obtainable in Germany at 2s. 6d. a ton cheaper than German coal, with the result that the bunkering trade of the ports of Bremen and Hamburg dwindled away to nothing, German ships preferring to take on British coal at Rotterdam."

The oldest story in politics traces the evolution of yesterday's dissenters into today's prophets and tomorrow's lawgivers —a process which projects Proust out of the pages of fiction and into the annals of intellectual and political history. For Proust, yesterday's courtesans are tomorrow's duchesses; and unrequited love for ladies unattainable in the present comes to fruition with their daughters—thanks to the tricks of time, which asserts itself as an instrument of revolution and as a measure of the evolutionary process. Thus, in the left-of-center American politics of mid-century, the dissenting opinions of Holmes, Brandeis, Cardozo and Stone became the political philosophy underlying first Roosevelt's and then Eisenhower's consensus. Angell's authority grew on a comparable scale: the more the world ignored his recommendations, the more it honored the man.

Just so, the book in which Angell leveled his indictment against the thought patterns and power structures of the world of 1910 was involved in a curious historical coincidence. By one of the most tragic ironies of time lost and unrecapturable, the year 1933, in which Hitler's rise to power transformed the crisis of imperialism from a theory into a condition, was also the year in which the Nobel Peace Prize went to Angell, by that time duly knighted. (Could Proust himself have written it better?) But whereas the first act in the Angell drama was a study in philosophic frustration, and the second act a black comedy, the third act produced a happy ending. Angell's strictures against the unprofitable and insupportable demands of imperialism before World War I gained acceptance as the blueprint for international reorganization after World War II.

In 1910, when the clouds prefiguring World War I were still below the horizon, that most representative of early twentieth-century Americans, William James, entered a plea for "a moral equivalent of war." Midway through the century, Europe, recoiling in horror from her latest ordeal by bloodshed, harnessed American aid to her own practical ingenuity and devised an economic equivalent of war. This is what the postwar "European Miracle" of prosperity without armaments has been.

2 : DE GAULLE'S DISENGAGEMENT

THE EUROPEAN MIRACLE that followed World War II has been bred and fed on imports of American ideas, practices and, not least, cold hard cash. Contrariwise, America's intellectual fashions, from the beginning, have had European origins. The standard approach for selling a new theory or a new technique in America has always been to demonstrate that it has worked on the other side of the Atlantic.

America's cultural propensity to import ideas from Europe has been apparent from the outset of her history, as Carl Becker showed in his classic study on the embryology of *The Declaration of Independence*. Its philosophy, as Becker put it, was "good old English doctrine newly formulated to meet a present emergency." American deference to European experience was still apparent during the depths of the Great Depression, when Marquis Childs introduced a demoralized American opinion to the institutions of the welfare state in his *Sweden: The Middle Way*. The sensation stirred up by this adventure in intellectual exploration soon became, in economists' terms, a "leading indicator" of subsequent improvisation here. Even more recently, Keynes's theory of economic management has found fertile ground in America, although, like the welfare state, it was worked out to meet a specific European problem and with no particular sensitivity to America's habit of inflating Europe's pragmatic expedients into institutionalized principles.

Both Keynes's theory and the theory of the welfare state have been somewhat transformed by their trans-Atlantic crossings. The welfare state, as introduced to America, carried few overtones of an authoritarian ruling class buying off a threatening proletariat. By the time Washington implemented Keynes's policies, the boom of World War II was off to a flying start and his original "stagnation thesis" had lost its relevance. Thus, the dominant theme of "American Exceptionalism" has continued to assert itself, to the frustration of European innovators and their American disciples—as Karl Marx discovered when he attempted to fit the American experiment into his grand historical design; and as Stalin discovered when he coined the phrase in order to discount the phenomenon.

But, turnabout being fair play, Europe also has become an importer since the end of World War II. Her post-1945 economic innovations, which made the European miracle possible, were imported from America, along with the investment capital needed to start postwar reconstruction and then to stage the post-reconstruction miracle. The adoption of mass production methods is only one of the dynamic results of Europe's economic discovery of America. The drive to Americanize living standards is another. Still another is the mechanization of agriculture and the conversion of diets to a protein basis. The entire concept of the Common Market, which American opinion has looked upon as a distinctively European breakthrough, is in fact an attempt to duplicate the structure and scale of the continental American economy, both as a means to prosperity and as a base for political influence.

But modern Europe's most important new borrowing from America is the oldest of native American themes: the interdependence of peace and prosperity, and the dependence of both upon isolationism—that is, upon a studied aloofness from other people's wars. George Washington's *Farewell Address* is the source of the repeated warning not to "entangle our peace and prosperity in the toils of European ambition, rivalship, interest, humour, or caprice." A century and a half later, another General built "Peace and Prosperity" into the platform on which he won the Presidency. Nevertheless, between Washington and Eisenhower, America's wars promoted her prosperity while she reiterated her commitment to peace. Over the same span of time, Europe—identified in American folklore as committed to war—first enjoyed a century of prosperous peace and then nearly destroyed herself, let alone her prosperity, in the two greatest wars in history.

No doubt a generous share of the credit for Europe's conversion to the belief that war does not pay should go to Russia. After World War II, Europe took to heart the Marxist–Leninist prediction that Communism would be the beneficiary of capitalism's wars. Overnight, Europe became convinced that the way to keep capitalism, and prosperity, was to keep the peace.

Europe's pragmatic reaction to the physical threat of Stalinist encroachment was in striking contrast with America's glandular reaction to the more indirect and philosophical confrontation of the Cold War. The original American response in the European arena, formulated by George Kennan and Dean Acheson, was both creative and effective. But the fresh thrust of the Truman Doctrine and the Marshall Plan deteriorated over the years. The Soviet threat gave Europe a compelling incentive to disprove the Marxist–Leninist thesis by turning away from imperialism and renouncing war as an instrument of diplomacy and armament as a short-cut to prosperity. Every country in Europe has joined in the continent's postwar commitment to peace as the best defense of capitalism, and every country has backed up this commitment with a mobilization of state powers to conserve and advance the interests of private wealth. But the effect of Soviet pressure on America has been to make us substitute reflex for reason. Instead of being wary of peripheral military involvements which squeeze the economy more than they serve the national interest, America plunged into a new colonial war in Vietnam. And the dynamics of this war dislocated and disrupted the functioning of American capitalism.

Thus, Europe has come to hold a balance-of-power position

between its passive Soviet enemy and its active American protector. For Europe has been able to play Russia as a market for the future and America as a banker in the present. And her freedom from the military burden which weighs down both America and Russia has allowed her to take economic advantage of her political position to build a new continental structure for her economy modeled along American lines. By commercializing her balance-of-power position, Europe has won respect from Russia and advantage over America. Europe's progressive political drift away from the Western alliance and into a balance-of-power position between East and West has coincided with America's progressive isolation in the Far East. At the same time as Europe was proving that peace held the key to prosperity in the new world of postwar realities, America was being drawn into an unplanned and seemingly endless military stalemate in Asia.

In the years after World War II, Europe demonstrated that she had learned the lesson that war does not pay by echoing the American slogan, "Peace and Prosperity." That peace and prosperity had never been causally linked in American experience as they were in American myth was only part of an ironic reversal. The other part was that Europe's explicit postwar commitment to peace as the road to prosperity was matched by America's tacit acceptance of war, limited and recurrent, as a way of life.

THE WORLD of 1945 was pregnant with revolution. But, by the late 1950's, the miracle of recovery by the vanquished—Germany, Italy and Japan—had become the success story of the century. Learning from the economic catastrophe which followed World War I, America underwrote the recovery of both her enemies and her allies after World War II. In Germany, particularly, the attainment within twenty years of a level of prosperity far beyond that of pre-World-War-II days recalled both France's recovery from defeat after the war of 1870 and her own formidable mobilization of industrial power in the 1930's.

The prophetic logic of Marxism has won many decisive battles with history, but it has also lost its share. From the day

Marx published the *Communist Manifesto,* Germany has been decisive in all Communist calculations. Germany's ripeness for socialism was suggested by the rapid growth of the Social Democratic Party (the world's largest pre-1917 Marxist political force), as well as of her industrial development. This was in contrast to Victorian England, whose economy Marx took as his original subject. Marx assumed a direct correlation between economic maturity and ripeness for revolution. By the Marxist calculus, therefore, Britain's political maturity had lagged disappointingly behind the leadership she attained in her drive to economic maturity. Marx and the Marxists, accordingly, regarded Germany as conforming to their rule of revolutionary development, and England as the great exception to it. But their disappointment with England's refusal to confirm their expectations was easily rationalized. For Marx and the Marxists could see, as readily as Napoleon, Bismarck or Hitler, that, in power terms, Germany was the key to the mastery of Europe.

An American political variant of the instinctive Communist sensitivity to the German factor was expressed by Franklin Roosevelt after his failure to purge the Democratic Party of his better-known critics in the 1938 primaries. He had, however, succeeded in laying low a long-since-forgotten New York Congressman with whom he had been having a vendetta. When FDR was up, his repertory of political vaudeville invariably prompted him to sneer at Harvard; when he was down, he was just as likely to invoke the withering mystique of Harvard snobbishness. On this occasion, he explained to one of his press conferences: "Harvard lost the schedule but won the Yale game." While Communists do not exactly approach takeovers of countries as if they were Ivy League sports classics, they have from the beginning regarded the fight for Germany as "the Yale Game"; and they still do.

The logic of Communism's dialectic is as inexorable as its politics are opportunistic. Lenin's apocalyptic theory of imperialism is based on the proposition that capitalism is so structured that it suffers from chronic malnutrition in its home markets; and, therefore, that it must forage abroad for colonies (which,

Marxist dogma insists, are crown jewels, in the financial as well as in the prestigious sense, and not burdens). Lenin's minor premise declares that imperialism unleashes an armaments race which turns into a race to use armaments: the economics of armaments fire up the politics of war which trigger the dynamics of Communist revolution. In the Marxist syllogism, the conclusion is inescapable that imperialism, which supposedly nurtures capitalism, is actually digging its grave.

By the time Stalin and Hitler confronted each other, their theories about Germany's imperialist needs had developed a convergent thrust. Both agreed that Germany needed colonies to feed on, and that she needed to make war to win them. Their only disagreement was over Hitler's ability to pull off a Napoleonic triumph against all opposition. Hitler was crazy enough to bet that he could. Stalin was too cautious to count on Hitler to repeat Napoleon's blunder of charging into a two-front war. So Stalin was shrewd enough to insure Russia against the danger that Hitler would keep his earlier promise to take his first plunge in the East. The Stalin–Hitler Pact of 1939, which seemed a bewildering sellout at the time to popular-front idealists, was, in fact, based on cold logic, as George Kennan has fully demonstrated.

Since Communism was an ideology before it commanded power, it must commit its arsenal of ideas, as well as its muscle, to tests of strength. To Lenin's generation of Marxists, Germany's failure to fulfill Marx's prophecy that it would lead the industrialized West into the first proletarian revolution was not easy to rationalize. On the contrary, it came as a traumatic shock and lingered as a source of acute intellectual and political embarrassment. No less disturbing to latter-day Soviet thought has been the contrast between the repetition of the Napoleonic miracle which Hitler tried to stage (and which Stalin took seriously enough to appease) and the actual German miracle that dazzled the world between 1945 and 1965.

If the imperialist assumptions which Lenin and Hitler held in common had applied, the truncated industrial federation of West Germany after World War II would have been foredoomed to a recurrence of the bankruptcy and civil disorder which followed World War I. The postwar partition of Potsdam cut the heavily industrialized western portion of Germany off from the eastern sector, thereby depriving West Germany of its traditional source of cheap food and labor, as well as of specialized productive facilities with considerable export earning power and technical sophistication, notably in optics. By the popular economic assumptions of the world whose doom Angell had foretold and Hitler had sealed, the Bonn regime could not have been subjected to more onerous penalties.

Deprived of self-sufficiency as to foodstuffs and raw materials, and barred from recourse to the familiar formula of stabilization through arms spending, West Germany, according to the convergent Communist–Nazi prognosis, was fated to lose population and, in addition, to suffer unemployment. Instead, people, needed to fill vacancies in West Germany's shortage-ridden labor market, became her most significant import from the late 1940's into the 1960's, even in face of the fact that her absorption of mass immigration increased her agricultural and raw materials import requirements.

Germany's achievements after World War II stand as a monument to Angell's thesis and as a living refutation of all the various theories of imperialism—especially of the successive Marxist versions. Altogether, after World War II, the seemingly impractical theory which Angell had formulated before World War I found complete vindication in the marketplace. For not only Germany, but Italy and Japan as well, scored triumphant economic recoveries—thanks to their being disarmed.

Before World War II, Japan's colonial empire had been a parasitic growth on her economy. Colonies spawned more colonies and loaded new burdens on the productive portion of her society. So long as imperialist dreams kept Japan bogged down on the continent of Asia and diverted from the rich markets awaiting her in the Americas and in Europe, she traveled a one-way street toward disaster. But after defeat in World War II freed the Japanese economy from its delusions of imperialist grandeur, Japan promptly developed the most dynamic growth

rate in the world. Her productivity, released from the distractions
of empire-building and from the burden of armaments required
to support it, began to pay national dividends big enough to
finance lower export prices and to attract foreign capital. By the
mid-1950's, Japan's invasion of the American market was fully
launched.

Italy's experience is parallel. Under Mussolini, the high cost
of militarism had bled her dry. Her lack of natural resources had
put her in the "have-not" category along with Japan. Like Japan,
too, her population pressures had seemed to make imperialism
plausible. Nevertheless, the moment defeat and disarmament put
her overpopulated and underfed economy on its own, Italy began
to run Japan a close second in the growth race.

Lest the redemption of the vanquished in World War II be
dismissed as a morality play in modern dress, the post-World-
War-II experience of the victors bears equally eloquent testimony
to the hypothesis that the economics of empire do not pay; that
the military cost of empire-building cannot be financed; and that,
to put the proposition positively, peace does pay. Of course,
much of the success of the vanquished in surpassing their prewar
economic performance is due to American financial aid, which
provided the money to do the job; to American military protection, which at the outset freed Europe to do her job of reconstruction; and to American investment, which gave her the
wherewithal for Americanization. Britain, too, was both financed
and protected by America. But Britain has so far proved incapable of making the psychological transition which defeat forced
upon her continental neighbors. The Common Market, after all,
is a "Losers' Club." And Britain seems unlikely to emulate its
single-minded devotion to economic progress until she admits
that, in all but moral terms, she too lost the war. A significant
step in the right direction was made by Prime Minister Harold
Wilson in July, 1967, when, over strong American protests, he
made clear his intention to reduce substantially Britain's overextended positions east of Suez.

Britain has remained burdened with all too many of the
"fruits of victory" for her own good. As Dean Acheson told the

British in 1962, England has lost an empire without having found a role. Certainly, the scorecard on England's performance in the postwar world has added up to what John Kennedy liked to call "a mixed bag." But she managed to limit her losses, to cover her retrenchment, and to make substantial progress in her transition from the big empire of the past to a key link between the European and Atlantic communities. Indeed, if Prime Minister Harold Wilson has his way, England will play a broker's role between America and Russia which corresponds to the economic balance Europe won with her renunciation of war and armaments as an instrument of policy. For the success of this essay in gradualism, England—and the world—can thank the progress she has made in divesting herself of her former colonies and in relieving herself of her former military responsibilities and their fiscal burdens.

But because Britain has not been entirely free of the shadow of her former imperial position, she has not been able to take anything like full advantage of the new flexibility which her colonial divestment has put within her reach. If she had been able to pursue her own interests alone, and to determine the extent of her continuing military commitment, she would long since have liquidated her joint security ventures with America as unproductive luxuries. The burden has been on Britain to separate present political realities from past political romanticism. Her American umbrella had shielded her from the consequences of her unpreparedness in 1914 and, again, in 1940: the war crisis of 1940 repeated the war crisis of 1914. Both worlds are now gone forever. Nevertheless, England has acquiesced in America's continuing insistence on saddling her economic transition with the costs of overpreparedness.

In any case, Britain's sensible commitment to imperial and military retrenchment after World War II has fallen afoul of her continuing American connection. Because of the dogmatism into which American policy has been frozen, we have taken advantage of Britain's acquiescence to complicate her problem and to block her progress. The fault lies not with Britain's American connection per se but, rather, with failures of American policy, which have frustrated America's purposes and weakened every country dependent on her.

Purely in terms of Britain's immediate national self-interest, the early pressure which De Gaulle put on her to divorce America and ally herself with Europe made practical sense—that is, to the extent that any formulation of Britain's self-interest in a vacuum insulated from her American connection can make sense. But when Britain balked at De Gaulle's ultimatum to renounce the American connection and then denied herself the benefits which Europe had gained, she admitted that her welfare was in the hands of American leadership. But America's leadership has impeded her progress toward the solution of her own accumulated problems. Harold Wilson's move to reactivate Britain's long-term interest in the Common Market late in 1966 and early in 1967 was in good part a warning to America to put less muscle behind her leadership and more wisdom.

From America's point of view, her postwar decision to underwrite Britain as the sick man of Europe—no longer an empire, but not yet a big Switzerland—has in the end proved self-defeating. Britain, in her holdover role as an adjunct to American overseas operations, has been overextended and over-involved both east of the Rhine and east of Suez. In response to American demands, Britain has accepted a slowdown in the rate and scale of her overseas military retrenchment. She has maintained costly overseas commitments as an accommodation to America's decision to hold every position everywhere at the same time.

In return, Washington has pumped money back into Britain, under the label of financial assistance, while draining it out under the label of military cooperation. America's investment in the cost of underwriting the pound (despite the devaluation in its reputation) brought her a return in public relations, but not in the realities of foreign policy. For the subsidized British connection has enabled America to avoid—or at least to delay—acknowledgment of the actual isolation into which she has gradually but steadily drifted. Britain has served as exhibit A for America's claim that she has not been isolated from the West by her unilateral military commitment in Vietnam, even though Britain has refused to join her militarily. Meanwhile, America has risked infecting the dollar with the ailments that afflict the pound. Gresham's law has its counterpart in subsidized markets: just as bad money drives out good, so money that is subsidized casts suspicion on the money that subsidizes it.

Certainly, the American economy, as well as the economy of the world, has been protected from disaster by Washington's successful commitment to stave off the devaluation of the pound. But both the American economy and the economy of the world would have been immeasurably better off if emergency injections of cash subsidies had not been needed to avoid that devaluation. During Britain's successive sterling crises, the Swiss bankers have muttered again and again that "the English must learn that Queen Victoria is dead." The English have known this for some time. Their real problem has reflected America's failure to realize that the day of John Foster Dulles is also over. Britain has been pressed into service to stand sentry duty over the outposts of his far-flung Maginot Lines—NATO, CENTO, SEATO—at uneconomic cost both to her and to America behind her.

American foreign policy has been playing a game of Penelope's Web on a world scale with Britain's economic progress, undoing it as fast as it has been achieved. Certainly the ailments which have beset sterling, even in spite of Britain's program of colonial divestment and of military retrenchment, indicate how great would have been the crisis awaiting her if she had moved any more slowly or if she had refused to move at all. Nonetheless, Britain's progress toward financial flexibility has been impeded by her continuing involvement in politically anachronistic and economically unsupportable commitments left over from her days of power. But Britain's acceptance of Washington's claims has deprived the British government of the freedom of choice which every government needs in order to deal effectively abroad and to meet its responsibilities at home. Worse still, as fast as British realism has moved to retreat from inherited positions recognized as no longer tenable, American romanticism has frozen her in her tracks.

The fact is that, by the time the great post-World-War-II boom was roaring on to its climax at the end of 1965, the modernized sector of the British economy was performing in very much more competitive fashion than widespread public criticism suggested. To be sure, the British economic landscape was still marred by the grazing of sacred cows; and even the most dynamic economies lose productivity because of the sacred cows whose grazing they must subsidize. But no inefficiencies responsible for productivity failures in the private sector of the British economy are more glaring or more costly than the stubborn, wasteful protection accorded by their own governments to American construction, to German agriculture and coal mining, to French manufacturing, or, for that matter, to Japanese industrial employment and even to Swiss banking.

Britain's partial progress has neither stilled the criticism, nor updated the wasteful practices, nor enlivened the inertia which have been responsible for her all-too-obvious domestic economic troubles. Financial and psychological erosion had proceeded so far by July, 1966, that the Wilson government, despite its overriding stake in Britain's prosperity, found itself forced to dramatize Britain's failures by resorting to deflationary shock therapy more drastic than any of Britain's foreign critics had ever presumed to suggest (or than any of them had dared apply in their own countries). In his emergency program to satisfy critics of the pound, Wilson decreed unemployment the specific cure for uncompetitiveness. Because America still refused to recognize that Dulles had died, England found herself forced to pretend that Keynes had never lived.

In direct contrast, the Strauss-dominated and De Gaulle-oriented government in West Germany moved in exactly the opposite direction less than six months later. Provoked by the 1966-7 slump into a form of the self-indulgence which De Gaulle and his fellow devotees of the gold cult had so long criticized Britain for subsidizing, she made money artificially easy and increased government welfare spending, while cutting back on defense. Thus England, Europe's laggard, took the decision to weaken her recovery vis-à-vis Germany, Europe's pacemaker. England found herself reduced to trying to persuade De Gaulle of her conversion to economic orthodoxy, while Germany was free to practice Keynesian heterodoxy and still enjoy the benefits of a backstairs deal with De Gaulle. Moreover, Britain absorbed the cost of a planned slump in 1967 while maintaining her token watch on the Rhine, which was meaningless as a military asset, but all too meaningful as a financial liability. But Germany cut back her defense expenditures as a recovery measure in support of her turn toward Keynesian remedies. Germany's new European priority system worked, and England's old, American-dominated system did not. Economic strength meant power; military show meant weakness.

The decisive difference between England's relative postwar inflexibility (despite her progress toward modernized productivity) and Germany's relative flexibility (despite her stubborn and self-indulgent commitment to her structure of subsidies) is accounted for by the superstructure of unfinanceable costs attributable to Britain's holdover military commitments abroad. These commitments, in turn, have been rooted in Britain's stubborn and understandable loyalty to her American connection. The progressive thrust of America's realistic internationalism during two world wars had saved Britain in 1917 and, again, in 1941. But the economic consequences of America's romantic internationalism since 1945 have weakened Britain. If only the British economy had been freed by Anglo–American policy to move forward as an economy, instead of as a bankrupt and impotent ghost of a dead empire, Britain would have done very much better than in fact she has done. Without the weight of a shadow-empire on her shoulders, Britain would certainly have done well enough to spare America any need to compromise the dollar in order to pay the high cost of maintaining sterling as a reserve currency. That Britain still retained some freedom of action, if she was willing to ignore American attitudinizing, became clear almost a year to the day after Harold Wilson's proclamation of the "great freeze" in July, 1966. The announcement that Britain would leave her bases in Malaysia and Singapore by the mid-1970's offered the hope that London's policy priorities were coming into line with the realities of the post-imperial world.

On the side of the victors, the case of France vindicates

Angell's thesis even more strongly than England's does. In fact, it fortifies Angell's argument as decisively as the prosperity which developed in Japan, Italy and Germany the moment defeat freed them from the financial and economic consequences of military drag. Between World War I and World War II, France was the official beneficiary, not the victim, of the Versailles system of reparations and war debts which sentenced Germany to turmoil; which caught England in a vise between Europe and America; and which, in the end, brought down the entire international structure of finance and credit.

But during France's days of protected and chauvinistic ascendancy at the top of the Versailles pyramid, she quivered with fear and bristled with protective armament. Security was the be-all and the end-all of French policy during the interwar years, and armament was not only her shield and her buckler but her substitute for any serious concern with financial and economic problems. Reparations from Germany, and American dollar advances to Germany to keep the reparations money coming, were her main concern. The collapse of the mark came as no surprise in view of the plight to which the Versailles system sentenced Germany. But the collapse of the franc scarcely attested to the dividends of victory. France, no less than Germany, turned out to be the prisoner and, financially speaking, the victim of the system which her victory had organized.

If France's failure to prosper during the decade of her domination over Europe constituted negative proof of the validity and durability of Angell's thesis, her travail and triumph during the second postwar period sealed the positive case for it all over again. Angell, after all, had made his reputation with his original exposé of France's achievement in converting military defeat into economic victory at Germany's expense during the 1870's. The 1950's found France bound down on two colonial war fronts where once she had held imperial assets. The first was Vietnam, the second was Algeria. Again and again, Europe's experiences anticipate America's; and they certainly did in Vietnam. For one thing, the French awakened long before the Americans to Saigon's vested interest in prolonging a state of war in order to support war profiteering by the Vietnamese uppercrust along the Paris–Saigon axis and with the enemy. Long before America felt the weight of the war burden she took over, France had found herself on the short end of the deal which inflated the business of war into Vietnam's big business.

When France passed the synthetic torch of empire in Vietnam over to America, she laid the basis for the turn from chaos to prosperity that she was to make under De Gaulle. But France found her feet again only after De Gaulle faced the storm over Algeria and disengaged France once and for all from the fight to dominate a colonial cauldron which could not be subdued politically and which, economically, would not have justified any more investment in pacification. The sun rose on *la gloire* the day it set on France's abandoned colonial empire. The financial and nuclear trappings of *la gloire* measure the extent of France's second liberation. For the growth of French living standards has been penalized by the perverse priority given to the accumulation of gold, and French resources have been diverted to produce the strategically meaningless *force de frappe*. Only France's liquidation of her Vietnamese and Algerian commitments has made room for the financing of both egocentric exercises in waste.

During the climactic phase of France's fight to cling to her rotting empire, Paris ceased to be safe for Frenchmen. But when France acted on the discovery that colonialism is a yoke borne by the imperial power, she pressed the magic button for the recovery which almost overnight enabled her to deal from strength with America. France's political position was on the ascendant and America's was on the decline during the decade after France's disengagement from her disastrous colonial wars in Vietnam and Algeria. For this was the period of America's unilateral rush into a protective stance over every country everywhere. When John Foster Dulles took over the direction of foreign policy for Eisenhower, he characterized American strategy as a search to develop "situations of strength." Instead, under Dulles's direction, unilateral American commitments to defend bastions of isolation proliferated to an extent that is incompatible with strength even for so powerful a country as America.

When, at the outset of the 1952 campaign, Eisenhower

guaranteed his victory with the electrifying announcement, "I will go to Korea," little did he, much less the relieved electorate, realize that while he was free not only to go there, but also to return, we were fated to remain—not only in Korea, but in Asia. When, as President-elect, Eisenhower did go to the front, the American military establishment urged him to accept the bloody price of victory and to move north to fight for it. Instead, he opted to seek the best of both worlds—a retreat to normalcy at home and a freezing of emergency on the Cold War front in Korea.

"Peace and Prosperity" was Eisenhower's slogan at home; Berlin and Seoul were his outposts at opposite ends of the world; and the broad base under the permanent defense budget, stabilized during his Administration at $40–50 billion a year, was his supporting fiscal commitment. The postwar boom began by making "peace and prosperity" not just a slogan but a living reality in the countries which had lost the war. At the same time that it enabled our European allies gradually to regain parity with the vanquished, it also gave Britain a belated start along the same road.

But America's unmatched economic power found itself under the yoke of an unfamiliar commitment to the maintenance of a permanent peacetime military sector within the economy. While Europe was striking out on the high road to domestic peace and prosperity which had been pioneered on the American continent, America was preparing to reenact the oldest tragedy in the repertory of European history. Indeed, the contrast goes deeper. For Europe's peace and prosperity flourished behind the American military shield. But the post-1945 American decision to provide that shield led us gradually but inexorably into an unthinking, uncontrollable commitment to provide a shield for every piece of real estate—however far its peace, let alone its prosperity, lay beyond the ability even of America to guarantee. By the time the Vietnamese tragedy ripened once again in the 1960's, the shrewd strategic selectivity America had shown during the early phase of the Cold War degenerated into a frenzied struggle against unforeseen entrapment.

3 : WASHINGTON'S
    : LEGACY

THE NATIVE American suspicion of Europe as a battlefield was born of experience but fed on myth and demagoguery. It began, of course, with idealism: with George Washington's appeal for isolationism in defense of American peace and prosperity and Jefferson's fear of authoritarian contamination. But even as this attitude was hardening in America, Europe was in fact moving into a long era of peace that America was not free or fated to share. Soon after America consolidated its revolution by beating off the British land grab in the War of 1812, Britain consolidated its leadership over the European counterrevolution by beating off Napoleon's power grab at Waterloo. And, while counterrevolutionary Europe settled down to enjoy the security of peace, revolutionary America, having withstood the inevitable test of counterrevolutionary intervention (which is what the War of 1812 was), set out to expand into a continental power by all the means at its command—including war.

The first objective of any political movement with survival potential—whether revolutionary or counterrevolutionary, whether progressive or reactionary—is necessarily power. Once a revolution succeeds, its chances of holding onto power depend on its ability to make a quick transition from the preliminary phase of violence, dominated by agitators, into the phase of consolidation, dominated by administrators with an eye to business and a sense of political survival. Thus, in the American Revolution, responsibility passed from Samuel Adams to Alexander Hamilton; in the French Revolution, from Danton to Napoleon; in the Russian Revolution, from Trotsky to Stalin; in the Nazi revolution, from Ernst Roehm to Hjalmar Schacht; and in the Spanish counterrevolution, which became a civil war, from José Primo de Rivera to Franco. Certainly each of these classic exercises in social transformation shared the same distinctive evolutionary characteristic. But, insofar as generalizations about social movements are valid, as soon as revolution evolves out of the takeover phase of violence into the phase of consolidation, it develops a second characteristic in common with counterrevolution. Just as any violent social movement—whether from below or above—seeks power during its phase of violence, so each commits itself to the politics of peace in the phase of consolidation which follows.

But if a quest for power and protestations of peace are common to both revolution and counterrevolution, there are also differences. With regard to the incentives to make war as an extension of the political game, the differences outweigh the similarities. Successful revolutionaries win an option on developing a stake in the new order, while counterrevolutionaries, by definition, have all along had a stake in the old order. Revolutions tend to become expansionist, and counterrevolutions tend to sit tight. Soviet Russia and Nazi Germany, the two pattern-making revolutionary administrations of the first half of the twentieth century, were expansionist. Franco's Spain, the prime counterrevolutionary regime, was anything but.

By the time revolutionaries taste power, they are often embittered, xenophobic and paranoid. They tend to remain sensitized to their memories of encirclement and intervention long after the danger subsides. Consequently, their antiforeign prejudices come to claim priority over their protestations of peace. Thus, the advertising which victorious revolutionaries give to their dedication to peace again and again turns out to be true only in the special, and tricky, sense of being isolationist. Certainly, nationalism, and isolationism as a function of nationalism, dominated the strategy of the American Revolution during the years when it outgrew its defensive stance against intervention from across the Atlantic and set out on its expansionist course to build a distinctive continental system of its own. The young republic expanded without aggression when it was possible, but with violence when it was necessary. Of crucial interest is the fact that the developing continental system suffered financial strain when the expansion was peaceful, but profited when war took over as the engine of expansion.

A revolution which has reached the phase of consolidation invariably proclaims its determination to dig in and protect the national frontier against counterrevolutionary intervention. But not only does it identify foreign powers as aggressors and accuse them of trespassing: it uses its own professed dedication to peace and internal security as a cover for its own trespassing. A revolutionary regime needs time and wants space. Peace, therefore, comes to mean expansion—in the name of defensive isolation. In fact, so long as *arrivistes* in power avoid risking general war against the establishment, they have everything to gain and nothing to lose by pushing the frontiers of revolution outward into buffer zones—by diplomacy if they can, by force if they must.

The French Revolution, in its radical, or Danton, phase, set out on a crusade to export the institutions of the new regime. As it evolved from Robespierre through Napoleon the Consul to Napoleon the Emperor, its determination to assert its sovereignty, to expand its national orbit of power and to thwart foreign encirclement hardened its commitment to war as the revolutionary way of life. The American Revolution certainly practiced expansionism from the outset, relying interchangeably on political bargaining, notably in the case of the Louisiana Purchase, and on straightforward aggression in the Indian and Mexican Wars. The Russian Revolution in this century followed the same pattern of expansionist nationalism as the American and the French Revolutions before it. For, as the Bolsheviks passed from the first flush of ardor in behalf of permanent revolution to reactivation of the traditional nationalistic stratagems of Czarist

diplomacy, their push to extend their power base and to neutralize possible bases for intervention against the new Socialist
Fatherland took on less of an international and more of a
Russian character. Hitler's expansionism took form after he
killed off his unruly Brownshirt "left wing" in the purge of
June 30, 1934. His first moves toward absorbing Austria followed later that year. The American Revolution, the French
Revolution and the Russian Revolution, each in its turn, justified
expansionism on the grounds of international security against
foreign—that is, counterrevolutionary—intervention. Nazi expansionism was more frankly nationalist and *revanchist*, justifying itself more on the basis of what had been done to Germany
at Versailles than on the basis of any contemporary threat of
intervention.

While revolution looks toward an enemy beyond its frontiers, counterrevolution, by contrast, turns inward. After Waterloo, European counterrevolution found itself demonstrating
devotion to peace, but with a different order of priorities: not
by breathing fire and brimstone against would-be aggressors
from without but, rather, by merchandising the benefits of order
and dramatizing vigilance against recurrences of violence by the
enemy within. Counterrevolutions are motivated by a commitment to peace that is genuine because directed solely toward self-
preservation—although, to be sure, at the price of subordinating
rudimentary civil liberties to armed authoritarianism. But
whether the thrust of counterrevolutionary regimes is reactionary
(as that of the Habsburgs was) or progressive (as the Pax
Britannica was under Disraeli and Gladstone), their interest runs
counter to that of revolutionaries struggling to stabilize themselves in power.

Counterrevolutionary regimes have everything to lose and
nothing to gain from starting wars of their own, much less from
involvement in other people's wars—as so many counterrevolutionary regimes have had to learn the hard way. The classic textbook case is that of Napoleon III's adventures, which fired up
Marx's limitless powers of moral invective, but which were really
more amateurish and self-defeating than, as Marx charged at the

time, "monstrous." The most politically impressive illustration of the overriding priority which a shrewdly led counterrevolution with an instinct for survival gives to peace comes from contemporary Spain. Thirty years ago, the Falange was generally linked with its backers abroad, Fascist Italy and Nazi Germany. And Fascist that movement certainly was. But before too long the world learned that Franco had never been a Falangist revolutionary, but was a nationalist counterrevolutionary. Long before Franco's twilight days, the Falange was downgraded until it meant very little in Spain. Franco, in power, mobilized force solely for domestic purposes. He illustrated the difference between rightist revolution and counterrevolution such as he directed by limiting his expressions of solidarity with his ideological brothers on the right, Hitler and Mussolini, to the most innocuous forms of lip service and the most disciplined commitment to neutrality. Spain, Switzerland and Sweden were the only nations on the continent of Europe which neither declared war nor were overrun during the course of World War II.

THE NEW American Revolutionary establishment practiced expansionism by force as earnestly as it preached isolationism for peace. Nevertheless, the tradition of American Revolutionary oratory fed on its famous criticism of Europe's division into armed camps. Our nineteenth-century orators exploited Europe's war-ridden past, comfortably ignoring our own warlike expansionist movement westward across the continent. For a hundred years, from Waterloo to Sarajevo, American opinion gave Europe no credit for having learned from its own bloody history, nor did Americans generally realize that in the Mexican War, the Civil War and the Spanish–American War they themselves were repeating that history.

Smug though the makers of the American Revolution became in their criticism of Europe, they nevertheless had good reason to be grateful for Europe's occupational commitment to war. For the war Europe happened to be fighting at the time of the American Revolution helped win peace for America by giving the French an incentive to hit the British on their exposed

American flank. This move was a consolation prize for the French and the lesser evil for the British, but it offered the Americans a decisive opportunity to swing the tide of battle in their favor; and they made the most of it.

The success of the American Revolution, as well as of the subsequent expansion of the new American Republic, froze the attitude of each generation of immigrants to America into the isolationist (but by no means pacifist) mold set by the Founding Fathers; and each successive wave of European immigrants put new force behind the American attitude that contact with Europe must be avoided because war was its native industry. The political commitment of our immigrants to American isolationism, and their economic involvement in the benefits of American continental expansionism, turned the descendants of Europe's refugees into even fiercer and more protective nationalists than the original members of the Order of the Cincinnati (whose reactionary prejudice against "hyphenated Americans" of recent foreign origin provoked the organization of Tammany Hall and other immigrant fraternal and political organizations as a defensive counterirritant). From George Washington to Joseph P. Kennedy, American isolationism saw war, not horse-racing, as the traditional sport of Europe's kings. Nineteenth-century European immigrants were more isolationist than the native social elite which had participated in the American Revolution, even though they came here as Europe was settling down to peace and America was becoming habituated to war.

George Washington, mythologized into a symbol of solemn schoolroom virtues, stood at the center of this classic drama of political ambiguity—proclaiming isolation from foreign involvements while, at the same time, mobilizing his countrymen for continental expansion. Washington's mentor was Hamilton who, like so many eminent lawyers (among his clients were patricians named Roosevelt) and practical financiers, was a naïve politician and, certainly, a candid one. His formula for a stable domestic social structure was to create a propertied class tied to the new government. Of course, any working Machiavellian could have warned him that the new apparatus of Federal power designed to further the interests of the "haves" was liable to be taken over by the "have-nots." When it soon was, Hamilton's formula for stability became a secure base for dynamic movement, social as well as geographic.

Nevertheless, the popular interpretation of Washington's *Farewell Address* is mistaken. Future generations confused America's commitment to continental isolationism with passivity in the use of power. As America reacted to European sorties and pretensions from across the Atlantic, it served her national purpose to be isolated and dominant within her continental sphere of interest (although, to be sure, her dominance did not go unchallenged). At the same time, as she expanded into her national frontiers, she was from the outset activist and aggressive, contrary to the image Washington left behind him. The Revolution in America came of age worried about intervention from Europe but flexing its muscles in military exercises on its own continent.

More than coincidence was involved in the interplay of forces between the Revolution in America, which unleashed the dynamics of continental expansionism, and the counterrevolution in Europe which, at least temporarily, demobilized and neutralized the instrumentalities of nationalistic aggression. When Europe settled down to its own version of peace and prosperity under the counterrevolutionary regime which followed the defeat of Napoleon, peaceful consolidation provided a broad and relatively firm base for sober commercial and industrial expansion. America benefited, receiving the capital she needed for industrialization and finding the farm markets she needed to pay for it. Britain's political retreat from the American military front after the War of 1812 was the necessary precondition for her advance on the economic front (with Europe not far behind). The achievement of our Revolution in winning the war against England, and of the War of 1812 in consolidating that victory, opened America to large-scale imports of capital and industrial goods at the very time when Europe's counterrevolution was winning her a new era of peace and enabling her to accumulate surplus capital and capacities—and requirements—for export.

America began to make its own history by repeating that of the old political economy of war on which Europe had depended before it recoiled from the carnage of the Napoleonic wars.

America made war, and it made war pay, just as Europe was making the new post-Napoleonic economics of peace pay. When Napoleon indicted England as "a nation of shopkeepers," Pitt entered a plea of guilty, and won his case. (Europe's great conversion after World War II to the doctrine that peace pays and that war does not was, at least in the case of England, a reconversion.) In fact, the fiscal burden carried over from the Napoleonic wars resulted in England's practicing what Hamilton had preached: the use of a large funded debt to tie the propertied classes to the government and to assure the economy of periodic injections of liquidity from interest on, trading in, and collateralization of government bonds through the banking system. Between 1792 and 1815, while Britain was fighting Napoleon, her expenditures exceeded $7 billion—a prodigious lot of money in those days. By the time of Napoleon's final defeat, Britain's public debt had quadrupled and her tax burden had become enough of a nuisance to the taxpaying electorate to give a century of politicians an irresistible incentive to make their careers by cutting taxes.

England's post-Napoleonic preview of Europe's recommitment after World War II to the political economy of peace lasted until imperialism and imperialist rivalries got out of control at the end of the nineteenth century. Between the Crimean War and the American Civil War, for example, when Disraeli was making his mark as Chancellor of the Exchequer, he set out to out-Gladstone Gladstone by resisting pressure from his own Tory colleagues to spend money on the modernization of the navy. He warned that the House of Commons would not tolerate the creation of new public debt in peacetime to pay for what he branded "bloated armaments."

The twentieth century remembers Disraeli as one of the founders of imperialism, but it has forgotten his stand for economy and against arms spending at the zenith of the Victorian era of peace and prosperity. When, nearly a century later, European Continentalists of Gaullist persuasion began to deal with England from strength during the successive crises of sterling after World War II, they took to sneering at Britain's anachronistic imperialist pretensions. They too had forgotten how well

England had done after she won her bet against Napoleon and before she placed her bet on imperialism. The disastrous subsequent experience of capitalism with imperialism everywhere goes far to vindicate the dissenting opinion of Joseph Schumpeter, entered during World War I, that capitalism depends on peace for its progress, and that imperialism and war represent regressions instead of, as Lenin claimed, the climax of capitalistic development.

Thanks to the special circumstances of America's historical development, American opinion, too, has remained confused about the nature and sources of the capitalist dynamic. America advanced to successively higher stages of capitalism by fighting successively bigger wars, until she became involved in her profitable small war in Korea and her unprofitable small war in Vietnam. Americans still believe in the modern myth that war pays because their experience of their own history has satisfied them again and again that their wars have triggered booms: all their wars have, until Vietnam backfired. While Schumpeter was a virtuoso economist, he was preeminent as the historian of economics—"historical sociology" was his term for the art. His classic essay on *Imperialism and Social Classes* lays down the rule that imperialism represents a more primitive stage of development than capitalism and, therefore, that the two cannot evolve together. But Schumpeter recognized America as the great exception. Capitalism did evolve *pari passu* with imperialism and by recourse to war because, as Schumpeter said, primitive imperialisms respond to "concrete interests" which "need not be economic in character" and, in fact, are more likely to be instinctive.

America's early continental expansionism past her old frontiers combined "concrete" (in Schumpeter's sense of pre-economic and, certainly, pre-capitalist) interests with the most explicit of economic drives propelled by capitalism. The frontier, whose role in American history was memorialized by Frederick Jackson Turner, embodied the forceful dynamics of Schumpeter's concrete interests. But capitalism's own dynamics first reinforced and then replaced more primitive motives for expansion. By the twentieth century, America had run out of continental frontier and faced diminishing returns on her militant expansionism. But the two World Wars and Korea allowed America the best of both worlds: sanctuary from being a battlefield and stimulus from being an arsenal. Only with the Vietnam War did America reach the stage at which the disruption and waste inherent in war outweighed war's short-run contribution to employment and its long-run potential for triggering booms.

By 1966, America's war in Vietnam had begun to reenact Europe's century-old experience of war: at best a distraction, at worst a blight. This war, which called a halt to social progress in America, unleashed the twentieth century upon Southeast Asia. It compressed into a few years of her bloody history the technological revolution which had taken generations to evolve in the West. If not for America's military intervention, this "takeoff" in the technology of communications, construction, transportation and medicine would certainly have taken generations more to reach Southeast Asia. From the day Commodore Perry and Townsend Harris opened the door to Japan in the 1850's, the dream of an Asiatic market big enough and rich enough to absorb the surplus capacities of the West has been a recurring mirage. (Absurd though the idea seems to hindsight, well into the twentieth century practical men of affairs in the West theorized that, if only the robe of each Chinese could be lengthened by one inch, the uneconomic mills of Lancashire and New England would enjoy permanent prosperity.)

But not until America's wars in Korea and Vietnam did the West invade the continent of Asia with modern implements of production on a mass scale. True to historical form, these high-powered resources, mobilized for destruction, have transformed the face of occupied Asia and saturated its wasteland without the slightest regard for human beings or the age-old social structure which had formed their attitudes and reactions. And because of the lavish scale on which America stepped up her commitment of modern military technology to Southeast Asia, the chances of eventual social adaptation there must await the emergence of regimes able to harness American technological installations to their own uses. Precisely because the military power America has injected into the area has been massive to the point of engineering a technological revolution, victory is bound to elude any attempt to govern by purely military means, without a political capability for harnessing the technological potential let loose there. The dictum of the age of infantrymen—"You can do anything with bayonets except sit on them"—is continuing to assert its force in the age of the missile and the laser.

It is ironic that America's military intervention in Southeast Asia should have begun to duplicate Europe's historical pattern of wartime technological progress and simultaneous social lag. For America's own experience of war has been altogether different from that which has frustrated Europe and is now convulsing Asia. Looking backward over the broad perspective of America's modern economic development, our wars have not been blights, marking social setbacks or disintegration. On the contrary, they stand out as the successive takeoff points in the history of our economic growth and social progress; and, conversely, the successive takeoff points in the history of our economic growth and social progress are marked by wars, or, more specifically, by the economic spillover from successful wars.

The Marxists have a special term for the American phenomenon: they identify its characteristics as "American Exceptionalism." The fact is that Marxist theory has been negated and Marxist predictions have been confounded by the stubborn and elusive exceptionalism of the American economic phenomenon. Many complicated and unfamiliar ingredients have contributed to the exceptionalism of the American phenomenon—most obviously, the frontier and the continental scale and scope, first, of economic expansion and, then, of economic operation. The American phenomenon took form as a unique "triple play" which combined large-scale manufacturing operations with a generous support from large-scale reserves of extractive materials and an agricultural economy of limitless productivity (endowed, more than incidentally, with exportable surpluses). Other ingredients of the exceptionalist mix were an internal reservoir of labor, inherited from slavery; external additions to the labor supply provided by the successive waves of immigration; the diffusion of incomes and liquid savings allowed by our political and social systems; and, last but not least, the expansive dynamic renewed by successive wars.

Nothing like this complex of exceptional complications had been taken into account as the raw material for analysis by the Europeans from whom America has taken its economic theories. Smith, Ricardo, Mill, Malthus, Marx, Marshall, Böhm-Bawerk, Schumpeter, Pareto, Rist, Cassell, Hawtrey, Hayek and Keynes were all Europeans; and they formed their theories within a European framework which, in every case, was altogether different from that created by American Exceptionalism and without making significant allowances for it.

American economic thinking has been and still is largely dominated by European theories which have not taken into account the peculiar institution of American Exceptionalism. European economic practice, by contrast, has in recent years been transformed by direct efforts, embodied above all in the Common Market, to duplicate the American economic structure. But American Exceptionalism is no recent development. On the contrary, the wonder is that theorists as intelligent and penetrating as the creators of Europe's living body of economic literature should have remained so largely insulated from the formative data responsible for the American phenomenon.

For America, the contrast with Europe's experience of war as the catalyst of nationhood and state power begins at the beginning. In Europe, war had more often than not partitioned old nations and gerrymandered new aggregates of state power; and, when the resultant dislocation and discontent called for redress, war had satisfied old grievances by manufacturing new ones. In some European countries, nationhood and state power evolved gradually and on different time scales. In others, the two crystallizations coincided as a happening. In still others, the birth of the nation-state came as a grant from above. Only in some did a simultaneous assertion of national solidarity and coequal state power develop as a direct product of war or a direct by-product of other people's wars. But for America, in the beginning was the shot and the sword. The Revolution was a war. The founding of America was a testament to the efficacy of war.

4 : JACKSON'S
HEIRS

BETWEEN THE consolidation of the Revolution in 1812 and the testing of the Union in 1860, American expansion was punctuated and spurred by the Mexican War. The war focused the political conflicts of a generation, both demonstrating and deepening the growing sectional split. Ultimately it fed the new force of industrialism in the North. Like the Korean War more than a century later, its political and economic impact was out of all proportion to its military scale.

The central economic contrast between Europe and America at the outset of the Industrial Revolution was that, as J. Franklin Jameson wrote in *The American Revolution Considered as a Social Movement,* "Land was so cheap and labor so much scarcer than in Europe. . . ." In time of war, both here and there, all belligerents took their turn at running out of money. In Europe, normal operating practice called for alliances which opened up foreign sources of war finance. Accordingly, no European regime of those days found itself forced to inflate on the same scale as the Continental Congress, until France's revolutionary government of 1789, which was ideologically isolated from established European wealth. But America in the 1780's

41

held one strategic ace-in-the-hole which no European monarch could match: when the money paid to Washington's troops became worthless, land was offered instead. In Europe, the same land was again and again drenched in blood. But the only attempt to base a currency upon it, the discredited *assignats* of the French Revolution, failed disastrously. In America, land became effective legal tender before the dollar did.

Not only did the Revolutionary veterans sell the land assigned to them by their states in lieu of pay: the states made large direct sales themselves in order to pay their debts. This practice of paying the troops, of distributing sections of land as bounty for military service and of financing state debt accruals by turning land into de facto legal tender, gave the normal process of war inflation a new twist; and it gave the postwar economy a new lift. (To this very day, the searching of titles for property transfers in what is now Cincinnati goes back to the original records of the sections paid as bounty for Revolutionary War service to the first settlers there.) Instead of flooding the country with worthless paper in the usual way, the monetization of free land established real estate as America's first authentic growth industry, and it endowed the still near-wild West with the new settlers the frontier needed. Monetized land made as rich a contribution to the opening of the West as did cheap money. In Europe, war had decapitalized countries. By contrast, the American Revolution gave a powerful send-off to the process of capital formation by the simple, desperate expedient of discharging debts owed to pauperized troops by bankrupt states through payment in cheap land. It was a classic bootstrap operation.

The Revolution enfranchised America commercially and industrially as well as politically. It ended the colonists' captivity to British mercantilism and enabled them to go into business for themselves. It opened America up to a degree of marketplace freedom which Europe has yet to attain in the era of the Common Market. Economic incentive is the mother of political principle. No argument against making war upon liberty-loving kith and kin weighed more impressively on British opinion than the warning that the war to hold the Crown's colonies would close the American market to British business. To be sure, as Jameson says, "Europeans believed that, when the artificial stimulus produced by the war was withdrawn, many [leading American manufacturers] would not continue to succeed." Of course, this standard illusion has misled European opinion during and after each and every one of our wars. (The most memorable expression of this illusion came from Stalin, who turned the inquisition loose on his Court economist, Varga, when he strayed from dogma. Varga's offense had been to warn that depression in America after World War II was neither inevitable nor, in fact, possible.)

In terms of the symbolism as well as the economics of our emergent nationhood, the War of 1812 is a second milestone. The roots of the war lay deep in the maritime and trading economy dominated by the established commercial interests in our Eastern port cities. At the same time, however, the war's geopolitical thrust, as well as its actual assertion of military strength, staked out our next stretch of frontier in the most primitive possible way: that is, by the battles that took their names, respectively, from Detroit and New Orleans. The hero of the Battle of New Orleans, General Andrew Jackson, was to be the most important figure of the next interwar period, and the political progenitor of the participants in the next war.

History often sets its pattern through the interplay of political economy and political sentiment, and each takes its turn as cause and effect. The original decision of the Constitutional Convention to locate the new Federal Capitol north of Virginia and south of Maryland was, of course, a practical experiment in the political arithmetic of compromise. But it is no exaggeration to say that after the British burned Washington in 1814, the reconstruction of the Capitol was a profound emotional experience in the history of the nation. Washington was no baronial base, and its selection had represented no victory for any factional group. But after the British blunder in burning Washington, sentiments which had been indifferent or cynical toward the purely political decision to locate the Capitol on the "mosquito-infested morass along the Potomac" were transformed during the city's reconstruction. (In March, 1967, an *Atlantic Monthly* "Report from Israel" found a striking contemporary parallel there with America after the War of 1812, when the energies and passions unleashed by war were also dedicated to the construction of a national center. "Whatever the rights and wrongs about the Suez War," *The Atlantic* reported, "it consolidated the security of the State of Israel much as the war of 1812 consolidated the independence of the young United States. It enabled the Israelis to turn the focus of their energies to the internal problems of the state and the building of a national economy.")

Before the Marxists enjoyed the maturing experience of power, they operated under the spell of the slogans of economic determinism. Yet Soviet history is studded with many chapters which commemorate the force of sentiment as a causative historic factor: Stalingrad offers one such example, and the self-subordination of Stalin's political victims in the front-line stand of the suicide troops against the Nazi invasion provides another. In our own history, the reconstruction of Washington as a prime postwar objective of the new Era of Good Feeling presided over by President James Monroe illustrates the contribution which our wars have made to our progress (and, what was so critical at that formative stage in our national development, to our cohesion). But the embryonic American economy was still hopelessly lacking a centralized Federal power base without which it had no hope of making a breakthrough to industrialization. On the one hand, the Jeffersonian party stood firm as a barrier against any extension of function at the Federal level; on the other, the Federalists, although anxious to participate in such an extension, were limited by a class and sectional stance. The political drive and the economic development which were destined to change the course of history awaited an emotional event, and the British staged it for us when they turned the rootless city of Washington into a national center.

The Mexican War provided the next milestone in our imperial development. In an unmistakable reference to this adventure, Schumpeter illustrates what he means by "concrete" (in his special sense of pre-capitalist) expressions of imperialism:

"When a planter aristocracy prevails upon its government," he says, "to seize some foreign base of operations for the slave trade, this too is explained by a real, concrete interest." The America of the Mexican War period was a mixed society, as indeed were all the capitalist societies of Europe at that time. The difference between the American "social mix" and the European—another instance of American Exceptionalism—is that Europe acquired its new layer of capitalism while it was still saddled with anachronistic legacies of feudalism and oligarchy. In America, slavery furnished the backward component of the social mix. But unlike any European feudal hangover, the American slaveocracy was as new and expansive a force as capitalism itself.

The fundamental conflict within America which the Mexican War brought to the surface was economic: expanding Northern capitalism versus expanding Southern slaveocracy. But the form the conflict took was political. The primary pressure for war came from the agricultural slave interest, which was anxious to extend its political reach in a nation on the verge of industrialization. Certainly the new capitalism seemed to have little to gain from war. All the incentives making for the commercial and industrial progress to which our future belonged were set against it. Henry Clay, for example, the spokesman of the new capitalism, opposed the Mexican War on practical grounds as a threat to his tripartite American System (which consisted of high tariffs to encourage industrial expansion; high land prices to keep labor from giving up low wages for cheap land; and internal improvements to recycle the revenues from high tariffs and land prices into accelerated industrial expansion).

Although the period prior to the war's outbreak had been marked by volatility of performance and conflict of purpose, its economic consequences produced, as Bray Hammond says in *Banks and Politics in America—From the Revolution to the Civil War,* "a remarkable series of events" which accelerated economic expansion and solidified financial strength. As Hammond points out, "The Mexican War . . . expanded American territory with a great, fresh sweep and intoxicating ease. Though the affair was carried through with a palpable hardening of the

heart and an idealism not of the traditional sort, the economy
was exhilarated by it and, like a strong man, rejoiced in its
strength. In the last previous war, that with Great Britain in
1812, the federal Treasury had been nearly paralyzed by the
difficulty of obtaining money that the economy either did not
have or would not trust it with. But now, such was the solid
accumulation of means within one generation, the government's
loans were taken at a premium and in specie. And this was before
the acquisition of California and the discovery two years later of
its gold."

Our new war, Hammond wrote, was, by contrast to the
War of 1812, much more profitable from its outset: "That the
economy in 1846 had been able to subscribe a war loan in
specie did not mean that it was itself beyond the need of borrowing. Far from it. The demand of business enterprise for credit
grew, because the successful use of borrowed money impelled
the debtor to ask for more and the creditor to let him have it."
In fiscal terms, the Mexican War was a success. Internal improvements, the subject of prewar political polemics, became an
engine of progress. The South had conceived the Mexican War
as an offset to the westward expansion of the railroads, of business and of free land and free labor. Ironically, the war speeded
up that expansion.

Some Southerners' extremism in defense of the slaveocracy
went so far as to call for the annexation of Mexico, but cooler
heads directed the expansionist thrust of our war aims westward.
Calhoun, for example, agreed with Clay that the North was
stronger than the South, and that the gap between them was
bound to widen. As Margaret Coit says, in her definitive biography of Calhoun, the symbolic spokesman of the slaveocracy
was realistic enough to recognize the South's need for a Fabian
tactic. He regarded Texas as the last objective which the slave
states could hope to achieve. Calhoun was willing to compromise
to get it into the Union; to divide it into four or six slave states;
and thus to bargain out a broadened base for the South within
the Senate. The pattern of modern political history has shown
that Calhoun's judgment was considerably calmer than the ring

of his rhetoric. In fact, by the middle of the twentieth century, the strategy which Calhoun had recommended to the South was working so well that it had come to dominate the American political balance, taking the form of the alliance which the South had formed with Texas at the height of Lyndon Johnson's ascendancy on Capitol Hill. For it was a modern version of Calhoun's pre-Mexican-War strategy which was vindicated during and after the cliff-hanger campaign of 1960: when first Johnson swung enough Southern support behind the Kennedy ticket to elect it; and, subsequently, when Kennedy subordinated his campaign pledges to push civil rights legislation in the interest of retaining his Southern alliance and holding his political base in the Senate without remaining dependent upon Vice President Johnson. The Kennedys' plan to drop Johnson from the ticket in 1964 required them to appease the South. By the same token, Johnson's first phase of greatness in the Presidency followed directly from his success in resolidifying the South's alliance with Texas and then confounding his critics by making good on Kennedy's lapsed civil rights pledges.

At the time, although the primary pressure for U.S. aggression against Mexico had come from the South, the North proved to be the prime beneficiary. The political representatives of the slave power soon discovered that its success had opened the way for the industrial power of the North to execute a flanking movement against it. For, once the new Southwest was annexed, the new industrial power of the North began to build a formidable offset to the entrenched political power of the South. The very fact of the incorporation of the new territories into the Federal system created a prodigious demand for capital dedicated to internal improvement—all the way from the river-and-road tending activities of the Army Engineers to railroad construction.

In the Age of Jackson, the running argument over the right and power of the Federal government to raise and spend money on turnpike construction had flared up into one of our recurrently traumatic conflicts over the economic activities of the Federal government. Van Buren, "the little magician," had won the Governorship of New York, a strategic bastion for the frontier-oriented Jacksonians, but had promptly resigned in order to accept the Secretaryship of State, which he turned into a headquarters for political showmanship calculated to please the home folks. He soon persuaded Jackson to make a stand against Federal spending for public works. In that distant decade, radicalism fought for repayment of the Federal debt and invoked the ethos of self-help, while the moneyed interests stood for spending, taxing and lending as their way of electing. To dramatize the issue against the "money power," Van Buren ferreted out an appropriation bill calling for the expenditure of Federal funds to build a highway across Kentucky, from Maysville to Lexington, the home of Henry Clay, who was the arch-champion of internal improvements and of the industrialization necessary to make them possible and to take advantage of them.

Jackson's veto message is a museum piece. Promising the liquidation of the national debt within four years if spending were restrained, Old Hickory rhapsodized: "How gratifying the effect of presenting to the world the sublime spectacle of a republic, of more than twelve millions of happy people, in the fifty-fourth year of her existence—after having passed through two protracted wars, the one for the acquisition and the other for the maintenance of liberty—free from debt, and with all her immense resources unfettered!"

Jackson invited the country to choose between lower tariffs and higher spending. The votes, stacked as they were on the side of agriculture and, particularly, of Southern agriculture, went for lower tariffs.

Jackson vetoed the Maysville Turnpike Bill; the veto stood; and, according to plan, the backwash of the fight helped sweep Van Buren into the Presidency. But the success of Van Buren's scheme involved him in a two-front war—first against the use of Federal money to provide an outlet for the industrial power, and then against the grant of bank charters to the money power to finance a Federal debt. He lost this second fight when the political backlash of the money panics of 1837 and 1839 cost him reelection. Van Buren, by contrast with "Old Tippecanoe" (political *nom de guerre* of General William Henry Harrison), was just a politician. The times were ripe for a nonpolitical general with clean hands, an open face and no brains.

The Jacksonians of the Middle Border controlled the party balance between the slavery and Free Soil factions. So impressed were they by the political appeal of prosperity and the popular allure of military heroism that they fell into line behind the slaveocracy and sought in the agitation over the proposed annexation of Texas a political attraction as great as Jackson himself had been. The struggle for Texas turned out to be the prelude to the Mexican War. But it also marks a decisive dividing line in American history, for the decision of the Jacksonians to deny Van Buren the chance he sought for a comeback reflects their acknowledgment that the "ins" must bear the political onus of hard times. General Jackson had succeeded in turning his fight for austerity against the money power into winning politics despite the belt-tightening his administration forced, and Van Buren had tried unsuccessfully to play the same game. But if the military heroes whom we again and again put into the White House have managed to avoid war, the purely political leaders who have taken over in their wake have tended to get involved militarily. Polk, the victor in 1844, was "just a politician," too. When he took over, he went to war against Mexico and, as a by-product, demonstrated to the country that he was one Jacksonian who was going to be a Prosperity President.

Van Buren had begun as a political conniver. But when, in 1844, he stood on Free Soil principle and opposed the annexation of Texas, his reward was to be ditched for good and all by the Democrats. His principles led him to the Free Soil candidacy for President in 1848. The coalition of industrialists and farmers he attempted to put together then was destined to take form as the Republican Party in 1854 and would go on to elect Lincoln President in 1860. The dual role Van Buren played in American history is as meaningful for our development as it is ironic politically. The climax of his career established him as the principal political beneficiary of the successful Jacksonian maneuver to stop the Federal financing of internal improvements that would have strengthened the relative positions of the industrial and financial interests of the North. Its anticlimax, half a generation later, turned him into the principal political victim of the power play which enabled the South to start the Mexican War.

Perhaps the Martin Van Burens, the Harry Trumans and the Lyndon Johnsons in our history sense the suspicion with which Americans habitually regard politicians. Therefore, as the Freudians would say, they may overcompensate by getting involved in fights over principle fiercer than professed idealists in public life feel obliged to take on. At any rate, Van Buren inserted himself into two historic fights in America's economic development—the one over Federal financing of internal improvements (which he won), and the other over the annexation of Texas and the Mexican War (which he lost). In each fight, he raised the Jacksonian banner against the march of economic progress as it gathered momentum from Federal spending—especially from Federal spending for war. Only in 1860 would an adhesion to principle like Van Buren's be vindicated politically. Then, Lincoln's stand on principle was backed by a new progressive force in America, the industrialism which was Van Buren's *bête noire*. Industrialism stood to benefit enormously by the war Lincoln's stand would force. The irony was complete.

When the Jacksonians turned away from Van Buren and, therefore, from his commitment to Free Soil expansionism, in favor of Polk, the favorite son of their war hero's native Tennessee, the annexation of Texas became inevitable. Texas taken, war for the Mexican territory west of Texas was next on the agenda. The economic consequences of the massive territorial annexations which followed the war ended the political and constitutional reverberations of the Maysville veto, except for historical discussion. It also transformed the controversy over the spending power of the Federal government from fashionable political theory, pro or con, into inescapable economic practice. For the new frontier of the Southwest, once annexed to the body of the Federal Republic, had to be connected with it. The age of capital investment in arterial expansion had been born, and the Mexican War was its midwife. If the causes of the Mexican War were pre-capitalist, its economic consequences were profound enough to unleash the revolutionary energies of America's emergent capitalism.

Meanwhile, the momentum of economic growth and supporting capital formation in America had been given a powerful push forward by the chain of events set in motion by one of America's more unfortunate exports. The potato disease of the early 1840's, having fed on excessive moisture in America, moved to southern England and then to Ireland. "This was serious enough for England," as Robert Blake says in his life of Disraeli, "but in Ireland, where half the eight million inhabitants lived exclusively on potatoes because they could not afford bread, it was a complete catastrophe. . . . Given the circumstances of the time," Blake writes, "it is doubtful whether anything could have prevented the great majority of the million deaths which ultimately resulted. The root of the trouble was the poverty of the Irish peasants, so great that, even if bread had been made as cheap as it could be by complete removal of import duties on grain, it would still have been far beyond their purchasing power. The only solution was state charity, outdoor relief on a huge scale, and, apart from the ideological difficulties which this raised with any government in those days, the sheer physical task of distribution would probably have been insuperable in a country of bogs and mountains, bad roads and no railways." The victims and survivors of the famine flocked to the ports and headed for America, and the import boom in cheap labor was on. Immigration was to prove such a potent and recurring source of renewal for the American growth rate from the eve of the Mexican War until the eve of World War I that its expansionist influence has been second only to that of our wars. Indeed, the popular reconstruction of our success story has underestimated the expansive economic impact of our wars in assigning the first instead of the second place to our successive waves of mass immigration.

Peel, then Prime Minister, committed England to what was for the time unprecedented emergency aid. Between grants-in-aid, public works and loans, his government put out no less than £700 million to meet the emergency created by the Irish Famine. It was nowhere near enough to cope with the tragedy, but the outlay of some $3½ billion at the classic exchange rate of $4.86 to the pound was eloquent testimony to England's accumulation of capital and, what is not necessarily the same thing, liquid wealth, during the generation of peace and prosperity following Waterloo. Of this endowment to Britain's foreign clients, customers and suppliers, America's share added up to precisely £105,256 8s. 8d.—all for grain—at the classic exchange rate, nearly half a billion dollars of hard cash farm export income. This was a proper Hamiltonian goal for capital accumulation, earned by Jefferson's farm constituency. An enduring by-product of this windfall was Peel's decision to seize on the Irish Famine as his pretext—he had been looking for just such an opportunity! —for repealing the Corn Laws and opening England up to free trade.

Thus, America was endowed not only with a rich cash fund in the present but with an even richer market for the future. Historically, America has prospered when American agriculture has prospered; American agriculture has prospered when America's agricultural exports have enjoyed a premium cash demand overseas; and the American dollar has strengthened when and as the export earnings of American agriculture have strengthened it. America's triumphant idealism might well humble itself before the historical fact that the one major experience of growth in nineteenth-century American economic history which did *not* involve a war encompassed a million deaths. Ireland's catastrophe boosted the American economy as only past and future wars had or would. It flushed half a billion dollars of hard sterling into America's ports and back onto her farms in the very prewar years when America needed this foreign cash windfall as margin on which to pyramid the gamble on war prosperity and postwar expansion which she was about to launch.

If the dollar was the prime financial beneficiary of the Mexican War, its political casualties were equally conspicuous. Van Buren, Clay and Calhoun were not the only political victims of our victory in the Mexican War, although they were by far the best-known ones. By the time the war broke out, the commercial life of the country had outgrown the coastal strip from

Boston to Baltimore. In keeping with the American way of importing theories and labels, the Federalists had grown into Whigs; and the Whigs, anticipating the ways of their Republican progeny, had split wide open over the war.

Clay, like Van Buren on the Democratic side, was a power broker to the backroom born. American folklore teaches us to suspect all who play the political game professionally as moral deficients, practicing or at least potential. Yet notwithstanding this prejudice (or, perhaps, in defiance of it), again and again in our history our professional politicians have turned away from their supposedly single-minded pursuit of the principles of politics and gambled instead on the politics of principle. Some of these gambles, to be sure, have been forced on politicians outmaneuvered in the continuous fight for party control and, consequently, driven to seek refuge in statesmanship or, depending on the point of view, in the nuisance value of opposition. But, by the same token, some such stands have represented free and conscious—indeed, sophisticated—decisions to buck the winds of prejudice and to risk unpopularity in the present for the sake of possible vindication in the future.

Talleyrand's famous dictum that treason is a matter of dates applies as well to ventures in the politics of principle. They are never more risky than when war fever is on the rise, as it was in 1846 when Clay and Van Buren converged in opposition to the Mexican War. Lincoln, then an obscure and unlikely first-term Whig Congressman, followed Clay. In fact, Lincoln followed Clay right into the crossfire between their party's Western Free Soilers and its Southern fellow travelers. In terms of political ethics, the stand of the Clay wing of the Whig Party against the war was aimed to point the country toward the mainstream of social and economic progress. But in terms of political arithmetic (all the way up from the precinct level), Whig statesmen marched their political followers into an ambush, which cost Clay the Presidency, the Whigs their claim on the future, and Lincoln his renomination for a second term in Congress.

In 1966, the Vietnam Doves found protective cover in the precedent of Lincoln's fight against the Mexican War. They had no way of knowing whether they were destined to suffer the same fate for challenging Johnson's War Presidency that Lincoln had for challenging Polk's. (The debacle of the Whigs in the Mexican War did put them on notice that premature political opposition to a War President is at best a very risky business—the more principled, the riskier.) Lincoln had echoed Clay when the Great Compromiser, notwithstanding his commitment to internal improvements and centralized financing for them, put on the mantle worn in our time by Senators Wayne Morse and J. W. Fulbright and interposed the voice of conscience against the march of "Manifest Destiny" (even though the Mexican War promised a prophetic acceleration of internal improvements and financial progress). "I am afraid," Clay charged, in the Latinesque rhetoric of the day, "that we do not now stand well in the opinion of other parts of Christendom. Repudiation has brought upon us much reproach. All the nations, I apprehend, look upon us, in the prosecution of the present war, as being actuated by a spirit of rapacity, and an inordinate desire for territorial aggrandizement."

Lincoln's supporting charge, as spelled out in his correspondence with Herndon, propelled the noninvolvement doctrine of Washington's *Farewell Address* forward into the new era of continental expansion and improvement. Capitalizing on the native American suspicion of war as Europe's, and therefore despotism's, native institution, Lincoln picked up where Washington before him had left off, arguing that "kings had always been involving and impoverishing their people in wars, pretending generally, if not always, that the good of the people was the object. This our convention understood to be the most oppressive of all kingly oppressions, and they resolved to so frame the Constitution that no one man should hold the power of bringing this oppression upon us."

But Lincoln's attack on the integrity of Polk's Mexican War commitment was a time bomb, fated not to explode with full force until the hour came for America to evaluate Johnson's Vietnam War commitment.

5 : LINCOLN'S
     : LUCK

AMERICANS HAVE been brought up to regard wars as emergency interruptions of political normalcy and as peripheral to the main course of our economic development. True, by the time Vietnam had begun to dominate economic as well as political considerations, American opinion had been conditioned to exaggerate the dependence of the American economy on military spending for prosperity and stability. But Vietnam came when America had outgrown any need to rely on war-related spending as a substitute for post-Keynesian national economic management. In the 150 years preceding Vietnam, however, war had substituted for the sort of peacetime intervention by government which Keynes advocated. And, for the U.S. at least, war had been made to pay as a substitute for economic management despite its inherent wastefulness and disruptiveness. Of no war was this more true than the American Civil War.

American history from the Mexican War on records the creeping polarization of attitudes and interests along North–South lines which culminated in the Civil War. As conflict became certain following the 1860 election, the North enjoyed two strategic advantages whose combined impact would prove decisive. American industrialization had been concentrated in the North, which was consequently far better physically equipped for war. This was a known factor, if too little appreciated at the time. But the second critical ingredient in Northern victory remained, in 1860, an unknown quantity. This was the political leadership which Abraham Lincoln would provide.

Lincoln's opportunity to provide such leadership could hardly have been foreseen fifteen years before his election. But his sacrifice of an immediate political future in the Mexican War debate positioned him for the greater debate over the greater issue which would follow in the late 1850's. Moreover, to hindsight, the line Lincoln took in developing his opposition to the Mexican War struck a new note in American history. It was one that would recur as the frontier of the original Union was absorbed into its expanding center, and as the country's influence reached out into areas formerly regarded as peripheral. That same note was destined to echo powerfully during the debate over the Vietnam War.

The liberal *New Republic* carried an article by Herbert Mitgang in February, 1967, on the contemporary relevance of Lincoln's Mexican War position, and found the conservative *Wall Street Journal* making the same point almost simultaneously. Lincoln criticized Polk for exactly the same error of omission for which Taft attacked Truman after 1950, and for which Senator Morse, in particular, attacked Johnson in 1966. In a speech on January 12, 1848, Lincoln charged that the war was "unnecessarily and unconstitutionally commenced," without clearance by Congress, which found itself confronted with a *fait accompli*. In eerie anticipation of the politics of the Vietnam War, Mitgang says that Lincoln found Polk guilty of trying "to twist every silent vote for supplies to support the army into an endorsement of the war itself." Lincoln found, Mitgang says, "a credibility gap in the President's first war message which declared that the soil was ours where hostilities began." This Lincoln called "the sheerest deception."

"Constructed almost in the form of a legal brief," Mitgang explains, "[Lincoln's] speech attempted to drive a wedge between the President and the Congress." Lincoln charged that the President "has swept on and on till, disappointed in his calculation of the ease with which Mexico might be subdued, he now finds himself he knows not where." And Lincoln went on, "As to the mode of terminating the war and securing peace, the President is equally wandering and indefinite. First, it is to be done by a more vigorous prosecution of the war in the vital parts of the enemy's country; and after apparently talking himself tired on this point, the President drops down into a half-despairing tone, and tells us that 'with a people distracted and divided by contending factions, and a government subject to constant changes by successive revolutions, the continued success of our arms may fail to secure a satisfactory peace.' " In concluding, Lincoln remarked that "it is a singular omission in this message that it nowhere intimates when the President expects the war to terminate." Thus did the central political issue of 1847 anticipate that of 1967.

In 1966, when the falling out between Johnson and his former Congressional allies provided a Washington second front to the Vietnam War, the dialogue between LBJ and his former associates degenerated into angry volleys and countervolleys. "After all, I'm President," Johnson snorted from the White House. "Papa knows best," the Congressional chorus lashed back. "Papa knows best" also sums up Lincoln's reply to the argument of his former partner, Herndon, that President Polk had invaded Mexico for a defensive purpose.

"Allow the President to invade a neighboring nation whenever he shall deem it necessary to repel an invasion," Lincoln wrote, "and you allow him to do so whenever he may choose to say he deems it necessary for such purpose, and you allow him to make war at pleasure. Study to see if you can fix any limit to his power in this respect, after having given him so much as you propose. If today he should choose to say he thinks it necessary to invade Canada to prevent the British from invading us, how could you stop him? You may say to him, 'I see no probability of the British invading us'; but he will say to you, 'Be silent: I see it, if you don't.' "

Mitgang goes on to say in his commentary: "The most startling section of Lincoln's speech seemed to give aid and comfort to the enemy. He preached a doctrine of people's revolution: 'Any people anywhere, being inclined and having the power, have the right to rise up, and shake off the existing government, and form a new one that suits them better. This is a most valuable—a most sacred right—a right, which we hope and believe, is to liberate the world.' "

Thus, the ghosts from Mexican War days came to dominate both sides of the fight over our Vietnam intervention. For while the Doves invoked the spirit and echoed the cry of Lincoln, Johnson gave himself up with increasing determination to the new incarnation of himself which his long-time adviser, James Rowe, aptly described as a projection of "the President's Sam Houston or Alamo complex." Although latter-day students of Johnson's Congressional record had come to take his native populism for granted, they were shocked to discover the atavistic drive with which he responded to the echo of the war-whoop in his political heritage. At the height of the Civil War, says Sandburg, Lincoln superseded slavery as the issue. Lincoln became the issue again at the height of the Vietnam War, when, in rebuttal of the Doves, Johnson recalled how unfair Lincoln's critics had been of his determination to do what was right.

The politico who was to grow into the martyred War President of 1865 enjoyed a charmed life—even in defeat. The Democratic politicians made and won their war. And the war fever they stirred up culminated in the traditional American ceremonial in which the opposition party, which had opposed the war, drafted a glamorous political nonentity from the available spillover of war heroes and marched down Pennsylvania Avenue behind him. General Zachary Taylor was the nonpartisan Eisenhower of the moment, and he quickly found a combination Sherman Adams, John Foster Dulles and George Humphrey in New York's aggressive Senator William H. Seward, who harnessed him to the Northern party yoke. Seward did so in such a provocatively factional way, in fact, that Clay had to be called on to save the Union again by negotiating the Compromise of

1850, although by that time his embitterment had already become a byword, and not just for his own time. ("If there were two Henry Clays," he had raged, "one of them would make the other president of the United States. . . . I am the most unfortunate man in the history of parties: always run by my friends when sure to be defeated, and now betrayed for a nomination when I, or any one, would be sure of an election.")

Seward's celebrated invocation of "a higher law" made him a marked man in the South and, therefore, a vulnerable Presidential candidate nationally. But before Seward had committed himself to the far-out prewar position on the antislavery issue, and thereby jeopardized his front-running chance for the Republican nomination in 1860, Lincoln's constituents had done him the favor of exiling him to political limbo during years in which no man conspicuous in public office could avoid a rendezvous with defeat. Lincoln's luck lay in losing before the onset of the crisis over slavery and secession, and on an issue which was to be obscured and deemphasized for fully 120 years. This explains the otherwise mysterious and certainly unique phenomenon of a one–term Congressman who failed to win renomination, who lost his only try at a Senate seat and who, at the time, was not a charismatic figure but "just" another politician—and an unsuccessful one at that—turning up as a "can't lose" Presidential nominee in a war year against a split opposition. Here indeed was a contrast to the jinx that haunted Clay. In all Lincoln lore, no accident is more revealing than the one which Sandburg relates as having occurred in the composing room of the Albany *Evening Journal* on the night Lincoln was nominated. The newspapers had just begun to learn how to transmit sound by tube. When the excited voice called through to report that "Abraham Lincoln is nominated for President on the third ballot," the printer on the receiving end called back, "S-a-y, what damn name was that you said was nominated for President?"

The Chicago Wigwam in which Lincoln won his Presidential nomination was symbolic of his political genius, for the tent he pitched was broad enough to house many wings. In terms of Lincoln's stand on the Mexican War, although his original indictment of Polk had bristled with allusions to "a higher law," he was lucky enough not to coin the actual phrase which Seward dramatized two years later. At the same time, Lincoln's defense of the sovereign right of a people "to rise up, and shake off the existing government, and form a new one that suits them better" lent itself, when directed at the South rather than at Mexico, to an implied indulgence of the slaveocracy's equal right to "counterrevolutionize" itself into secession. At the time, of course, Lincoln's ambiguity on slavery itself—opposing its extension, yet pledged to defend its existence where already established—was of greater immediate impact. Meanwhile, by 1860, Polk and the Mexican War were past and forgotten, and the industrial and commercial progress of the decade after the Mexican War gave the North a practical incentive to avoid secession and civil conflict. Certainly, the humiliation Lincoln suffered after his fiasco in the House chastened him. As Randall emphasizes in his *Lincoln the President*, "He was always careful in later years to add that he had supported supply bills and measures favorable to officers, soldiers, and their families." (This was to be exactly the position the Vietnam Doves took against Johnson.)

The Mexican War was fought in part to protect and extend the political interests of the slaveocracy. Its aftermath blended into the preliminaries to the Civil War. As the Civil War was soon to show, America paid dearly for the Mexican War. But, meanwhile, the Mexican War paid. Indeed, it paid so well that it generated the wherewithal to bear the enormous cost burden of the Civil War. Readers of Horace Greeley's *New York Daily Tribune* were told by its correspondent Karl Marx that the Civil War was "the first grand war of contemporaneous history." No doubt they were more impressed by the publication, which had been a household staple for years, than by its correspondent, who in 1861 was still just another name although he had published the *Communist Manifesto* thirteen years before.

At the outset of the century that began with Waterloo, the trend of world history was made in Europe, and the initiative in its making was held by Europeans. At the end of this hundred-year span, the outbreak of World War I provided grim testimony to the same state of affairs. Halfway through the period, otherwise dominated by unprecedented continuity of peace and economic and social progress, the American Civil War tore apart the original fabric of American life and its aftermath lingered on as an obstruction to the evolution of a modern fabric to replace it. But the American Civil War was primarily an American tragedy. Its impact did not jolt European experience, nor did its repercussions change European opinion. Even in America the influence of the Civil War, while enormous, was fragmentary; American opinion continued to be made and molded in Europe. And Europe, during this century of general peace marred only by local wars of short duration, felt a profound revulsion for war, which was fortified by the spread of prosperity. Memories of the toll of human life taken by the Napoleonic wars were mingled with relief that Europe had put those wars behind her.

Current historical thinking has added a moral imperative on the political side to the traditional view that the Civil War was inevitable for economic reasons. Slavery as an economic institution—in conflict with the emergent, dynamic capitalism of the North—could be overthrown only by the shock therapy of war. But the moral enormity which slavery represented had, by the 1850's, imprinted itself on every aspect of American political life. The fact that slave-holding was strictly limited geographically meant that the polarization which took place would be overwhelmingly along sectional lines. And the fact that the basic split in the American Union was by section, rather than by class, meant that the possibility of civil war was far more real in mid-century America than it was even in a Europe whose industrialization was sharpening class conflict to the point of peril. In the end, America's Civil War was unique in the century from Waterloo to Sarajevo. Only in the Paris Commune of 1871 did class conflict become military conflict, and then the forces of reaction swiftly and brutally triumphed.

In the decade before the Civil War erupted, the combined potential of Northern and Western resources built up to irresistible proportions, hemming in the slaveocracy and foredooming it to military defeat in the impending confrontation. The Mexican

War had precipitated a preliminary confrontation between a relatively modern economic apparatus and a backward industrial society. To this extent, it provided a trial run for the Civil War. But, ironically, in exploiting its political advantage in Washington to press for the small Mexican War, the South opened the way for the North to gain the economic advantage which was to prove decisive in the big war for sectional domination.

If the South wanted room to extend its political base in the 1840's and 1850's, the North was making room for its own expanding industrial base. And the dynamics—geographic as well as economic—of industrial growth were far stronger than those of the cotton culture. In the years before 1860, the South had fallen farther and farther behind. One key indicator of industrial development and military strength is railway mileage. Before 1820, both North and South had begun to develop what would prove the number-one factor in continental war. By 1860, the North had built some 22,000 miles of railroad track as compared with the mere 9,000 miles of the South (much of which was second-rate in quality and all of which was handicapped as a unified system by a multitude of different gauges). This factor enabled the North to nullify the South's "internal lines" and wage an active two-front war in the East and West. Railroads tied the Midwest to the East economically and shifted the lines of economic interest and political alliance from North–South down the Mississippi Valley to East–West. The states of the old Northwest, once hotbeds of anti-Abolitionist agitation, stayed with the Union in 1860 with barely a murmur. And it was the West whose farm boys and farm produce, joined with the weapons of war produced in the East, provided the margin of victory.

The strategic question at issue in the Civil War was whether the North would win by not losing. The South was incapable of conquering the North; it could win only by being allowed to do so by the North. If political leadership could hold together the extraordinary coalition—it was scarcely a consensus—that dominated the politics of the North, then Northern economic supremacy must sooner or later assert itself. Lincoln's Presidency offers perhaps the finest example of virtuoso political creativity in American history. Operating under the cover of the first Lincoln myth—that he was merely a vulgar, uncultured "baboon"—Lincoln played interests and issues off against each other with one aim only: the preservation of the Union. His manipulations and maneuverings were sufficient. The negative prescription for victory—that the North not admit defeat—was fulfilled. And this allowed the fulfillment of the positive prescription: that the North's economic supremacy be brought to bear on the primitive South.

In fact, in a remarkable preview of the history of economic mobilization to come during the twentieth century, the North won the Civil War in exactly the same way as industrial America has won all her subsequent wars—by the sheer momentum of the war production and the war-supporting production generated behind the lines in the economy. Hindenburg's rueful comment in his memoirs about America's secret but decisive weapon in World War I—"Her brilliant, if pitiless, war industry," he wrote, "had entered the service of patriotism and had not failed it"—applied as well to the way the North won the Civil War.

On a larger scale, our victory in World War II was achieved in the same way. As I summarized America's strategy of victory in World War II in *The Struggle for Survival*: "It was because we began to win the war as a war of production that we did not have to fight it as a war of fully coordinated mobilization. Therefore, we did not. . . . The militaristic totalitarianism of Roosevelt's period seemed at the time to be an omnipotent masterpiece of organization. To organize its defeat, he put his faith in the unorganized momentum of American democracy." The magnitude of Roosevelt's gamble on economic momentum to power America's military push may have obscured its family resemblance to the pattern-making strategy Lincoln adopted eighty years earlier. In fact, Eisenhower laid siege to Europe in the same exasperatingly slow, deadly methodical way in which Grant dug in to take Richmond—and on the same Gargantuan scale.

$$6 : \begin{array}{l} \text{CARNEGIE'S} \\ \text{CAVALRY} \end{array}$$

ECONOMISTS THEORIZE about growth, statisticians measure it and politicians brag about it. But whether or not the leadership principle applies to history in general, it certainly applies to the making of economic history: the pace of economic growth is set by the growth industries which lead the economy onward. The economy depends on its emergent growth industries to ignite the spark which generates its forward momentum.

What the rudimentary functions of shipping, shoemaking, cotton spinning and iron founding were to our revolutionary period; what steel, electrification, and the automobile and the truck were to the age of transition marked by World War I; what aviation would be to World War II, and aluminum and electronics to the Korean and Vietnam Wars; what land speculation and real estate development were to each period of wartime expansion in its day; railroading was to the Civil War.

The number-one item of rail traffic was agricultural produce. It was no coincidence that a war-generated railway boom should have coincided with and fed on a war-generated farm boom. In fact, during each of our historic cycles of wartime economic expansion, agriculture prospered in gear with industry. Growth has become the watchword of contemporary economic analysis; and, in the age of Keynes and affluence, its lure has obliterated the traditional concern about where the money was to come from to finance it and to keep it financed. Historically, our periods of industrial growth have generated demands for capital faster than our ability to create or import it. But our periods of farm growth have always generated hard cash earnings from abroad.

Our inherited perspective on history has conditioned our ways of evaluating our successive economic cycles. We have underestimated the economic consequences of our wars. Until Pearl Harbor, we looked back on the Civil War as the definitive military emergency in our history—as if it had not also been the definitive economic experience of the era before we came of age internationally. We also looked forward to each new fight over money as the normal source of political conflict; and we expected a farm slump to sound the call to battle against the money power. Because the economic role of war has been subordinated instead of acknowledged as the driving force which has again and again paced our historical cycles of expansion, we have been conditioned to associate the troubles of our farm economy with domestic credit strains and resultant political disturbances. That is to say, we have been sensitized to the impact of our farm slumps on our domestic fights about money, and we have been desensitized to the impact of our wars upon our farm booms and to the reciprocal impact of our farm booms upon our wars and their successful financing.

The fact is that each and every one of our war booms brought a farm boom with it. These successive wartime farm booms have literally been worth their weight in gold because they have paid for themselves in gold, while contributing significantly to the financing of each war and of each round of wartime industrial expansion. Conversely, our historic sieges of farm contraction have fallen within peacetime fluctuations in the industrial and financial cycles. The double base on which the American economy stands, combining world leadership in farm production with world leadership in industrial production, has from the beginning given it a distinctive advantage in world competition.

Even when the Civil War divided America and put her on the defensive at a time when she was still dependent on capital imports, she found herself in a commanding international economic position. In fact, the construction of this unique industrial–agricultural base explains America's ability to offset the obvious diplomatic disadvantage to which the Civil War put her and, at the same time, to finance her prodigious capital import requirements.

The Crimean War—England's one military exercise between the era of counterrevolution in which the Napoleonic wars culminated and the era of imperialism which culminated in World War I—gave American agriculture its second expansive opportunity. (The Irish Famine had been the first.) Russia had been England's principal source of grain imports, and the combined impact of Britain's industrialization and free-trade policies was steadily increasing her grain import requirements. Simultaneously, Britain was demonstrating her financial ability to outgrow the primitive nationalistic practices of mercantilism and to improve her living standards and broaden her prosperity by increasing imports. In going to war against Russia, England and France had violated, or at least gambled with, the first principle of military prudence laid down in Caesar's classic manual: the emphasis on *frumenta*, the grain supply, as the necessary support for any military undertaking. The Industrial Revolution had magnified the gamble by multiplying the requirements of the Anglo–French alliance for overseas grain imports. England needed America as a reliable alternative source of wheat in order to fortify herself against the Russian Bear in the coming years of imperialist expansion.

But if the leaders of mid-Victorian England ignored Caesar's injunction to give wartime priority to the food supply, they passed muster under Cicero's rule that the first quality of successful generals is luck. In fact, their calculations in this period of mounting British power were every bit as feckless and reckless as the calculations of their successors a century later when they presided over the disintegration of British power. Not only did Britain go to war against its eastern granary in 1854; it then came close to compounding the blunder within a decade by lining up against its alternative western source of food supply in the northern United States. It was an open secret that the outbreak of the Civil War found the British government not only betting on the South but tempted and, indeed, poised to line up with it—as if the grand strategy of neutralizing and flanking Russia had not made Britain dependent on American agriculture.

If ever the writers of history have interposed their frustrations between their art and its subject matter to confuse the students of history, Henry Adams did. His masterpiece of perversity, *The Education of Henry Adams*, effected a mystic confluence between the Adams legend and Civil War folklore when he showed his father at work in Lincoln's London embassy striving and scheming to insure continued British neutrality, benevolent or otherwise. However engaging the veil of Adams's prose has been over the years, very little attention to economic realities is needed, as the lawyers say, to pierce it. The British were not long in awakening to a realization of the jeopardy in which they were placing themselves by their political alignment with the South. When they did realize that their bread literally depended on the grain being harvested in the North, they pulled back so abruptly into a neutral stance that no diplomatic blunders on the part of Lincoln's ambassador could have driven them into support of the South.

If the failure of the British to put first things first was surprising, the shallow overconfidence of the leaders of the Confederacy was even more so. At least the British discovered where their economic interest lay and retacked toward neutrality. But the leaders of the Confederacy were so disoriented from economic reality that they counted on cotton to win intervention on their side from Europe. So deep-rooted were the agrarian preconceptions of the Southern strategists that they were incapable of recognizing the division of labor which obliges fundamentally industrial societies—which, by definition, the Confederacy's European cotton customers were—to give an overriding priority to their food import requirements.

Charles and Mary Beard, in their *Rise of American Civilization*, tell how the fundamentals of food supply took priority over commercial calculations in the minds of European politicians. "During the Civil War," they say, "the increase in the wheat export to England furnished an offset to the stoppage of southern cotton, helping to turn the balance in the mind of English statesmen against any open action in favor of the Confederacy. In economic terms, the choice lay between cotton and bread and bread won. The total export of wheat in 1860 was 17 million bushels; it rose three years later to 58 million . . ."—supporting the Beards' judgment that "the flow of American agricultural produce to the Old World in the latter part of the nineteenth century made a revolution in its economy comparable to that produced by the flow of gold and silver in the age that succeeded the discoveries of Columbus." The price of grains, the income from producing and marketing them, and the export earnings of the economy spiraled upward together.

The first Presidential appointee to head the new wartime Bureau of Agriculture happened to bear the name of the discoverer of the law of gravity; and, appropriately, the reports of Commissioner Isaac Newton measured the workings of the new wartime law of economic gravity. During the Civil War, 1861 through 1865, America's hard cash earnings from wheat alone brought in a tidy $178 million for some 138 million bushels. The open market value of the "greenback" dollar on the world currency exchange reflected America's net gold intake during the Civil War and the years which followed until specie payments were resumed in 1879. The value of the wartime greenbacks was bolstered as a direct result of the surge in farm export income. The normal reaction to wartime inflation in the cost of living is to deplore it as a hidden capital levy. But, paradoxical though it may seem, and unprecedented though it was at the time, the wartime inflation of food crop prices between 1861 and 1865 fortified the economy and, certainly, demonstrated that a rising spiral of prices can on occasion strengthen the currency while also furthering the process of capital accumulation.

The ability of America to sustain the loss and cost of a major war on its own soil and, at the same time, to finance it by filling Europe's peacetime food deficiencies marked a new epoch in economic history. It also foretold the decisive westward shift of future political power and military potential. Up to that point in economic history, the outbreak of war had automatically turned every belligerent into a forager for food. The American Civil War turned the normal historical rule upside down: the belligerent fed the neutral.

No originality of research is needed to ferret out the conclusion that the Civil War, like its predecessors, strengthened our economy and sped it on its forward progress—not least because of the sensational push it gave to Northern agriculture. Many writers of perspicacity and sophistication have seen the point and made it in terms of specific chapters of our history, if not for our history as a whole. Burton J. Hendrick wrote as early as 1921 that "The Civil War in America did more than free the negro slave: it freed the white man as well." In his *The Age of Big Business,* he pointed out that "In the Civil War agriculture, for the first time in history, ceased to be exclusively a manual art. ... Many as have been America's contributions to civilization, hardly any have exerted greater influence in promoting human welfare than her gift of agricultural machinery."

The evidence invited historians and publicists to draw the conclusion that the American Civil War, like the wars fought before it and the wars fought after it, paid; and, in paying, served as an engine of expansion and as a catalyst of progress. Hendrick followed the evidence to its conclusion. "Europe gazed in astonishment," he said, "at a new spectacle in history; that of a nation fighting the greatest war which had been known up to that time, employing the greater part of her young and vigorous men in the armies, and yet growing infinitely richer in the process." But while Hendrick has been widely read, and while the story as he told it was there for all to see, what he wrote was taken simply as one man's literate observation of a familiar situation. It was not taken to heart, as on its merits it was entitled to be, for the lesson it taught and the moral it pointed regarding our history as a whole.

No doubt the reason is that, at the time Hendrick delivered himself of this essay in realism, American opinion was looking the other way. In 1921, the country had had its fill of war; it was in the throes of a sharp postwar depression; the crusade for the League of Nations had gone up in smoke; and America wanted to be left alone in order to return to "Normalcy"—Harding's immortal malapropism caught the spirit of war weariness. Hendrick's view of the Civil War had touched on the dominant theme of our history, but at a time when readers were not ready to credit or accept it. Only after Vietnam began to teach us that war had ceased to pay, and after Europe had abandoned it as an instrument of policy, did the winds of crisis blow the mist away and free our vision to recognize the reality that has always been there.

Idealistic isolationism in the Washington tradition has obscured the brutal fundamental *realpolitik* that, once war becomes inescapable for a country, the lesser evil among possible wars is a foreign war—not least because a foreign war can erupt into a civil war behind the enemy's lines. Domestic wars have always been more wasteful and destructive than foreign wars, even before Lenin noted the tendency for wars to turn into civil war and civil wars to turn into Communist revolutions. Washington's *Farewell Address*, with its hard backward look at the age of continental jeopardy which America would soon outgrow, can be taken as the political equivalent of the wills of legendary Massachusetts millionaires who, in the age of rugged individualism, drew them up with the intent of dominating the lives of their grandchildren from the grave. In fact, it took the traumatic bloodbath of the American Civil War to enter a pragmatic dissent to Washington's isolationist premise. Nevertheless, the doctrine based on that premise continued to dominate American thinking about the outside world.

Costly and horrible though the American Civil War was, it also brought unprecedented benefits to the economy. Not that this was its purpose. But the economic consequences of the American Civil War provide the sharpest possible contrast to the toll taken by Europe's wars. Both before our Civil War and after it, Europe's wars were merely costly and horrible. The Civil War not only stimulated and supported a record postwar boom; it also propelled our railroads and our farms into their historic role of joint economic leadership. What is more, our Civil War acted as an instrument of social emancipation and progress, supported by a simultaneous self-financing prosperity. In Europe, by contrast, the Napoleonic wars did not start until after the French Revolution had completed its emancipating mission and turned expansionist. Europe's various localized conflicts were merely exercises in the nationalistic tug of war and mobilized no progressive social forces behind the lines.

Within the American Civil War economy, agriculture was the prime earning asset and railroading the major claimant for the resulting availability of capital. The leadership of railroading in expanding the industrial economy, and in building a firm base under the structure of finance and credit, measured not only the ability of agriculture to prosper but of the country to fight what Marx had been quick to identify as a modern war. As John W. Barriger writes in his *Railroads and the Civil War*, "The war came at that period when railroads were first beginning to have a substantial effect on the American economy. Railroads not only affected the outcome of the war, but the war also affected the development of the railroads and molded the men who shaped the railroad system we know today."

Lincoln was subjected to a great deal of criticism as War President for the lackluster performance of his generals and for his apparent lack of incisiveness in overcoming the advantage which the South seized when she took the professional leadership and most of the apparatus of the Army into secession with her. But Lincoln—old frontier railroad lawyer that he was—could not have been more incisive in grasping the advantage which the North's superior railroad system gave to it or in exploiting the decisive military asset which this constituted. Like all shrewd politicians, Lincoln was willing to accept criticism as a lesser evil to catastrophe where he did not command the tactical advantage, as he most certainly did not in the field against Lee—at least not until the beginning of the end. But where he did, as in the mobilization of the railroad system of the North against the horsetrails of the South, he knew that he had the whip hand. As a shrewd politician always does, he played it hard.

The evidence Barriger gathered leaves no doubt that Lin-

coln knew that in the railroads, and just as much in the railroad
men of the North, he had a formidable, perhaps decisive, military asset. He mobilized it promptly and effectively. In August,
1861, within a month after the first battle of Bull Run, he took
the unusual step of appointing Thomas A. Scott, vice-president
of the Pennsylvania Railroad (by then well on its way to becoming the largest corporation in the North), as Assistant Secretary
of War. Scott was charged with military control over railroad
lines and telegraph communications, in both the area of behind-
the-lines support for military operations and in the zone of conflict,
and he immediately picked a superintendent on the Pennsylvania
named Andrew Carnegie to be his assistant. It was a seemingly
minor delegation of responsibility, but one fated to exert major
influence on the conduct of the war as well as on the history of
the entire postwar generation.

The appointment of the Scott–Carnegie team inspired both
confidence and controversy. In the first place, the Pennsylvania
was itself a ward, or at least a beneficiary, of the public bounty.
Its main line had been built by the state of Pennsylvania and
operated at a loss until the road's engineering staff bought it, as
if led by a prophetic vision of the wartime premium soon to be
enjoyed by its facilities. Scott and Carnegie found themselves
serving under the benign patronage of Secretary of War Simon
P. Cameron, Chase's highly political representative in the war
setup. In his *Lincoln's War Cabinet,* Burton J. Hendrick notes
the taint of corruption attaching to Cameron's activities and
awards. Though Lincoln was obligated for his nomination to
Cameron, he eventually had to exile him to the American embassy in Russia which, at that point in history, before Seward
bought Alaska, was East Nowhere. As Hendrick says, the favors
which Cameron consistently bestowed upon Pennsylvania Republicans "occasioned widespread criticism. . . . No one questioned the abilities of Thomas A. Scott . . . but the fact that he
continued his post as vice-president of the Pennsylvania Railroad—without salary, it is true—a corporation with which he
was constantly making contracts for transporting troops and
supplies, caused much criticism. The charges exacted for moving
soldiers—two cents a mile in boxcars—seemed excessive."

The conflict of interest was glaring. The Secretary of War had been caught time and again dipping into the pork barrel. His Assistant Secretary was the railroad magnate who kept it full for him. The Secretary was the shipper, and he was subservient to his Assistant Secretary who ran the carrier serving him. Morality was outraged. War costs were inflated. Nevertheless, the arrangement fit into Lincoln's scheme of things: he needed to enlist the wartime participation and know-how of the business establishment of the day, and these were the rules that then prevailed. More than incidentally, the arrangement sped the genetic processes of capital formation; and it opened the opportunities of industrial empire to the young operating member of the Scott–Carnegie team.

During the Civil War, finance was the critical link between the military apparatus and the economic resources under mobilization. The Lincoln Administration, nullifying the Jacksonian taboo against a chosen instrument to finance the Treasury, designated Jay Cooke & Co. as the fiscal agent of the United States. The selection of Jay Cooke & Co., the institutional heir of the Biddle tradition of Philadelphia private bankers who had been anathema to the Jeffersonians and the Jacksonians, reinforced the Administration's dependence upon the Pennsylvania Railroad in dealing not only with the military side of the mobilization problem but with the financial side as well. It also set an important precedent. During World War I, when procurement and pricing were sensitive problems on the civilian side, Wilson, prodded by his grey eminence Mr. Justice Brandeis, made a bold effort to balance the grant of war economic powers. He recommended Bernard Baruch for the Chairmanship of the War Industries Board precisely because he was a speculator who could be counted on to know the score. During World War II, production was the problem, and Roosevelt, after a brief and futile attempt to achieve a public relations balance between management and labor on the civilian side of the problem, faced up to the realities and reverted to the Civil War pattern, relying on industrialists and financiers to run war production and to coordinate it with the mobilization base in the economy.

At the outset of the Civil War, Lincoln moved decisively—

as neither Wilson nor Roosevelt felt obliged to do—to subordinate the military men to the businessmen within the military hierarchy. Rediscovering Talleyrand's maxim that "war is much too serious a thing to be left to military men," the Lincoln Administration implemented that philosophy in the famous order of the Secretary of War directing that "no Officer, whatever may be his rank, will interfere with the running of cars, as directed by the superintendent of the road, under penalty of being dismissed." The second disaster at Bull Run had shown Lincoln that defeat was too close to the Capitol for the economic side of war to be left to the generals.

As Barriger points out, "The northern states were well supplied with the metal working furnaces, mills and factories to produce the equipment and supplies required for railroad construction, maintenance and operation. The south," he adds, "was virtually devoid of them. . . ." The Confederates' only chance of limiting the long odds against them in the distribution of potential military power behind the lines was to fight as the Chinese and Vietnamese Communist guerrillas learned to do nearly a century later—by arming themselves with equipment captured by raiding and encircling the invader. But the Communist guerrillas had less trouble foraging for shot and shell than the frayed Confederate horse brigades had in making off with locomotives and cars which, once captured, turned out as often as not to be unusable on the narrow-gauge tracks of many Southern lines and spurs. Moreover, secession found the South with nothing but wood-burning locomotives, and she was hopelessly lacking in the industrial plant to convert to the new and more efficient coal-burners, as the North had managed to do.

During the years of Union humiliation and fumbling on the battlefield, all that showed to the naked eye were the failures of Lincoln's generals. Behind the lines, however, the South's powers of resistance and replenishment were being drained from it; and the momentum of the Union's wartime industrial advances quickened the process of attrition. Barriger notes that "coal was first used successfully as locomotive fuel in an experimental way in 1853. The general transition to coal-burning locomotives had begun in the North on the Pennsylvania Railroad, around 1859. By 1862, all PRR freight locomotives were coal-burning engines. Two years later, all of its locomotives could burn coal."

This achievement is no more than an interesting footnote to our understanding of the economic advantages which the North exploited in order to clinch its victory. But it demonstrates conclusively the catalytic role which the Civil War played in expanding and enriching our economy and modernizing its technology. Measured in terms of wartime capital formation and postwar economic growth, the conversion of our mushrooming railroad plant from a wood-burning to a coal-burning basis stands as a more meaningful historical milestone and a more impressive technological achievement than the conversion of our military air fleet from propeller to jet engines under the stress of World War II.

The political history of the Civil War years, as it has been institutionalized for us by accepted legend and received belief, has distracted us from formative economic realities. It has centered on personalities and glamorized even such a fundamentally ordinary figure as Grant. On the other side of the lines, if the South had won the war, the horse would have galloped into history as its symbol. In fact, it was the iron horses of the North that did the job.

Industrially, the logistical revolution wrought by the great advance in wartime railroading not only put industry and transportation on a coal-burning basis; it also switched its basic material content from iron to steel. In fact, the American Civil War effected this transition in railroad engineering at just about the same time as the parallel evolution of German military metallurgy was enabling Krupp to switch new artillery from the conventional brass to the new steel basis. (This evolution contributed as importantly as the failure of leadership on the French side to the momentum of the German juggernaut in the Franco–Prussian War.)

The new metallurgy revolutionized the technology of war at sea as well as on land. The British launched their first ironclad ship in 1860, and they were simultaneously delighted and dismayed to discover, as Robert Blake says in his *Disraeli,* that it "could have sunk single-handed every battleship built before the Crimean War." The *Merrimac,* which the Confederacy had captured and converted, quickly confirmed this judgment in the test of battle. No sooner did steam power iron to ram and sink wood than the *Monitor* and the *Merrimac* put on their prophetic demonstration of the special ability to steam into stalemate which floating sea power developed between the American Civil War and World War I.

Politically, the outcome of the Civil War hoisted "the bloody shirt" as a banner and unleashed the Grand Army of the Republic as the reigning institution for a generation to come. But the economic aftereffects of the Civil War, while less conspicuous, were more fruitful. Not only did the Civil War equip America to start her new era of postwar expansion with a new elite corps of experienced rail transportation personnel at a time when, as Carnegie's subsequent career was to show, railroad technology held the key to industrial progress; it also enabled the North to keep right on moving. As Barriger says, "The war led to the provision of interline fast freight service and important forward strides in railway mail service coextensive with the railway map." These prodigious advances in industrial logistics and in the engineering and production of transportation support—especially from the steel industry—called for money, and lots of it. The economic revolution brought about by the Civil War dethroned King Cotton and established in its place the democracy of demand for money to be put to every kind of work. It endowed people of all kinds with new assets and earning power sufficient to qualify their demand as "effective" in the marketplace.

The Civil War, like every other war we have fought, created prodigious new appetites for goods and services, and it provided the money to satisfy them. It is axiomatic that a big war, while it lasts, whips up demands faster than the economy is able to supply them. One of the remarkable economic characteristics of the Civil War is that the wartime demands it generated carried over into the postwar period on their own momentum after the pump-priming impetus of the war had been spent and after battle damage had been repaired. The Mexican War, to be sure, had done so too, but it was a small, short affair fought out beyond the fringes of an economy which was still largely unindustrialized. World War II also developed the same powerful carryover of effective demand into the postwar period, but this parallel is complicated by the fact that Franklin Roosevelt came to his War Presidency bursting with criticism which bordered on contempt for the mismanagement Wilson had permitted of our first world-war economy, and determined to do better. FDR's plan for post-war prosperity was incomparably better conceived and executed than his more ambitious vision of world peace. In contrast with the post-World-War-II boom which carried over from Hiroshima, the expansion that accelerated after Grant told Lee that his men could keep their horses was entirely unplanned. Certainly, horses had ceased to be the economy's prime source of horsepower.

7 : CHASE'S SOMERSAULT

THE TWO GREAT secular booms in American economic history have been those following the Civil War and World War II. In each case, expansion of output and increase in real income continued almost unbroken. The financial disturbances after the Civil War and the cyclical reactions after World War II proved to be merely temporary resting periods in the long-term drive to unprecedented new standards of living. Total war in each case provided both the basic dynamic for real growth and the means to finance that growth. America emerged from both the Civil War and World War II with unparalleled opportunities for investment and with a comparably greater store of liquid savings to pump into the investment opportunities which war had opened up.

The Civil War determined the future economic experience of the Republic in four critical areas. First, the war endowed the nation with a supply of money ample enough to prevent monetary constraint from choking off postwar expansion before it could get under way. Second, the war laid the foundation for the growth sectors which would lead the American economy to world industrial leadership within a generation. Third, the direction of that industrialization, and the formidable rise in living standards which accompanied it, set the pattern for the organization of American labor and went far to determine its distinctive nonpolitical approach. Fourth, the North's success was based on its ability to match the industrial expansion necessary to win the war with the agricultural expansion required to finance the victory through food exports. This unique achievement of balanced agricultural and industrial growth was to characterize America's continuing post-Civil-War drive to economic maturity.

In a negative way, the public career of Salmon P. Chase symbolized America's domestic economic experience in the last third of the nineteenth century. As Secretary of the Treasury, Chase bumbled his way into the expedient, which first paid for the war and then underwrote the peace, of printing the greenback paper dollars which became famous as the postwar symbol of easy money. As Chief Justice of the Supreme Court five years later, Chase precipitated a financial and political crisis by declaring his own wartime expedient unconstitutional. The domestic money issue in all its forms—greenbacks, silver, the gold standard, and the banking system—was a burning political issue right up to World War I. Chase was largely responsible for setting it afire. But neither the political irresponsibility of Chase nor the financial instability from which America suffered in the late nineteenth century could significantly brake the dynamism of the American economy. In historical perspective, the real significance of Chase's somersault is how insignificant was the impact on the real economic achievement during the post-Civil-War generation of the political struggle over money and the recurrent financial breakdowns which kept the political pot boiling.

The Civil War had been fought over the issue of Federal power. As one side-effect, the Federal government had successfully asserted its wartime power to put the money of the Union onto the greenback standard. The central issue of the postwar period had been pre-formed, as it were, by the wartime use of Federal power to supersede the gold standard with fiat money. The question of whether or not the Federal government had the power to set the value of the dollar had by this time become academic: once the wartime precedent had been set, all that remained to be settled in the postwar period was which political pressure group in the country would use the power. Business was anxious to put the country on the gold standard, while business's debtors and customers were fighting to keep it on the greenback standard.

At the outset of *A Treatise on Money,* which appeared in 1930, Keynes declared that money is what the state says it is. He added that the state "claimed the right not only to enforce the dictionary but also to write the dictionary." Keynes's genius was more than analytical. He was a master dramatist in the mobilization of words with intent to shock. Shock certainly was the effect on the shaken establishment of his laconic, matter-of-fact remark in support of his dictum that the State sets the value of money. "This right," Keynes said, as casually as if he were invoking a self-evident axiom, "is claimed by all modern States and has been so claimed for some 4,000 years at least." But if conventional thinking in the world of 1930 was not attuned to this fact, the history of the American Civil War serves as a forceful reminder of it.

Lincoln's practice anticipated Keynes's theory: the government asserted its right to issue money and, therefore, the government set its value; the activity of the Bureau of Engraving and the Mint superseded the free workings of the gold market. Once a government which is fighting to vindicate its claims to sovereignty subordinates its needs within its area of sovereignty to the workings of an abstract and arbitrary market standard, it jeopardizes its chances of survival. By the same token, when any government commits itself to make war, it comes under pressure to run markets—beginning with the money market, which is the market of markets. Lincoln's War Administration was prompt and incisive in acting as if it knew that economic mobilization begins with the mobilization of the money market. It suspended the domestic convertibility of specie in the first year of the war and, for the duration, committed the Union to greenbacks, close to $450 million of which were issued.

The printing of greenbacks to pay the Treasury's bills and

to reimburse state governments for their advances was not the only wartime policy which, deliberately or not, filled the liquidity reservoir. The Federal government also paid bonuses in cash to demobilized veterans. In a paper published in *The American Historical Review* for April, 1919, Professor C. R. Fish estimated that final payments averaged about $250 per Union soldier, all paid in lump sums on discharge. And, as Fish says, "A small amount of money in 1865 smoothed a good deal of rough road." The Northern veterans who joined the Grand Army of the Republic became the most potent political lobby in the country and probably the most frankly predatory, a remarkable accomplishment considering the competitive bidding of the day. Fish makes the point that, in the absence of any system of social security in those days, the pensions which the GAR bludgeoned out of the government during the postwar generation contributed significantly to offsetting the lags and inadequacies of aggregate demand. They certainly supplemented the limited operations of government in a prophetic way.

War finance endowed America with a "monetary overcoat," to use Schumpeter's phrase, with plenty of room for the productive apparatus to grow up inside it. But the monetary factor alone cannot explain the generation of growth that followed. During the period of transition immediately following the war, however, the spillover of greenbacks made the difference. It bought the time needed for the cumulative momentum of economic development to become self-sustaining. The positive factors which thrust the American economy forward were those which both stimulated demand and increased the economy's capacity to meet that demand at a rate of growth that was not only unprecedented by economic standards, but revolutionary in social terms. By and large, the maintenance of an adequate pressure of demand was not a problem for post-Civil-War America because of the ample opportunities for profitable investment. In addition to the increases in output generated by investment in postwar economic modernization (notably in railroading), a variety of other factors added to the unprecedented growth in productive capacity. Free immigration increased the supply of

labor; technological innovation accelerated (especially in communications); and the new lands in the West offered easy opportunities for dramatic increases in crop production. In a classic
demonstration of self-sustaining growth, economic advance came
to feed on itself.

So great was the expansion on the supply side of the American economy that the price level fell even as overall demand rose.
The dynamism of American growth was so great that the normally depressant effect of a falling price level was more than
offset. Orthodox thinking associates economic growth with rising
prices. In fact, when prices are rising in response to increased
demand, and not merely reacting to a cost push from below, the
increased profits thereby generated obviously reinforce the pressures working for economic expansion. This has certainly been
the pattern of twentieth-century economic growth (nowhere
more dramatically, for example, than in post-World-War-II
Japan). But post-Civil-War America reversed the familiar rule.
Rising profits contributed to a historic economic breakthrough
while prices fell. Costs of production fell even more quickly and
substantially.

The monetary factor did provide a big bonus for the economy in the international sphere. Postwar expansion enjoyed the
practical benefit of a double standard. Until the return to the
gold standard in 1879, the greenback dollar exchanged at a
discount below the prewar gold parity. But, because of the impressive political support behind the conservative push to resume
convertibility, no one could count on the permanence of the
discount. America's exports were cheap but, so it seemed, only
for the moment—a telling "buy now" sales point. The promise
of a return to the gold dollar exposed America's export customers to the hazard that prices quoted in dollars would rise.

On the capital-importing side of the dollar equation, the
softness of the dollar created incentives too, and for the same
reason—that softness seemed merely temporary. Foreigners who
took the risk of investing the hard money America needed bought
greenbacks all the more readily because the chances of coming
out in gold with a double profit, on their investments as well as

on their greenbacks, seemed within ready reach. While the Civil War was still on, the discount on the dollar reflected the Union's inflated import requirements during a period of export deflation, and not any flight of capital. On the contrary, the discount on the dollar attracted money into the country. Milton Friedman, in his monumental *Monetary History of the United States,* credits the ability of the war economy to offset its cotton export losses and to pay for its emergency requirements to the large inflow of foreign money. The fact is that, although the domestic price level doubled between the outset of the Civil War and its end, the accompanying de facto devaluation of the international gold dollar was only 20 per cent—an eloquent testimonial to the strong and steady foreign gold demand for paper dollars during the worst of the war. Moreover, despite the demand pressures arising from government borrowing, the rise in interest rates was moderate. No doubt the favorable experience of foreign money in the face of wartime risks encouraged it to speculate on post-war doubts about the dollar when the fight over resumption created opportunities.

In the country's industrial plant, the carryover of wartime momentum was impressive. Railroads linked the coasts by 1869. On top of the dynamic railroad expansion during the decade preceding the Civil War, track mileage and traffic doubled again between 1867 and 1879. Friedman notes that "despite a decline in prices, exports of finished manufactures were nearly 2½ times as large in gold values and 1¾ times as large in greenback values in 1879 as in 1867." John Moody recalls that, as late as the early 1870's, "when Cornelius Vanderbilt substituted steel for iron on the New York Central, he had to import the new material from England." Soon after, iron track was torn up all over the country and steel rail laid in its place. By 1890, America had passed all the countries of Europe combined in railroad mileage. And, as the Beards say, the capitalization of the railroad industry alone added up to almost $10 billion, or about one-sixth of the estimated national wealth—"easily twice the value of all the slaves on whose labor the planting aristocracy of the South had once built its political power." In iron and steel production, too,

America had outstripped England and France combined and already accounted for more than one-third of the world's total annual supply. Andrew Carnegie boasted that the iron crown had been placed on the brow of Pennsylvania, but he need not have limited his boast to iron or to Pennsylvania. Although America was still an importer of capital and, even more, of labor, and although she therefore depended more heavily than ever on the export of crops to balance her capital accounts, she had already forged into world industrial leadership.

As fast as American industry took over the American market and expanded apace with it, it won world market leadership too. Allan Nevins wrote in *The Emergence of Modern America, 1865–1878*: "It was an era in which new lands were being fast developed. . . . American manufactures had a special adaptability to such lands. Our locomotives and railway cars were the only ones really suited to many freshly opened regions. American agricultural machinery went naturally to all countries where large-scale farming was practiced, and the New Zealand farmer guided a South Bend plow while the Russian peasant drove a Chicago reaper. Indeed, the American iron and steel products broke into the European field in a way that alarmed Britons."

The Civil War also influenced the structure of the incipient labor movement of the postwar era. Labor was slower to develop into an economic and political force in America than in Europe —not only because the fluidity of American society offered such rich and varied opportunities to graduate from the bench, but because the rise in real incomes neutralized the pressures which normally drive labor to organize. But when labor organization did begin to catch up with industrial organization, it concentrated on precisely those industries into which the war had channeled capital investment. Railroads to win the war and coal mined to run the railroads had paced the wartime industrial expansion and set its pattern. This historic evolution was repeated in the labor revolution which exploded in the 1870's and 1880's.

Labor organization in America received its first forward impetus when the financial panic of 1873 saw those industries which had made the biggest contribution to employment make the biggest contribution to unemployment and to the misery and privation that were synonymous with unemployment in those hardy days on the old economic frontier. Railroading was the vanguard of organized labor in America, and coal mining provided its militant shock troops. Thus, the influence of the Civil War on the structure of labor organization in the American economy stretched into the future far beyond the closing decades of the nineteenth century. For, when the day of Big Labor finally dawned, it was the holdover nucleus of railroad and coal union organization which provided both the cadres and the leadership.

The early evolution of an American labor movement provides a striking and indicative example of American Exceptionalism. In the developing industrial states of Western Europe, the 1880's and 1890's saw the foundation and growth of the Marxist Social Democratic movement under the auspices of the Second International. Marxism has never been more than a fringe movement among the unions in Britain. There, instead, "Lib-Labism" had included organized labor merely as an interest group within the Liberal Party. The turn of the century saw this loose and amorphous liberal coalition break down as labor launched its preliminary move toward an independent bid for political power. In the U.S., by contrast, labor was barely a recognized interest group, let alone a political movement. While European labor was moving toward political power and quarreling over the efficacy of evolution versus revolution, American labor was just trying to get organized. Before World War I, the American labor movement certainly never developed beyond the stage of being an interest group. And it had no program more specific than the famous "more" of Samuel Gompers, founder of the AF of L.

The relative backwardness of the American labor movement by no means reflected only the opportunities for individual advance which American society offered outside of organized interest groups. Freebooting, laissez-faire capitalism, as symbolized by the robber barons, levied its unquestioned and immeasurable social cost as offsets to its obvious economic benefits. The imbalance in American society between economic health and social sickness was most apparent, of course, in the late-nineteenth-century betrayal of the promise implied by the Emancipation Proclamation. But neither white industrial workers in the

Northern cities, nor Negro tenant farmers in the rural South, had yet begun to share in the dividends produced by America's dynamic prosperity.

The excesses of American industrialization obviously offered themselves to Marxist interpretation. And the threat no doubt existed that "contradictions" inherent in the development process might disrupt the social fabric, although the strains generated by economic growth in America's fluid situation were much less onerous than those apparent in the rigid hierarchical societies in Europe.

Economic growth, in America as elsewhere, was a race against time—that is, a race between the social tensions and strains created and exacerbated by economic growth on the one hand and the economy's ability to deliver the goods on the other. In nineteenth-century America, the race was won handily (and Marxist analysis as to the inevitability of its being lost was controverted). Perhaps the most critical reason for this success was that the obvious imbalance between the economic and social sides of America was offset by an extraordinary balance within the economic sphere.

Westward railroad expansion, eastward crop movement and industrial development along the way all made a great leap forward when the government put into practice its policy for postwar adjustment. It was a simple policy, pragmatically designed to fit the needs and the social mechanism of the day. "At the close of the Civil War," the Beards wrote, "when thousands of able-bodied young men anxious to win economic independence were released from the armies, the federal government encouraged them to go West by allowing them to count their term of military service as a part of the five years' occupancy required for the permanent possession of a free homestead under the act of 1862."

Rich endowments of free land for free labor was the government's formula for insuring postwar expansion. It worked better than any exercise in planning or any experiments in government spending or financing could possibly have done at that stage of development. The Homestead Act of 1862 and the introduction of a protective tariff were the legislative payoffs for the farmers and businessmen whose alliance underlay the Republican Party. Thus, business, the potent new force in political life, lent its weight to the opening of the West in behalf of free land and free labor, the oldest economic and political interests in America.

In economic behavior, familiarity tends to breed confidence. The Revolutionary War had tried and tested a system of land bounties. The end of the Civil War found the system ready-to-hand for a repeat performance. Wholesale land giveaways to veterans had started the country moving, and now, after the Civil War, the same device gave it a new impetus. As the Beards wrote, "More than one-half of the whole area of the country, to be exact, 1,048,111,608 acres, belonged to the government in 1860—a benevolent government in the hands of friends, ready to sell its holdings for a song, to give them away, or to let them pass by mere occupation." Individuals were, of course, not the only beneficiaries of the bonanza of land giveaways. Railroad financing was giving a great forward push to American expansion. The railroads being promoted during those years were land companies before they became railroad companies, and they remained land companies after they had become railroad companies.

Free land was made available at a time when money was still scarce and industry was still in its infant state. Accordingly, land became a prime vehicle for capital accumulation in America. The contrast with eighteenth- and nineteenth-century Europe, where potentially productive capital was wasted by a privileged class of hereditary landowners, was great—as great as the contrast with the stratified cultures of twentieth-century underdeveloped countries where unproductive land is accumulated as a status symbol and no economic gain results. In mid-nineteenth-century America, capital invested in cheap land generated both the high rates of return and the liquidity which are prime conditions of economic expansion. Moreover, the economic development of the West, made possible by free land, stepped up the growth of the American home market, just as America's infant industries grew able to supply that market. America's industrial evolution during the nineteenth century, behind the walls of Republican tariffs, vindicated the number-one exception to the free trade dogma: the "infant industry" argument that tariffs can be justified to the extent that they allow domestic industry to become capable of meeting established foreign competition. But by the time American industry had grown this far at the end of the century, the growth of the home market had made the international arena relatively unimportant to American industry. For the opening of the West and the growth of farm produce as an exportable, cash return on investment in land proceeded step by step with the growth of industry. Nineteenth-century America presents the classic case of economic growth based on the balanced development of industry and agriculture.

The groundswell of America's drive toward economic leadership dominated the last third of the nineteenth century. Monetary disturbance and banking panic were to an extraordinary extent merely the froth on the wave. The political impact of the cycle of boom and bust was far greater than its economic effect. The wonder of the post-Civil-War period is not that its recurrent panics produced such violent political conflicts on the money front, but that the cycles of money panic and the extremism of contemporary money politics should have run their troublesome course during an era of unprecedented secular expansion. The difficulties of the post-Civil-War generation did not reflect failures of understanding and coordination between our business system and our political system. Such differences were simply ignored. The leaders in each walk of life habitually went their separate ways until national crisis knocked their heads together, as it did with the monotonous regularity of the downbeats and the upbeats of the business cycle.

The Federal government did not manage the national economy, saw no reason to manage the national economy, and would surely have been adjudged unconstitutional had it attempted to manage the national economy. Intervention in the economy by the government tended to be unpremeditated. It might take the form of a payoff to an important segment of a political coalition, as in the case of the Homestead Act, which also basically altered the economic structure of the country. Or the government might influence economic events for years as the incidental result of a decision to pay its wartime bills in greenbacks. Just how incidental and accidental was this event is pointed up by the fact that it was Secretary of the Treasury Chase who authorized the greenback issue, and Chief Justice Chase who eight years later wrote the opinion which declared his own act unconstitutional. It is too bad that the habitual British ignorance of American history hid this interesting reversal from the knowledge of Gilbert and Sullivan, for they surely would have enjoyed working it into one of the Savoy operas.

It was not Chase's fault that the expedient to which he was forced by the exigencies of war finance, the printing of green-backs, paid an unexpected dividend at a critical time in the postwar expansion. Nonetheless, Chase had been responsible for the decision. Lincoln, however, moved to safeguard the currency by jeopardizing the judiciary, and kicked his chief Cabinet troublemaker upstairs to the Chief Justiceship. Chase then, in 1870, displayed a degree of inconsistency remarkable even for him, and cast the swing vote in the Court against the constitu-tionality of his own greenbacks, explaining: "It is not surprising that amid the tumult of the late civil war . . . almost universal, different views, never before entertained by American statesmen or jurists, were adopted by many," meaning primarily himself. His opinion for the Court majority goes on to argue that "the time was not favorable to considerate reflection upon the consti-tutional limits of Legislative or Executive authority. . . . Not a few who then insisted upon its necessity, or acquiesced in that view, have, since the return of peace, and under the influence of the calmer time, reconsidered their conclusions." With a few Gilbert rhymes and a Sullivan tune, it would almost sing itself.

Dissenting Supreme Court opinions have a way of antici-pating political majorities, and the dissenting opinion of Chase's brethren in the legal tender case did. "This law," they said, "was a necessity, in the most stringent sense in which that word can be used." Within months, Grant threatened to start a fight to pack the Court. In fact, Congress passed a bill restoring the membership of the Court from seven (to which it had been reduced during Congress's fight with Andrew Johnson) to nine and authorizing a tenth place. Grant's appointees provided the margin by which the Court reversed its reversal—within only fifteen months of the original decision.

The Chase Court's repudiation of the Chase greenback contributed not only to short-run financial instability. The money issue took center stage for the duration of the century. At a time when radicalism in Europe was moving leftward toward the slogans and the substance of the class struggle, radicalism in America reflected the conflict between creditors and debtors. The radical movement that started up after the Civil War called itself the Greenback Labor Movement. When it was launched in the late 1870's, its leadership came from the farmers of the West with their easy-money, debtors' bias; and it was to their easy-money slogans and their attack on the entrenched money power of the East that the radicals and militants of the infant labor movement rallied. By the time labor began to raise its first cries from the periphery of American politics, the economy was well on its way toward modernity, and the radicals of American agriculture were firmly established as the leaders of the opposition, with easy money as their rallying cry and labor their lesser ally. As late as the mid-1920's, the order of seniority and priority implied in the designation of the Minnesota Farmer–Labor Party faithfully reproduced these political realities.

The political realities of the late nineteenth century reflected to a very great extent the economic facts of life at the time. Capitalism proved successful in its American habitat. From the Civil War to the turn of the century, America grew from the world's leading undeveloped frontier to the threshold of world industrial leadership. The great postwar boom of the Gilded Age endowed America with the economic resources for world influence. The boom of the post-Civil-War era ranks only with that following World War II as a generator of sustained increases in real income. Both postwar booms shared another characteristic: they carried domestic dynamism into the international arena. But, whereas the post-Civil-War boom left America poised for successful imperialist adventures in Cuba and the Philippines, the post-World-War-II boom ended by springing an unwanted and treacherous trap in Vietnam. Economic growth, instead of providing the material basis for strategic operations, wound up sacrificed to strategic oversight.

8 : MORGAN'S MISSION

IN THE TWENTIETH century, two world wars shattered the delicate structure of international finance upon which international economic relationships depend. Each postwar period consequently has provided an opportunity for creating a system of world finance almost from scratch. The key requirement in both 1919 and 1945, necessary for the stability of any new world money system, was that America accept its responsibility—in its own self-interest, above all—to provide capital for the world.

In 1865, America emerged from the Civil War into a world which Britain dominated financially as well as economically and strategically. Consequently, America's post-Civil-War international problem stands in sharp contrast to her problems of leadership after World War I and World War II. For after 1865, America needed Britain to play the role in America's postwar expansion that she herself would be called upon to play after the great wars of the coming century.

Horace Greeley's advice to the proverbial young man to "go west" has been overworked as the cliché that explains where America's future lay. William Graham Sumner offered a more realistic exhortation (as was appropriate for the chief academic apologist of the Gilded Age): "Get capital." For, by 1865, capital had replaced labor as the critical, limiting constraint on growth. Irish immigration had begun to relieve the shortage of population at the same time as the productivity of labor began to take off. Simultaneously, the drive to industrialize created ever-increasing needs for capital of all kinds and for all purposes. The free land which the Homestead Act provided relieved some of the competing demand for capital by reducing the amount required for investment in land. Nonetheless, the capital requirements of America's industrialization were far beyond the capacity of America alone to finance. The domestic supply of savings was inadequate to maintain the tempo of economic advance that would come within ready reach once the capital constraint was lifted.

The way to lift the constraint of capital shortage on growth, for America in 1865 as for the developing countries a century later, was to tap the savings of the more developed countries. In 1865, the place to go for capital was London. And the way to get capital—the only way in an age which had never dreamed of foreign aid—was to mobilize it through the mechanism of the private market. This meant that the investment community was likely to become dominant over the business community, even as the business community demonstrated its dominance over the country's political leadership. For if business had what the politicians needed to deliver—the means to prosperity—the bankers had, or knew where to find, what business required— capital. Moreover, the need for foreign capital provided an external sanction to back up the bankers' influence.

The young man who was to emerge as the most powerful and creative figure in the coming era of American primacy in the world was a disciple of Sumner, not of Greeley. It was his mission to link the mechanisms of American finance to Europe, first by exploiting America's dependence on Europe, and then by becoming the medium through which Europe developed its subsequent dependence upon America. His name was J. P. Morgan.

Morgan first asserted his command over the situation by virtue of the London connection he had developed during the wartime crisis of the dollar. The more lurid essays in Morgan muckraking have made much of the shabby business which first brought the brash young jobber-on-the-make into prominence. He had backed an obscure trafficker in surplus goods—in this case, rifles declared defective after the outbreak of the war—which the government had auctioned off for a song and which the shadowy buyer and his domineering banker then turned right around and sold back to the government at a markup appropriately rich even by the freebooting standards of the day. (The incorrigible Gold Dust Twins of the Gilded Age, Jay Gould and Jim Fiske, when they fought the first battle for control of the Erie with Morgan, summed up the morals of corporate piracy in telling their cohorts, after the dust had cleared, "Nothing is lost save honor.") The select Congressional Committee of 1862 which investigated Morgan's gun deal deployed no midget to sit upon the knee of the star witness, as its successor was to do to his son in 1933. But its report was every bit as dramatic: "The Government not only sold one day for $17,486 arms which it had agreed the day before to repurchase for $109,912—making a loss to the United States of $92,426—but virtually furnished the money to pay itself the $17,486 which it received."

Petty larceny, however, was not Morgan's game; and, indeed, the Court of Claims eventually gave his jobbing client the satisfaction of a judgment in full against the government. The meaningful chapter in Morgan's Civil War career was written when he first showed his hand in London. In 1861, after the defeat at Bull Run, Lincoln's hapless Secretary of the Treasury, Salmon P. Chase, had carried the spirit of panic from the northern end of Virginia to the southern tip of Manhattan Island. Chase appealed to the bankers of the New York Clearing House Association to stand by the government in its hour of emergency. As Morgan's friendly biographer Carl Hovey told the story, Chase said: "There is really more need of gold right now than of troops. The Confederacy expects to secure gold by sending cotton to Europe; and, until we can build a navy, we can barely interfere with the export. We of the North have no cotton. What are we to do? I am not a financier; I can only administer funds. You bankers of New York must show the Federal Government

how to get this gold, or we shall go on the rocks together!"
Clearly the North had won the war with its muscle and not with
its management. As Chase was too amateurish to understand
(but as Simon Newcomb, who was America's most creative professional astronomer and perspicacious amateur economist of the
day, pointed out), a Southern decision to squander its scarce
export earnings on gold was almost too much to hope for.
Newcomb was passionately dedicated to the principles of classical
economics, but he was realist enough to recognize that war
imposes its own laws on the marketplace. The South needed
munitions, not specie.

In fact, Chase's panic quickly produced the blueprint for
Morgan's program. Operating through another obscure front—
Ketchum by name—Morgan became a quiet and steady buyer of
gold, for his own account, but also in his professional capacity
as scout and adviser to the established banking house of Peabody
& Company (which the Morgan firm was soon to supersede).
"All at once," as Frederick Lewis Allen wrote in *The Great
Pierpont Morgan*, "they conspicuously shipped abroad half of
what they had acquired, in order to lift the price and sell the
remainder of their hoard at a handsome profit. The scheme
worked. . . . From one point of view this was a legitimate, if
crafty, speculative coup . . . it seemed reprehensible to people
distant from the exchanges but quite acceptable to people engaged
in the constant push-and-pull of speculative trade. Yet from another and larger point of view this gold deal was a shabby operation, since it was in effect an attempt to depreciate, at least
temporarily, the national currency in time of acute emergency."
Moreover, it succeeded; for, by the winter of 1862–3, the Union's
20-year, 6 per cent bonds were selling at a discount of 20 to
30 per cent while, by 1864, they had fallen below 50 cents on
the dollar.

The big money is made by the big players who know how
to play both sides of the table at once. Morgan did. In the
famous diplomatic passage-at-arms in which Ambassador Charles
Francis Adams negotiated the British into a breach of their con-
tract to build ships for the Confederacy, the consideration on

which the British government insisted was a prompt prepayment of a million pounds in gold. Adams, with five days' notice to put up or shut up, made an intensive canvass of the city of London—to no avail. Hovey relates, however, how the situation was saved by the timely and effective use of the gold Morgan had had the foresight to move out of New York and into London. Adams, Hovey writes, "received in secret a representative of Peabody & Co., who brought the information that the American firm was ready to advance him five million dollars in gold, and would do it immediately, upon the sole condition that the transaction should be absolutely confidential. No one else, except President Lincoln and Secretary Seward, was to know one word about it. The only security asked was Mr. Adams's receipt, signed as American minister. The gold was, within a day, delivered." Not for nothing did Morgan come to be called "The Magnificent." Even his raids turned into constructive achievements—to be sure, at high cost to the public and at staggering profit to himself in the dollar terms of the day.

The requirements of westward expansion after the Civil War forced the country to look abroad for capital. Foreign capital, which had been able to demand gold and get it in settlement of obligations during the worst of the greenback-issuing period, insisted on nothing less now. Morgan had made his mark running gold out of New York to London in wartime. If those who organized raids against the Union dollar were chair-borne, their operations were at least as effective as those of Jeb Stuart's cavalry-borne raiders against the Union infantry. The stresses of war had revealed gold as the need of the hour: London was the place to find it, and Morgan was the man who could get it. Now the requirements of postwar expansion made it Morgan's mission to bring the refugee gold back to America and to pile up new reserves behind it.

No doubt the wartime run of gold out of New York and into London would have developed even if no leadership had arisen to channel and consolidate it. The fact is that it did so in the person of Morgan. When he exploited the opportunity and dramatized the achievement, he also put his mark upon the

course of history. The new era of railroad finance opened up a
second opportunity for him to lead the inevitable movement of
gold back into America and, once it moved back again, to represent the European interests which had sent it.

"The original reason for Morgan's active participation in
railroad finance," Edwards wrote in *The Evolution of Finance
Capitalism,* "was primarily due to his realization of the need of
protecting the interests of the investors, particularly foreign investors, in American railroad securities." Following through on
his wartime success in taking over the Peabody connection in
London, Morgan first formed what was to prove an enduring
alliance with the Drexel interests in Philadelphia, Jay Cooke's
main rival; and he then proceeded to challenge the presumed
monopoly over government financing which Cooke had established during the Civil War. Drexel was involved in the financial
management of the Northern Pacific, and Morgan's aggressive
tactics resulted in Cooke's getting overextended in both railroad
finance and government underwriting. Cooke had seen the
Treasury through the whole of the Civil War, and he had therefore assumed that he would enjoy a continuing monopoly. Soon
after the war, Congress, impatient to get the war paid for, had
authorized the refunding of $500 million. But Cooke ran into
stiff resistance in selling the issue to the public and ended by
placing most of it abroad. In 1873, consequently, the time was
right for Morgan to break Cooke's monopoly. And his increasingly formidable Washington operation succeeded, as the admir-
ing Hovey says, by "getting the ear of President Grant."

In the end, after a great deal of procrastination and public
display, Secretary of the Treasury George Boutwell formalized
Cooke's loss of monopoly influence by dividing the patronage
between Cooke and Morgan (who, meanwhile, had taken advantage of his new position in the world to persuade the Rothschilds
to share their favors, heretofore reserved exclusively for Cooke,
with him as well: the Rothschilds dominated the international
gold market). The loss of confidence in Cooke; Cooke's loss of
control over the distribution of securities in a market saturated
with new offerings; the competitive tug of railroad finance; the
stress which always follows a delay in cleaning up a visible

accumulation of heavy financing requirements—all these factors combined to intensify one of the recurrent financial storms which would have proved troublesome even if arrangements in the realm of political finance had remained serene. Whether Cooke could have survived what turned into the panic of 1873 if his monopoly had remained undisturbed, no one will ever know. For, notwithstanding the fact that the opening of the door to competition had reduced his responsibility, the loss of his monopoly had fatally increased his vulnerability. In any case, the deed was done. Cooke went under with such a crash that two days later the New York Stock Exchange had to be shut down.

It was a case of "the king is dead, long live the king." Randall records that "commercial failures for the year 1873 exceeded 5,000, with liabilities of $228 million. These losses outnumbered those of 1872 by more than a hundred million; yet there was worse to follow. Failures in 1876 numbered 9,000, those of 1877 about the same, those of 1878 over ten thousand." The distress advertised the need of Europe's shaken investment community for an authoritative and reliable American representative to look after its claims. As Edwards says, "In 1876 39 percent of all the railroad bonds were in default, while in 1879, 65 roads with capitalization of $234 million were sold under foreclosure. As a result of these conditions, the European market for American railway securities was practically closed, and the free flow of capital from Europe to America was checked."

Morgan was probably the most important single figure in the history of America between Lincoln and Theodore Roosevelt. His disdain of politics and politicians reached the point of treating public distress as if it were merely an exaggerated case of private irresponsibility. Governments and the countries for which they bore responsibility he regarded as fair game in the jungle. "Send your man to see my man" had been his contemptuous way of telling President Grover Cleveland to instruct the Secretary of the Treasury to wait on the firm's lawyer in order to receive the terms on which enough gold would again be sent back to New York to formalize the end of the panic of 1893–5.

Yet one should give the devil his due. Anathema though Morgan was to the Populist opposition, distasteful though he was to the governments to whom he dictated terms, and exorbitant though his terms were, the fact is that once he imposed them, they stuck. In the case of his coup and dictat of 1895, his terms stipulated that not an ounce of gold was to be withdrawn from the Treasury for five months, and not an ounce was. By the time of the 1893–5 panic, no intelligence or conditioned reflexes more sophisticated than those of Pavlov's dog were needed to recognize the monotonous rhythm in which gold ran out of New York when confidence in the dollar sagged and ran back to New York when confidence returned.

The first post-Civil-War panic in 1873 was also the first to originate in America, an indication of our growing importance in the international scheme of things. And it was the first panic in which Morgan played a significant role. From that time until the outset of World War I, both American business and government had to carry on with a sword held over their heads; and Morgan held the sword. Morgan was the decisive power in the New York money market because he controlled its link to London. Whenever a political ruckus shook confidence in New York, money could threaten to take the gold road to London; the condition for its return was a return of confidence in New York. In effect, therefore, the rating which political leadership enjoyed on the New York money market was the pre-World-War-I equivalent of the contemporary public opinion polls.

Money retained its veto power over politics so long as it had somewhere else to go. But when World War I closed down the money markets of Europe, another historic irony asserted itself: New York gained financial primacy in the world at the same time as it lost its veto over politics at home. Fifty years elapsed before foreign financial opinion again became an influence in American decision-making.

Before World War I eliminated Morgan's ultimate sanction by closing the escape hatch for gold to Europe, the country's confidence in the currency shifted with the Wall Street weather. Morgan was Wall Street's chief authority and principal rain-maker. Just as his moods reflected great passions, his moves were made in the grand manner, with the bargaining table as a battlefield. His way of dealing with the American government each time it fell afoul of the workings of the gold market involved a flexing of muscles and a brandishing of brass knuckles which conjured up the legendary image of Bismarck beating a disarmed and defenseless enemy government to its knees in 1871 and refusing to accept its surrender unless first it acquiesced to his terms. Morgan was a Bismarckian figure. And, because the country whose historic pattern he helped to forge was headed for world ascendancy whereas Bismarck's Germany was not, it was dramatically appropriate that Morgan died a dominant figure and that Bismarck wound up his career an exile from power.

It was altogether in character that this commanding magnifico in American public life personified not so much money as the money power. Morgan deserves to be ranked with the great conscienceless European power politicians of the age as one of the nineteenth century's presiding geniuses. No doubt Bismarck, Palmerston and Disraeli were all more authentically creatures of their times because they felt obliged to compromise with the rising demand for freedom and reform. Morgan personified the money power in its function as pure power. Although he became an immensely wealthy man, the fortune he made was incidental to the power he wielded. His importance for his time and for history stems not from his wealth but, rather, from the power which his domination of the money world brought to him in the political world. He was not interested in or conversant with the tortuous methods of politics; but his mobilization of money dominated politics because it dominated finance. In Morgan's day, the structure of political power rested on power arrangements in the world of finance.

Morgan's career personified yet another reversal of dramatic role in the continuing European–American relationship. America, which pioneered the nineteenth century's evolution toward freedom and reform, and whose ideals and progress toward realizing them won even Marx's respect, produced in Morgan the one uncompromising figure who stood for pure power as measured by money and nothing else. His successful European counterparts, by contrast, for all their reactionary bent, found it the better part of valor to sway with the wind and to swim with the current. Disraeli and Bismarck, although reactionaries in principle, were pioneering practitioners of reform. But the commanding power figure produced by nineteenth-century America had no patience with reform and felt no compulsion to compromise with it. Instead, he dominated the world of money politics. There he reflected the emergent source of America's irresistible claim to world leadership—with, as he saw it, no nonsense about welfare or even about giving generous accommodation to his own government in distress.

In Morgan's career, the road from New York to Washington (from the time he first dictated the terms on which gold would support the dollar) and from New York to Pittsburgh (when the time came for him to put the U.S. Steel merger together) always went by way of London. By keeping open the line of retreat for gold to London, he was able to guarantee instant success for his forays when he deemed it auspicious to sound the "all clear" for gold to come home again and to bring new foreign money behind it. But Morgan's success in his mission as financial plenipotentiary between America and Europe went further. Because of it, he became commandingly influential in setting the pattern both for the reorganization of American government finance (when the time came to go back on the gold standard) and for the reorganization of corporate finance (when the time came to begin putting the trusts together after the Spanish War).

Morgan's success symbolized that extraordinary operation, the pre-1914 gold standard. The old gold standard was never self-adjusting; and gold had never, in theory or in practice, embodied any intrinsically immutable value as a benchmark for all other values (any more than did Marx's equally metaphysical concept, labor). The old gold standard was managed, but it was managed by men like Morgan. Above all, it was managed by the Bank of England, then very much a private organization. The Morgans of the world's financial centers achieved what no public agency, national or international, could have achieved at that time: a functioning system of international financial relationships that operated for the public on the basis of private relationships.

Morgan's career encompassed America's rise to world financial parity with Britain—or, rather, New York's rise to parity with London. World War I destroyed the old gold standard. Britain's postwar efforts to restore it culminated in the crash of 1929–32. Britain could not lead alone, and the question was whether America would share the burden with her. By 1931, the answer to that question was no. By 1945, America had learned enough from the interwar fiasco to take the lead in establishing a new international monetary system. But when, in the mid-1960's, the weaknesses inherent in that system revealed it as no more than a stopgap, America hesitated. Only America could recoup the opportunity that had been lost in 1945; whether she would or not was a dangerously open question. It could never have been said of Morgan that he hesitated when the opportunities of leadership were his.

9 : MCKINLEY'S
PRAYER

SUCCESSFUL WARS are short and sweet. For the victors, they are
invariably small wars; they are fought on foreign soil; they com-
bine limited immediate risks with unlimited prospective rewards;
and they are won conclusively. America's war against Spain
qualified on all counts. In February, 1898, the sinking of the
Maine found America isolated from Europe and isolationist in
her attitude toward developments beyond the water's edge.
Eleven months later, the Treaty of Paris, which ceded Cuba,
Puerto Rico, Guam and the Philippines (the latter not yet con-
quered) to America, left her a two-ocean power, with a triumphant navy to prove it. The feat of the *Oregon* in steaming 14,000
miles in 68 days set a new record in the application of modern
technology to the ancient art of seamanship and excited the
imagination of the country. It also demonstrated that the Spanish
Empire was not to be the only victim of the war: ocean distances
were being annihilated too.

Half a century later, Korea reminded America that a small
war can exert immense political leverage—not only at the time,
but well into the future. For the Korean War contained the seed
of the Vietnam War and the world crisis to which it led. But the

Spanish–American War was more epochal than epic. Not only was it America's first offshore exercise in belligerence and, if only for that reason, a milestone in modern history; it also gave the world its first view of a two-ocean war.

The Spanish–American War, World War I and World War II all reproduced, each in its turn, a similar cycle of wartime expansion and postwar consolidation, of war won by the American economy and of peace dominated by it. None of these three wars was so much a victory for American statesmanship as it was a victory for the American economy (even though the aftermath of World War I brought a severe depression of far-reaching importance). On the smaller scale of intra-European competition, it was possible and perhaps inevitable after 1871 for Germany, having won her war with France, to lose out in the subsequent peacetime competition against her. But for the America of the Spanish War, of World War I and of World War II, postwar victory was unalloyed and uncomplicated—at least so far as the leadership role of the economy in the world was concerned. Indeed, America's victory was so decisive in the economic competition that it not only offset but concealed the failures of statesmanship to take advantage of the political opportunities opened up to it.

No mystery need surround the causal connection in American history, from the Revolution through the Korean War, between military victories and great leaps forward by the economy. The economics of war is the economics of destruction. The ability of a national economy to prosper despite the destructive toll of war reduces itself to an essay in quantification, in which the aggregates of destruction are balanced against the aggregates of productivity racing to replace and offset what is destroyed. America has never had to fight a total war. Nor has the industrial pace of the American economy ever been subjected to the ordeal of a scorched-earth offensive. In the only application of scorched-earth firepower on the North American continent, it was the industrial states of the North which scorched the earth, first of the agricultural states in the South and then of the frontier Indian territories in the West.

Joseph Schumpeter, who as a European had known total war at first hand, took it for granted that war cripples a capitalist economy, and that total war cripples it totally. "The national economy as a whole, of course," he wrote, "is impoverished by the tremendous excess in consumption brought on by war." Alfred Marshall, the synthesizer of pre-Keynesian economics, agreed that military spending was economically wasteful. In his *Principles of Economics*, Marshall identified the defense burden as the prime offset against the economic advantages of Britain's international involvement. "The naval and military expenditure," he explained, "which would be necessary to make the country fairly secure against this last risk [a great war], would appreciably diminish the benefits that she derives from the action of the law of increasing return."

Schumpeter and Marshall were merely using their common sense and expressing a truism when they asserted that resources used up in war are wasted because they are diverted from peacetime consumption. But the common sense even of great economists does not always go far enough. The dynamic impact of America's wars more than made up for the immediate and obvious waste of resources, human as well as material. In fact, if any contemporary American economic historian of the Civil War, the Spanish War, World War I or World War II were privileged to view from heaven the workings of the new economics on earth, he would no doubt be inspired to recall that in the good old days, America pioneered its own natural version of what the new economics has tried to accomplish deliberately. Instead of relying on alternating currents of monetary expansion and contraction to raise and to lower prices, to accelerate business activity and to stabilize it, to expand the scale of the economy and to consolidate its growth, America relied on war to harness and leaven the natural forces at work in the economy.

American imperialism became an active force during McKinley's Presidency. But the embodiment of the spirit of American imperialism, and the catalyst of its activation, was Theodore Roosevelt. The history of Republican politics after the Civil War was one of strong barons designating weak nominees for the Presidency. These nonentities, uniformly sanctimonious and dull, offered standing invitations for the ridicule which George Bernard Shaw leveled at middle-class morality. Theodore Roosevelt was neither a conformist nor a fool, although it was only as a policy-making influence, and not as an office-holding politician, that he survived (which means that in terms of the political trade he ended as a failure). Paul Warburg, at the climax of his crusade for the modern banking system which was to take form as the Federal Reserve Board, wrote of being asked to lunch in 1912 with ex-President Roosevelt and some twenty bankers and economists, and being seated next to TR. "Two things," he recalled, "impressed me immediately: (1) the lack of information with which Mr. Roosevelt approached the subject, and (2) the amazing keenness and rapidity with which he filled in the gaps in his knowledge of the matter." Diverse strands of aristocracy, eccentricity, opportunism and a native erratic radicalism combined to make Theodore Roosevelt the type-cast juvenile lead who could dramatize the new American spirit of imperialistic idealism on the world stage and of expansive reform at home.

McKinley nourished an evangelical desire for peace which tended to degenerate into a timorous preference for avoiding trouble. He had hesitated long before yielding to the persistent persuasions of Henry Cabot Lodge to appoint TR Assistant Secretary of the Navy because of TR's provocative jingoism. Scooping Hearst, TR had told Lodge, as early as December, 1895, "This country needs a war," adding that only the "timidity of wealth," with its commitment to "peace at any price," was frustrating the national drive to achieve "real greatness." Before McKinley acquiesced in the appointment, he required a sincere assurance from Lodge that Roosevelt did not mean a word of it. When McKinley and the bosses acquiesced in Roosevelt's nomination as Vice President, they did so after Mark Hanna, as ever rational, ethical and resistant to the jingoes, had warned: "Don't any of you realize that there's only one life between this madman and the White House?"

But Theodore Roosevelt's exercises in muscular juvenility

won respect and affection from an appreciative international audience. Moreover, the powers on whose toes he trod invariably turned up leading the applause. More than his charismatic posturing and prancing seems to have been involved in establishing America's up-and-coming role as a factor in world affairs. President Grover Cleveland before him had scarcely been a posturing political vaudevillian. On the contrary, he had been a plodding, four-square, "stand-up" independent. As a Democratic President, he stood up to labor; as an advocate of free-trade internationalism, he stood up to Britain's claims in Monroe Doctrine waters; and as the ex-President who had presided over the conception of American imperialism, he opposed the Spanish War. When he issued his famous ultimatum to Britain in the Venezuelan boundary dispute a decade earlier, the favorable reaction abroad prompted Carl Russell Fish to write: "So far was Cleveland's message from provoking war that it caused the people of Great Britain vitally to realize for the first time the importance of friendship with the United States. . . . Not that hostility was converted into affection, but a former condescension gave way to an appreciative friendliness towards the people of the United States."

As William Graham Sumner, in his capacity as the official historical sociologist of the folklore of American capitalism, had put it: "Within a few years the United States has been affected by an ambition to be a world power. (A world power is a state which expects to have a share in the settlement of every clash of interests and collision of state policies which occurs anywhere on the globe.) There is no reason to wonder at this action of a democracy, for a democracy is sure to resent any suggestion that it is limited in its functions, as compared with other political forms. At the same time that the United States has moved towards the character of a world power it has become militant."

American militancy found popular expression in the jingo politicking of Roosevelt and in the jingo editorializing of Hearst. Hearst boasted of having spent $3,000,000 in promoting the Spanish–American War. TR's contribution to the cause was perhaps the most blatant usurpation of authority in the history of the American Executive: he contrived both to give Admiral

Dewey advance orders to attack the Philippines and to keep them secret even from President McKinley. When Roosevelt's name had come up for consideration as Assistant Secretary of the Navy, he had asked his ally, Senator Henry Cabot Lodge, to send word to assure McKinley's new Secretary of the Navy, John D. Long, that "I shall stay at Washington, hot weather or any other weather, whenever he wants me to stay there, and go wherever he sends me, and my aim should be solely to make his administration a success." Secretary Long then proceeded to commit the fatal error of leaving the store unguarded, with his ebullient Assistant Secretary in charge. TR's promise was, in fact, a warning.

Even while America was spoiling for a fight, she enjoyed the public-relations benefit—if only as a salve for her own historic idealism—of self-righteousness at the top. When the time came for McKinley to decide whether to stand up to the war hysteria or to succumb to it, instead of facing both ways as was his wont, he knelt in prayer—which was his way of bowing before it. Later, McKinley recalled to a gathering of his fellow Methodists the way he came to his decision: "I walked the floor of the White House night after night," he said, "and I am not ashamed to tell you, gentlemen, that I went down on my knees and prayed Almighty God for light and guidance more than one night. And one night late it came to me this way—I don't know how it was, but it came. . . . There was nothing left for us to do but to take them all, and to educate the Filipinos, and uplift and civilize and Christianize them, and by God's grace do the very best we could by them as our fellow-men for whom Christ also died. And then I went to bed, and went to sleep and slept soundly." Although Lyndon Johnson has not in private been a frequent quoter of Scripture, he reenacted this exercise in self-centered sanctimoniousness on the celebrated occasion when, after warning his voluble daughter Luci that "her daddy might go down in history as the man who started World War III," he went praying with her and then back to the White House where, like McKinley before him, he slept soundly through the night.

Finley Peter Dunne did not live long enough to give himself and his audience the pleasure of enjoying LBJ at work twisting the arm of God, but the spectacle of McKinley's naïvely self-righteous cant prompted his Mr. Dooley to remark: "Me own idee is that war is not a matther iv prayers so much as a matther iv punchin'; an' th' on'y place a prayer book stops a bullet is in th' story books," and "I've heerd that th' Prisident is arrangin' a knee dhrill, with th' idee iv prayin' th' villyans to th' divvil."

Healthy though Mr. Dooley's ridicule was, America's venture in imperialism was no laughing matter, and it certainly did not make a laughingstock of America. On the contrary, the Spanish–American War qualified Washington overnight for acceptance not merely as a new force but as a major power. The other powers, far from resenting the upstart, were appropriately impressed when TR, now President, sent the Great White Fleet around the world. TR not only succeeded in staring down a resentful Congress (which opposed the trip at first), an alarmed Europe and a chauvinistic Japan, but his aggressive assertion of America's place in the world was also qualifying him to serve as peacemaker extraordinary. His mediation between Russia and Japan won him the Nobel Peace Prize in 1906. In the first glow of manly exploration, America was setting off on the grand tour. So long as the British Navy dominated world sea power, it was a harmless mission. But just because Britain's lines were already drawn thinner than her resources were deep, its very appearance of harmless redundance made it formidable.

The lurid origins of the Spanish–American War have distracted attention from the profound geopolitical consequences of the process which it set in motion around the world—understandably so, since horror headlines aimed to push sales of the yellow press have no necessary connection with the aims of national policy. The fact that Hearst did well out of the war has been taken to mean that it was a wrong war for America to fight. No doubt it was—in moral terms, like the Mexican War before it. But in power terms, America did well from this war too. Probably America would have done well in any case, but the fact remains that the way America did well at that particular time in history was through the Spanish War. And, thanks to it, America did very well indeed—particularly during the fateful years of drift toward world war which followed. By the Marxist standard of economic determinism, the Spanish–American War, reactionary and immoral though it was, served as thoroughly "progressive" a purpose as the Civil War itself—that is, in the Marxist sense of pushing capitalism into the higher stages which are supposed to precede its Götterdämmerung at the hands of the proletariat.

As the nineteenth century drew to a close, the new technology as well as the new politics and the new economics all combined to shrink the world. The Spanish–American War accelerated the process. Not only did the war supersede the political statics of the Monroe Doctrine with a new power-oriented activism. In addition, the political process which opened up the Southern Hemisphere in America to the power drives of the new capitalism simultaneously opened the Southern Hemisphere of Asia to them. By the middle of the twentieth century, the vision of a world united into one had become idealistic and forward-looking. But at the turn of the century, progress took the form of drawing together many worlds still insulated from one another. The strong and rich Western powers, along with Japan, armed with the new technology and with the capital it generated, reached out to penetrate and dominate the backward nations of Latin America, Africa and Asia. The very process which brought them together also drove them into conflict.

It was more than coincidence that the year of the Spanish–American War was the very year in which England, France and Germany intensified their historic race, sometimes competitively against one another and sometimes in cooperation with one another, to stake out spheres of influence in China and in Africa; that, moreover, in the same year Russia entered into the competition against all of them; and that, finally, also in the same year, Germany undertook its naval race against England. The Industrial Revolution had passed over into a capitalistic counterrevolution of its own: imperialism was in bloom all over the world. It had emerged as the movement of the time—in the democracies as well as in the autocracies, without regard to ideology or to the domestic commitment of each industrial power to social responsibility.

"One world" had become a fact of life by the middle of the

twentieth century, although it sometimes seemed that the peoples of the world had drawn closer together the better to fight one another. But no such idealistic internationalism had caught the popular imagination at the end of the nineteenth century. On the contrary, the nineteenth century from Waterloo onward was an age of nationalism which nevertheless had also been an age of peacekeeping, if not of pacifism, marred only by occasional conflicts which remained localized. Suddenly, history began to anticipate technology and the destructive political thrust which technology would soon make possible. (In 1905, Einstein's formulation of the Special Theory of Relativity made its own contribution to the process which would produce the nuclear weapons and the politics of midcentury.) The new imperialism was able to annihilate space and compress time, and, thereby, to break down the rigidity of colonial customs. The explosion which sent the *Maine* to the bottom of Havana harbor really was a "shot heard 'round the world." For, to anticipate the jargon of the atomic age, it triggered a violent chain reaction throughout the entire political atmosphere.

The contemporary nuclear race was prefigured sixty years ago by the contest for sea power. The great fleets of the European states continued for years to serve as mutual deterrents. It was the peripheral sea powers which exchanged shots. The first major naval confrontations since the time of Nelson took place successively in the Caribbean, the Philippine sea, off the shores of the African land mass, and back again in the South China Sea and the Sea of Japan. Only in 1914 did the heavyweight contenders move into the ring.

The progressive buildup of imperialism put a new premium on British sea power. The world was changing at what then seemed a whirlwind rate; and the more it changed, the more Britain came under pressure to hold the line against change. Cast in a conservative role, with more to lose from changes in the status quo than any other power, Britain unwittingly took the initiative in upsetting the balance of power more abruptly and more decisively than the imperialistic ferment was upsetting it anyway. Worried because the compression of the world had stretched her lines of defense, she freed herself to concentrate her strength against the new German naval challenge in Europe and to flank the old Russian challenge along the trade routes to Asia by entering into a naval alliance with Japan. Moreover, her former satellite, Spain, had been eliminated as a force in Asiatic waters by America's assertion of muscle.

The naval alliance Britain made with Japan twelve years before World War I reflected a decision on her part to assign number-one priority to Europe and a subordinate role to Asia. Beyond the immediate strategic significance of that decision, it also became a contributing cause to World War II. For, when Britain determined that her prime sphere of influence lay in Europe, she invited Japan to find her equivalent sphere of influence in Asia. Moreover, she set the pattern of priorities which was recognized again in World War II: even though that was truly a two-front war, it was fought by the Anglo–American alliance primarily as a European war and only secondarily as an Asiatic war. In 1902, America was still a spectator, although a rambunctious and articulate one. But the consequences of Britain's agonizing appraisal, which freed her to face west during the two World Wars, ended by costing Britain her empire and, then, by costing America her options. Once Britain admitted her inability to police both oceans at once, it became only a matter of time before America had to fight on both oceans at once.

After World War II, America came to stand in Britain's shoes. As she fought in Korea and Vietnam, while still committed to maintaining her power position in Europe, she began to learn at first hand what a study of British history between the Boer War and World War I might have taught her. But between Britain's overextension early in the century and America's in the second half of the century, there was one fundamental difference. Britain had been able to look to America to play a supporting role in relief of her depleted power. America, however, had no strong new ally on the make to fall back on.

The imperialist dramas at the turn of the century were slow to change America's direct participation in world power arrangements, but they were quick to change her world standing and political role. Whereas the big civil war America suffered in the middle of the nineteenth century had earned the support and admiration of progressives and even of radicals in Europe, the mischievous little war she started at the turn of the century provoked the denunciation of moderates and earned her the labels "reactionary" and "imperialist." In the progressive war of the midcentury, American idealism fell victim to aggression. In the reactionary war that saw the century out, American cynicism practiced it.

The swift coups by which emergent American imperialism dethroned the two encrusted oligarchic empires that stood in its way also prophesied the political finance of the coming century. Both Spain and the American South had institutionalized an ancient commitment to treasure as the hard core of power. Before slave labor picked cotton on American plantations, it dug silver and gold in Spanish mines. Spain's predatory colonialism had taken form as an exercise in metallic imperialism. Its mercantilist preoccupation with stripping gold and silver from its colonies had blinded it to the industrial possibilities of raw material development and to the commercial potential of export trade. In her primitive and predatory rapacity, Spain never tried to prove Lenin's latter-day charge that the spoils of imperialism spread the wealth in the mother country in order to purchase the allegiance of the leaders of the industrial proletariat. She had no industry and no proletariat, and she made no effort to push beyond feudalism. When defeat drove the Spanish Empire back on its undeveloped and poverty-ridden continental base, the ghost of the old metallic imperialism faded from relevant history into historical romance.

The disintegration of the Spanish Empire marked the beginning of Europe's transition from the silver to the gold standard. Thereafter, as now, gold became a status symbol for nations seeking financial respectability; and Britain, the first modern nation rich enough to afford a gold standard, set the financial fashion. The substitution of gold for silver facilitated the concentration of banking reserves which made the central control of the money system possible. Thus, the changeover to gold was a prerequisite for monetary modernization in that period.

The two great regimes which were left on the silver standard were India and China. Their continued adherence to silver paralleled their isolation from the unifying and modernizing forces at work in the world. It took the Communist victory in 1949 to free China from the century-long influence of "silver bullets"—the silver coins which had bought and sold the armies of the warlords and had represented the Middle Kingdom's collapse into corruption and anarchy. India, right through the twentieth century, continued to pay a price in blood for the anachronistic use of silver as a store of wealth. The failure of the Indian government to mobilize the vast amounts of privately hoarded silver provided the measure of its failure at the fundamental job of feeding its people, let alone at the far more difficult task of promoting economic development. Only in post-Civil-War America did silver become the symbol of progressive social forces. Its monetization was advocated as an inflationary addition to the money supply: coining silver was conceived of as the equivalent of printing greenbacks. The silver standard had no connotations of financial feudalism in America.

American imperialism became a force by destroying the last of the pre-capitalist colonial empires. The new imperialism, based on industrialization and reflecting the energy of triumphant capitalism, had liquidated the old. The prophets and apologists of the new imperialism, such as William Graham Sumner, were not alone in recognizing the contrast. Lenin, while still an obscure leader of a splinter of the Russian Marxist movement, undertook to provide a revolutionary counter to the new worldwide force of imperialism.

Marx had attempted to demonstrate capitalism's ultimate vulnerability within a domestic framework. As capitalism had become international during the nineteenth century, so Lenin at the start of the twentieth century internationalized Marx's analysis of it. He termed imperialism "the last stage of capitalism": it allowed the bourgeoisie to put off the day of reckoning with the revolutionary proletariat and, as well, provided a new mechanism for capitalism's final catastrophe. Lenin accepted the view that imperialism was in the short-term interest of the imperialists, for the wealth expropriated from colonies could be used to buy off the top stratum of the working class. With the same grasp of the realities of power which would win him the dictatorship of the Soviet proletariat, Lenin saw that the wages of imperialism were wars among the imperialists. Capitalism had to go imperialist, and imperialism had to go to war: such was Lenin's law.

As the basis for pragmatic action, Lenin's development of Marxism was more than adequate. For the capitalist powers had in fact gone imperialist, and imperialist rivalries were in fact about to culminate in world war. And war, Lenin saw, gave revolutionaries their opportunity—as France's collapse in 1871 and Russia's in 1905 had done. With tireless repetition he pounded at his thesis: revolutionaries have no incentive to support their governments in time of war because victory in modern war makes revolution impossible, but defeat makes it inescapable.

Lenin suffered from Marx's propensity to transform an insight about the workings of the system into an immutable law of history. As dogma, Lenin's theory of imperialism suffered from the misconception which Norman Angell had clarified: speculations in imperialism in the real world cost the imperialist powers more than they earned. But the trouble with imperialism went deeper than mere cost accounting, for the political scope of imperialism was inflated out of proportion to its economic scale. Because its whole conception was uneconomic to begin with, it could not be made to pay. Economic growth in the imperialist countries had inflated the scale on which external power could be meaningful well beyond the capacity of modern colonies to produce it. The politics of imperialism was for those who could afford it, and only for as long as they could. No one could afford the economics of imperialism, and no one could win its wars. By definition, any country big enough to bear the burden had to have an economy so big that the necessarily small returns from imperialism would not matter.

This was the real answer to Lenin's indictment, just as it was the answer—sixty years later—to the simplistic rationalization that America's military spending to back up her global commitments was necessary for her economic prosperity.

10 : BISMARCK'S BREAKTHROUGH

AMERICA'S DEEPENING involvement in Vietnam dramatized once again, as all twentieth-century wars have done, the potential conflict between guns and butter. The "butter" programs of Johnson's Great Society Presidency could not be turned off when he moved to his War Presidency—any more than the new drives toward social progress could have been put back on the shelf during Franklin Roosevelt's War Presidency, when "Dr. Win-the-War" replaced "Dr. New Deal." By the 1960's, it was clear that war was no substitute for reform, and that the pursuit of national security was no substitute for progress toward social security. Before the relationship of welfare and warfare became clear in America, it had had a long and illuminating history in Europe.

America's turn-of-the-century adventures in imperialism had set the stage for her entry into global power politics, and her declaration of war against Germany in 1917 formalized her participation. It was a truism at the time that our intervention in what had begun as a European war raised the threat of infection by dangerous ideas and crippling custom. Isolationism died hard as a moral and idealistic force: the burden was on internationalists to prove that isolationism was not the indispensable prerequisite for the maintenance of democracy and freedom. Idealism, no doubt, was as much the instrument as the inspiration of those who succeeded in reasserting America's political isolation from Europe after World War I. But, in an ironic way, the fears of the idealists seemed to justify isolation.

First, the international economic collapse of 1929–32 and, then, Hitler's seizure of power in Europe was taken as arguing for isolationism in strategic as well as in economic terms. But no matter how resolutely America set out to isolate herself from Europe's problems, she could not and did not isolate herself from European ideas, European political thinking and European experiments with social reform. Our first international war endowed us with an international heritage. While America had been enjoying a century of exceptionalism, Europe had been devising solutions for its own problems, which were soon to be America's problems. One solution was the welfare state.

As with all major social change, no single individual can be identified as solely responsible. But the time, the place and the daring innovator came together in Germany in the 1870's. Bismarck was the man. His goal was the establishment of a German nation-state, and he understood that the internal and external conditions for its existence were interdependent and equally indispensable. He saw that the rise of the modern nation-state was creating new demands on it for social responsibility, and that the parallel rise of industrialism was creating a crisis of social stability. He resolved to use each of these problems to solve the other. Only a Germany with domestic social cohesion could maintain itself internationally. Only a Germany whose international goals were limited, and therefore attainable, could enjoy social peace. Thus, Bismarck resisted imperialist adventures and invented social insurance.

The German nation-state was created as the Industrial Revolution was transforming European social relations. Bismarck faced not only regional differences and foreign suspicion, but domestic class conflict as well. Bismarck and Marx, it is worth remembering, were born only three years apart: the rise of an industrial proletariat with distinctive interests and concrete demands was as evident to the leader of the establishment as it was to the prophet of the revolution.

Bismarck was not the only conservative statesman to recognize the challenge to conservatism which industrialization presented. In Britain, Disraeli sought to frustrate both radicals and revolutionaries by providing conservatism with a mass base. Even before the revolutionary year of 1848, Disraeli had definitely identified the political challenge for his generation of European statesmen. He did so in his guise of political novelist. The following passage from *Sybil* added a new phrase to the English language:

" 'Well society may be in its infancy,' said Egremont [the noble hero] slightly smiling; 'but, say what you will, our Queen reigns over the greatest nation that ever existed.'

" 'Which nation?' asked the younger stranger, 'for she reigns over two.' The stranger paused; Egremont was silent but looked inquiringly.

" 'Yes,' resumed the younger stranger after a moment's interval. 'Two nations between whom there is no intercourse and no sympathy; who are as ignorant of each other's habits, thoughts, and feelings, as if they were dwellers in different zones or inhabitants of different planets; who are formed by a different breeding, are fed by a different food, are ordered by different manners, and are not governed by the same laws.'

" 'You speak of—' said Egremont hesitatingly.

" 'The rich and the poor.' "

Both Bismarck and Disraeli began by extending the suffrage to include the top layer of the working class. As Robert Blake remarks in his biography of Disraeli, the workers "were no use as allies if they had no votes." Disraeli, intoxicated as ever with his own magic, almost blundered into an excess of enthusiasm for his own expedient. In his maneuvering for the Reform Bill of 1867, which tied voting to qualifications, he went so far as to toy with an amendment calculated to give two votes to anyone combining certain qualifications. But Disraeli's technique for winning the support of the new electorate was to provide them with imperialist circuses. Bismarck chose to provide bread.

"Of course," A. J. P. Taylor noted in his biography of Bismarck, "Bismarck did not promote social reform out of love for the German workers. Sympathy and affection had never been his strong points. His object was to make the workers less discontented or, to use a harsher phrase, more subservient." As Bismarck put it himself: "Whoever has a pension for his old age is far more content and far easier to handle than one who has no such prospect." Bismarck revolutionized the operations of government at home in order to maintain the status quo in the underlying power relationships. Internationally, by contrast, Bismarck exercised moderation in order to achieve a fundamental transformation of power relations: the rise of the German Empire to primacy on the European continent.

Bismarck limited his exercises in militarism to starting local wars he knew he could win quickly and cheaply. Within ten years, he fought three short, limited and successful wars—against Denmark, Austria and France. By 1871, he had achieved his positive aim. Thereafter, his foreign policy was dedicated to the negative purpose of not dissipating the gains he had so shrewdly consolidated. The spectacle of France writhing in revolution after her defeat in 1871 impressed the mature Bismarck as profoundly as it later did the young Lenin. Bismarck, therefore, cast a cold eye on Germany's emergent imperial interests. "He had an occasional tiff with the British over Zanzibar," writes Taylor, "just to keep his hand in, but usually he spoke of colonies with his old contempt. Germany had acquired a vast African empire which Bismarck did nothing to develop. Indeed, in 1889, he tried to give German South-West Africa away to the British. It was, he said, a burden and an expense, and he would like to saddle someone else with it." If Bismarck anticipated Lenin in his understanding of the wages of war for the defeated, he also anticipated Angell in his understanding of the wages of imperialism for the successful.

The purpose of Bismarck's social policy had been to stabilize and cement the foundation underlying first the Prussian state and then the German Empire. He was careful never to push the bread-and-butter alliance he had forged with the working class too far by burdening it with the strains of total war. The young Kaiser Wilhelm II thought he knew better and, in 1890, dismissed Bismarck as Chancellor. Twenty-five years later, Germany faced the very crisis Bismarck had feared. The testimonial to Bismarck's national achievement came in 1914, when the Social Democrats overwhelmingly joined the moderates and conservatives in voting for the credits to finance the war. The testimonial to Bismarck's social foresight came in 1918, when defeat of the German armies in the field was matched by revolution behind the lines. The empire which Bismarck put together fell apart before a single Allied soldier set foot on German soil.

Bismarck created the welfare state. The man who translated the concept into English was David Lloyd George. Lloyd George was not himself unconscious of the link between his own program and Bismarck's social legislation. In 1937, in the twilight of his career, he told C. P. Snow that he had picked up his first administrative ideas in Prussia. But Lloyd George's creative improvisations were responses to specifically British conditions, as Bismarck's had been to specifically German ones.

Britain's historic ability to avoid revolution has for centuries been critically dependent upon the achievement of moderate reform before agitation boiled up into insurrection. The gradual extension of the franchise throughout the nineteenth and early twentieth centuries reflected the realism of the upper crust as much as the ferment among the lower orders. Die-hard reactionaries and dewy-eyed reformers both believed that real political and economic power would follow the ballot. Disraeli knew better. In the century since his Reform Bill of 1867, Britain has fallen from world leadership status to being the sick man of Europe, has fought two World Wars, and has been a leader in developing the welfare state. During these same hundred years, the Conservative Party has kept effective political control for more than seventy years. And Labour's interludes in office have done more for conservatism than conservatism has dared do for itself.

Throughout the nineteenth century, reform ventured no further than to offer a political voice to those who already had gained an economic stake in the existing social system. By the turn of the century, however, class privilege and economic inequality came under direct and widespread attack. In 1900, the imperialist appeal of the Boer War was still potent enough to win a sweeping victory for the Tories. But, as early as the 1870's, Joseph Chamberlain—already the radical leader of Birmingham but not yet the prophet of imperialism—had warned that property would have "to pay ransom" in order to retain its privilege. In the decade before World War I, the bill came due.

By the turn of the century, Lloyd George had succeeded Chamberlain as the radical leader of the left wing of the Liberal Party. His program of reform—taxation of land, national insurance, recognition of trade unions—reflected an inherited radical concern for social justice as well as a practical recognition of the competitive threat posed by the fast-growing labor movement. But in 1906, British labor still represented only an interest group, not yet an alternative government. The alternative to Lloyd George's radical social reform was the imperialist "tariff reform" program of Joseph Chamberlain, by then converted into the firebrand of the Tories. The great Liberal victory of 1906 was primarily an emotional endorsement of the free-trade policy, which had, in the popular mind, made Britain great. But it was also an invitation to Lloyd George.

The establishment which ruled England before World War I was bipartisan: Liberals could be as staunch in opposition to radicalism, let alone to socialism, as could Conservatives. The establishment's characteristically shrewd method of dealing with Lloyd George was to make him Chancellor of the Exchequer: the aim was to make the prophet of reform bear the onus of having to finance it. Lloyd George's response was a masterstroke. He shifted the subject at issue from the price of social reform to the principle of democratic responsibility by focusing the spotlight on the hereditary House of Lords. He invited the Lords to veto the will of the people's representatives.

On April 29, 1909, Lloyd George introduced his "People's Budget" with the words: "This is a War Budget. It is for raising money to wage implacable warfare against poverty and squalidness." Lloyd George's precedent-setting declaration of war on poverty was doomed to frustration. Anticipating the pattern of America's Democratic reform Presidents, from Wilson through Johnson, the Liberal reform government which Lloyd George dominated was superseded by the Liberal war government in 1914. In the short run, however, Lloyd George turned the tables on the establishment by the arrogation of domestic war-making powers. Once the overwhelming Tory majority in the Lords blundered into Lloyd George's trap, the conflict could have only one outcome. The realities of power were reestablished by the Parliament Act of 1911, which effectively stripped the House of Lords of its anachronistic pretensions.

The passage-at-arms of 1910–11 was a triumph for Lloyd George. But it demonstrated his ability to handle power more conclusively than it demonstrated his commitment to social reform. The National Insurance Act of 1911, although taken as revolutionary by the Right, seemed little more than tokenism to the Left. Unlike Bismarck, Lloyd George had not succeeded in cementing an alliance with the upper levels of the working class. All that he had done—and it was an impressive achievement—was to spring the trap which the establishment had prepared for him. The base from which he launched his personal bid for administrative power was the Treasury, which had been intended to be his prison. But Lloyd George's lack of a base broad enough to suit the times foredoomed his bid for the leadership of a Radical–Labor alliance outside Parliament and the machinery of government.

Lloyd George was the first political leader of modern times with a mass appeal who was able to make the machinery of government do double duty as his electioneering organization. World War I gave him his chance. The Prime Minister, Asquith, was an old school-tie Liberal and an heir of Gladstone with a built-in bias against government intervention in the economy. He also, as Lloyd George remarked to C. P. Snow some twenty years later, "hated war." A government attempting to wage total war on the principles of laissez-faire was bound to be a target for those intent on winning the war at any cost, including the cost of abandoning their own laissez-faire principles.

It was only a matter of time before drift and deadlock made clear the dependence of the establishment on the supposedly captive custodian of the purse. Before the war, the establishment had put Lloyd George into the Treasury to tone down his radical promises to the masses and to keep him busy raising money instead of manipulating the administrative levers of government. In the midst of the war, the establishment put him at the head of the nation because only he could inflame the masses and, at the same time, galvanize government into "war socialism." The requirements of militarism were met by the techniques of radicalism. Asquith's government fell in December, 1916, and Lloyd George became Prime Minister of a coalition government in which his main support came from "win-the-war" Conservatives. Lloyd George's prewar attempt to develop a new political base for himself had failed. Now, in climbing to the top of what Disraeli called "the greasy pole," he destroyed the old power base that he might have been able to make his own. For the Liberal Party split down the middle with half its Parliamentary representation staying loyal to Asquith. The split was fatal.

Lloyd George was made Prime Minister to win the war, and win it he did. The "Coupon Election" of 1918 was a triumph for bloody-shirt demagoguery: "Hang the Kaiser" was the war cry. But it was a tragedy for Lloyd George. He retained power at the sole discretion of the Tories, who had the votes in Parliament to form their own government whenever they decided that the emergency was over and that the time was ripe to be rid of the Pied Piper. Meanwhile, having won the war for the nation, Lloyd George was tolerated in power in order to win the peace for the establishment. Thus, the British establishment demonstrated once again its ability to absorb even the most provocative of its challengers and to employ the talents of even the most vociferous of its critics.

Labor's new postwar militancy had begun with a record outbreak of industrial unrest before the war, had intensified and spread throughout the war years, and had become formalized in the new Socialist constitution of the Labor party in 1918. The outbreak of peace was the signal for a showdown between the government and labor, which demanded delivery on the wartime promise of "homes fit for heroes" and the rest of Lloyd George's package of slogans. Labor, with its membership doubled and aglow with a new Socialist faith, set out to see whether the peace had been worth fighting for. More important still, it was temporarily freed from the inhibiting presence of its moderate Parliamentary leaders who had been crushed in the 1918 election because of their pacifist sentiments. Lloyd George met the challenge with demagoguery and distractions; he played a waiting game until the concentrated militancy of the war years had been dissipated. By 1922, it was all over; and, as soon as it was, so was Lloyd George's tenure in power. The Tories dismissed him as coldly as Wilhelm II had dismissed Bismarck.

In the British context, the primitive welfare state which Lloyd George had promoted was not sufficient to divert labor from its drive for independent power. But it unquestionably moderated the terms of the social conflict and helped keep potentially revolutionary drives within the confines of Parliamentary politics. World War I sped up the revolution in expectations which accompanied the Industrial Revolution and which took political form as an increasingly militant demand for social reform. Bismarck's breakthrough had been to weld the internal divisions of the nation-state by making it a welfare state as well. Defeat in World War I destroyed his work: the bankrupt Weimar Republic could not pay the continuing price of social solidarity. When Hitler picked up the pieces, the only way he could put them together again was by selling his brand of nationalism as socialism. In Britain, where Lloyd George's breakthrough followed Bismarck's and paralleled it, the historic pattern remained essentially the same. The pressure for victory gave labor bargaining power, political as well as industrial, on a hitherto unknown scale. If one lesson of modern history is that revolution is the price of defeat in total war, another is that reform is the price of victory. If revolution is the retribution a society exacts from an elite which exposes it to defeat, reform is the dividend society demands on its investment in victory. The refusal by a victorious elite to pay society's price opens the way for internal conflict to take over from external conflict. Worse still, the failure of a war economy to promise plenty while producing victory is a guarantee of defeat.

Britain's failure to pay the price that her people had earned in World War I dammed up social progress and cooperation during twenty years of bitterness and class antagonism. Only the pressures of World War II brought Britain's welfare state to its highest development. Lloyd George's heritage was transmitted by Ernest Bevin, the founder of Britain's largest union (the Transport Workers), who was to become Foreign Secretary during the Cold War. Bevin had witnessed both the promises with which Lloyd George had wooed labor during World War I and the way he had avoided keeping them after the war. He had a long memory. As the strong man of the labor movement and wartime Minister of Labor in World War II, Bevin saw to it that history would not repeat itself. The full-fledged welfare state which emerged from World War II was the final fulfillment of the bargain which Lloyd George had offered a generation before.

Bismarck's invention of the welfare state and Lloyd George's adaptation of it had each in turn provided the domestic prerequisite for giving those in power the freedom they needed to act internationally. Bismarck had, in fact, planned it that way. Lloyd George, characteristically, reached the same result by improvisation. In each case, the economics of welfare ended by being sacrificed to the politics of World War I. Among all the belligerents, the demands of war produced promises of postwar reform—promises which the defeated could not, and the victors would not, keep. In America, where social reform had not yet matured to the point reached in Europe, the pattern was the same. The contrast with the social consequences of World War II was complete.

Woodrow Wilson shared several crucial characteristics with

Lloyd George. Each came from a personal and geographic base outside the central political power structure: Lloyd George was a Welshman from the declining rural community; Wilson was a displaced Southern intellectual turned New Jersey academic. Each aroused hatreds and commanded loyalties far beyond the ordinary run of political relationships. Each reached power as the leader of a radical reform movement and each found himself heading a war machine more enormous than any other ever seen. But the essential difference between them was identified for all time by the young John Maynard Keynes, who recorded their confrontation at the Versailles Peace Conference.

"The first glance at the President," Keynes wrote in *The Economic Consequences of the Peace*, "suggested not only that, whatever else he might be, his temperament was not primarily that of the student or the scholar. . . . But more serious than this, he was not only insensitive to his surroundings in the external sense, he was not sensitive to his environment at all. What chance could such a man have against Mr. Lloyd George's unerring, almost medium-like, sensibility to every one immediately round him? To see the British Prime Minister watching the company, with six or seven senses not available to ordinary men, judging character, motive, and subconscious impulse, perceiving what each was thinking and even what each was going to say next, and compounding with telepathic instinct the argument or appeal best suited to the vanity, weakness, or self-interest of his immediate auditor, was to realize that the poor President would be playing blind man's buff in that party. Never could a man have stepped into the parlor a more perfect and predestined victim to the finished accomplishments of the Prime Minister. The Old World was tough in wickedness anyhow; the Old World's heart of stone might blunt the sharpest blade of the bravest knight-errant. But this blind and deaf Don Quixote was entering a cavern where the swift and glittering blade was in the hands of the adversary."

Lloyd George's masterful manipulations at Versailles were devoted, in Keynes's words, to "bamboozling" the President into accepting the "Carthaginian peace," notwithstanding the fact that

Wilson had made his international reputation by denouncing it in advance. But Lloyd George's success with Wilson had even more far-reaching implications than his contemporaneous success in bamboozling the British Labor movement. The role of sucker is not a sympathetic one: it is likely to produce what psychologists speak of as an "avoidance reaction" in the onlooker. There was in America's repudiation of Wilson and plunge back into isolationism in 1920 not only resentment directed against European "slickers," but also the mean, if human, desire to dissociate herself from a loser—a loser, moreover, who had let himself be euchred out of the prerogatives he had won.

Wilson's tragedy had its own aura of meanness. The attempt to conceal his disability from the public, and the greed with which those around him hung onto power in the last year of his Presidency, seemed better suited to a tyrant's court than to the American democratic process. The result was to discredit not only Wilson's own idealism, but idealism in general. The Golden Age of the twenties carried echoes of the decade that followed the Civil War, and a retreat from social responsibility was one of the major themes reprised.

As in Britain, the promises of social reform to make the war worth fighting, at least in retrospect, were swiftly forgotten. And the excesses of reaction which began before Harding's election formalized the defeat of "The New Freedom" at the hands of "Normalcy." It was A. Mitchell Palmer, Wilson's Attorney General, who set off a "Red scare" in 1919 that far outdid the McCarthy era's disregard for the decencies of conduct, let alone the sanctity of the constitutional process. It was in 1919, too, that the great steel strike was crushed; the failure began the reversal of the gains in terms both of wages and benefits and of union recognition that the needs of war had forced. In the 1920's, union-busting superseded the trust-busting of the prewar era.

Only after the Great Depression had shaken American society for three disastrous years did Washington finally turn toward the concept of the welfare state—and then with a profoundly nationalistic commitment to save America first. Only when economic catastrophe threatened to replace social mobility with class conflict—for the first time in American history—did America appreciate the pragmatic good sense and visionary foresight of Bismarck and Lloyd George. In the next generation, the challenge to speed social reform in order to head off social conflict would once more appear when America finally undertook to make good on the promise of the Emancipation Proclamation.

Even in the 1960's, and especially as social reform once again was in danger of being sacrificed to war, the lesson of Bismarck and Lloyd George remained relevant. In the 1920's, Germany's unemployed veterans of World War I had become Hitler's Storm Troopers, and Britain's disillusioned Tommies had made their last attempt at sharing in the promised rewards of peace in the General Strike of 1926. In the 1960's, when violence racked America's cities at the height of the Vietnam War, Washington was put on notice that the cost of deferring reform would not wait until peace came. Certainly, the men from the North and the South who had been drafted to make Asia safe for the ideals of the West were not likely to accept the terms of the *status quo ante* on their return. The ghosts of Bismarck and Lloyd George stood smiling in attendance as Lyndon Johnson fought to preserve a place for his Great Society in the Vietnam War.

11: WARBURG'S AMERICANIZATION

THE NUMBER-ONE political issue in America as Europe prepared to plunge into World War I was the establishment of the Federal Reserve System. America's Industrial Revolution spanned three-quarters of the century from the Mexican War to World War I, and it took place without benefit of a central bank or a centralized, manageable money system. By comparison with Europe, America's backwardness in the structure of her monetary system paralleled her backwardness in social reform. The New Freedom of Woodrow Wilson managed to make good the first deficiency, even while it fell short of its more specific dedication to making good the second.

In many ways, the fight to modernize the domestic American banking system during the years leading up to World War I provided a preview of the later fight to modernize the world banking system, which started after World War II and came to a head along with the Vietnam crisis. The objectives were the same—only the frames of reference were different. In each case, the idea was to create credit reserves tied to business activity, and to give these new credit instruments the elasticity needed to finance continuity in the flow of goods. Gold would continue to serve as a credit base but the credit base would no longer be limited to gold. The commercial system would, therefore, outgrow its age-old susceptibility to periodic liquidity drought: gold would cease to be the cyclical commercial equivalent of peasant hoardings and its periodic flights would no longer demonetize the channels of trade. The purpose of modernization—not only on the domestic scene before World War I but also internationally after World War II—was to insure the industrial mechanism against stoppages by providing a flow of liquidity as elastic as the operations of the economy and unaffected by the whims of gold owners.

America's domestic difficulties in the monetary area since the adoption of the Federal Reserve System in 1913, like the difficulties its monetary operations have periodically made for Europe, have arisen from the management of the system, not from its structure and mechanism. Institutionally, these difficulties have developed as the result of the inherent resistance of our economic society to managerial regulation by monetary controls. The crescendo of debate since 1945 over the creation of a modern international counterpart for the Federal Reserve principle gives more than historical relevance to the premises and purposes of America's original banking reform in 1913. In each fight—for domestic reform before 1913, for international reform after 1945 and particularly after the dollar troubles of the mid-1960's—the requirements of war finance intruded upon the requirements of reserve banking.

Despite America's entry into the imperialist race at the turn of the century, the center of gravity of American affairs remained domestic from the Spanish–American War until World War I. As late as 1912, Woodrow Wilson was elected on a platform promising domestic social reform. Even Pershing's chase into Mexico after Pancho Villa in 1916 was just a sideshow for Woodrow Wilson's New Freedom. The New Freedom was formally concerned with international relations in the economic sphere—because Wilson's Administration, like all Democratic administrations, pursued a tariff-cutting policy. But the political appeal of the ethics of tariff reduction was directed less to foreign competitors than to domestic consumers, to whom it promised the benefits of lower living costs. Democratic advocacy of lower tariffs, lower living costs and lower interest rates was all of a piece, and it invited a standard Republican riposte in the direction of higher tariffs, higher interest rates and high income scales which offered a more direct pocketbook appeal to labor than did the party of easy money. The substantial following enjoyed by the Republicans among labor groups attests to the failure of the easy money forces to win broad labor support.

For decades, the political cycle of Republican tariff increases and Democratic tariff cuts had paralleled the swings of the economic cycle. The Republican claim to be the party of prosperity had assumed protectionism and, of course, a tightening of hard money. The Democratic claim to be the party of reform had assumed freer trade and an easing of paper money. The Wilson Administration, however, promised a more comprehensive attack on the entrenched abuses of privilege, and, from the moment it took over, no one could deny that it began to live up to its word. The Clayton Anti-Trust Act, forbidding corporations to engage in the common European practice of buying the stock of competitors, was passed in October, 1914. The Supreme Court upheld the constitutionality of the income tax in January, 1916. The Federal Trade Commission Act—the crowning achievement of the New Freedom in its drive to regulate business and to protect the little man—was passed in the same year. Reform made progress as if it had rendezvous with war.

Although America had instigated the Spanish–American War, she remained remote and preoccupied with her own domestic problems while Europe was traveling the road from imperialism toward world war. In Europe, the forces of the left were the most articulate internationalists; but their American counterparts concentrated instead on old problems and new business close to home—above all, on the drive to restrict immigration. Moreover, American reform politics was winning politics only so long as it remained bread-and-butter politics close to home. But when war came to Europe, pressures from across the Atlantic intervened in the American political contest before America intervened in the European political conflict. When American intervention came, the makers of European strategy were not surprised, but the practitioners of American reform politics were.

The Democrats approached office in 1912 confident in their philosophy that tariff reform would ameliorate international tensions. To their surprise, however, Wilson's distinctive achievement when he settled down to govern lay in the domestic area of banking reform. In fact, the one structural reform of the New Freedom destined to find a timely and central war role and to emerge from the war in an institutionalized position was the Federal Reserve System.

If any episode in American history illustrates America's propensity to import ideas from Europe, the adoption of the principle which was to become embodied in the Federal Reserve System certainly does. A generation later, in the troubled years leading up to World War II, Franklin Roosevelt found his New Deal deficits subjected to withering criticism from Virginia's Senator Carter Glass, who, then nearing the end of his career, had come to personify the spirit of conservatism. But at the height of the New Freedom, before our entry into World War I, the same Carter Glass, as Chairman of the House Banking and Currency Committee, had crusaded for a system of financial reform calculated to make the banking system workable in periods of stress when, historically, temporary spasms of illiquidity had become indistinguishable from insolvency. So provocative had Glass been to the Republican right that its leader, Senator Nelson Aldrich, had denounced the original bill he sponsored in the House on the grounds that (as Aldrich put it with characteristic force) "it appeals to the Populists [by] adopting their plan of note issues; to the socialists by seeking to place the management of the most important private business of the country in the hands of the government; it seeks the support of bankers in great centers by its unexpected discrimination in their favor . . . it threatens to upset business and to produce the evil results which it was projected to cure."

But, while Glass and Aldrich debated the politics of a modern American reserve banking system, the most effective and

sophisticated crusader in its behalf was Paul M. Warburg, the
Hamburg-born banker who had migrated to this country in 1902
to become a partner of Kuhn, Loeb & Co. More than any other
single participant in the great debate of that day, he is entitled
to be regarded as the father of the Federal Reserve System. To
Wilson's credit, he appointed Warburg a charter member of the
Board, despite deep-seated traditional political opposition to
bankers of any origin, and especially to international Jewish
bankers. (In 1913, not anticipating the war, neither Wilson nor
the antibanker group pressuring him from the left suspected that
more provocative than either Warburg's profession or his Jewish-
ness might be his German origins and affiliations.) Warburg's
subsequent account of his approach to the assignment leaves no
doubt of his own concern over the charge that he might be trying
to foist a version of European central banking disciplines upon
America's decentralized and essentially undisciplined new frontier. In fact, when he showed his initial memorandum to his
partner, Jacob H. Schiff, he encountered the most violent resistance and found himself sworn to an almost conspiratorial degree
of silence. "Mr. Schiff read the paper with interest," Warburg
recalls, "and . . . while theoretically he agreed with most of the
thoughts expressed . . . he warned me to be careful not to have
the memorandum go any further, lest, having just arrived from
Europe, I might impair my standing in the banking community
by creating the impression that I was urging a system which, in
the final analysis, would have to be built around a central banking organization."

Stand-patism was, of course, the principal source of resistance to banking modernization. Warburg described its smugness
and its susceptibility to panic in telling of an encounter in 1903
with James A. Stillman, President of the National City Bank of
New York. "Why not leave things alone?" Stillman had asked.
"It was not without hesitation," Warburg reminisced, "that I
replied, 'Your bank is so big and so powerful, Mr. Stillman, that,
when the next panic comes, you will wish your responsibilities
were smaller.' At this," Warburg continued, "Mr. Stillman told
me that I was entirely wrong, that I had the mistaken notion

that Europe's banking methods were the most advanced, while, as a matter of fact, American methods represented an improvement upon, and an evolution of, the European system, America having already discarded its central bank. He had no doubt that progress would have to be sought, not by copying European methods, but by elaborating our own.

"Four years later," Warburg concluded, "in the midst of the panic, I found Mr. Stillman once more standing over my desk; and when I looked up, he asked, 'Warburg, where is your paper?'

"I said to him, 'Too late now, Mr. Stillman. What has to be done cannot be done in a hurry. If reform is to be secured, it will take years of educational work to bring it about.'" By that time, as Warburg said, "although we had no war scare, [and] the country was full of gold in 1907, . . . rates of 50 to 100 per cent could not bring money, because our system—or rather our lack of system—had killed our confidence in our own credit."

In fact, the entire period from the Panic of 1907 to the eve of World War I was needed to do the educational job; so that the Federal Reserve System was not only conceived in panic, but born to crisis. Warburg says of his own approach to the problem that he "was trained in the practices of a banking system which under varying forms had worked satisfactorily in almost every industrially advanced country, except the United States." Here, certainly, was impressive testimony to the impracticality of economic and monetary theorizing (then and subsequently) which is not careful to make allowance for the contrast between the traditional requirements of European economies and those of America's quite distinctive productive apparatus and financial structure. Warburg was quick to see the difference, explaining that "from the time of my arrival in America I felt impelled to urge the adoption of the fundamental principles upon which [Europe's] established and proven system was based, and by submitting several plans I tried to demonstrate the possibility of a practical adaptation of this system to American conditions."

The all-powerful legislative arbiter of financial disputes in those days was Senator Aldrich, the arch-protectionist, who was not only Carter Glass's opponent but John D. Rockefeller's brother-in-law. Warburg's missionary efforts soon brought him first into a confrontation and then into a working relationship with Aldrich. Aldrich's initial reaction to the suggested central reserve system was to confuse it with an American model of a European central bank of issue which would be, as he said, "in effect a central clearing house with very limited banking functions, under government control"; and therefore, he opposed the idea.

Aldrich's original stand stemmed directly from the classic Hamiltonian formula of "bond-secured currency." Historically, the difference between the conservatives and the radicals on the money issue had centered on the question of whether currency would be backed by deposits of government bonds or redeemable in gold (except, of course, when emergencies forced suspension). The concept of currency expanding and contracting elastically with the requirements of business activity, financing it and being secured by it, was altogether novel and alien. The even more extreme idea of deliberately managing the monetary system in order to damp down and iron out the fluctuations and excesses of the business cycle was barely envisioned, except in the writings of such missionaries as Professor Irving Fisher of Yale. Two full generations after astronomer-economist Simon Newcomb lowered his sights from the planets to people and identified a bond-secured currency as a monetized debt, even the staunchest of conservatives were not aware that the debt can be no safer than the currency, and the currency no sounder than the debt. Neither can be safe or sound so long as the banking system forces the economy to shift for itself instead of lubricating its machinery with orderly money flows.

Aldrich himself saw the light. The Senator, buttonholing Warburg after he had made an intensive on-the-spot study of how the European banking system really worked, told him: "I like your ideas. I have only one fault to find with them. . . . You are too timid about it. . . . You say we cannot have a central bank, and I say we can." Bankers are notorious for their bad judgments about politicians, and Jacob Schiff's sense of caution had led Warburg to underestimate the educational effect of panics spaced closely enough to make the fear of panic a constant. Both Schiff and Warburg had also underestimated the willingness of intelligent conservatives to compromise with accepted principle in order to save the system.

Once Warburg converted Aldrich from the neo-Hamiltonian position which advocated many national banks issuing bond-backed currency, rather than just one, the Republican party appeared to be in firm possession of the issue of banking reform. In fact, the Republicans had won the election of 1908 despite their vulnerability to blame, as the "in" party, for the Panic of 1907. Aldrich had done enough in the direction of banking reform to show that the Republican party was determined to free the country from the chronic fear of panic.

But the Taft Administration, having failed to perform legislatively or to maintain prosperity, was the loser in the Congressional election of 1912. Wilson was the beneficiary of the pocketbook issue, and, as he prepared to take office, he moved incisively to consolidate his advantage. By taking over the Republican position on banking reform, Wilson acted to seize a double advantage: first, he had a chance to show that he could translate promises into performance; second, he could turn the fact of his performance into a defense against the various "funny money" schemes agitated by William Jennings Bryan and the debtor-oriented factions within the loosely knit Democratic coalition. The conspicuous and effective way to implement this strategy was to draft the missionary who had converted Aldrich himself to the nonpartisan cause. This Wilson did, using the very able Henry Morgenthau, Sr., father of Franklin Roosevelt's Secretary of the Treasury, as his emissary.

The Woodrow Wilson who mediated the doctrinal and political disputes over the Banking Act which the country wanted in 1913, and who negotiated the working compromise between all of them, was a different man from the cold, aloof, scornful and uncompromising dogmatist of 1919 whose temper, pride and inflexibility provoked the traumatic Senate repudiation of his plan for the peace the world wanted. The bathetic contrast between the opening and closing performances of Wilson's Presi-

dential personality was so extreme as to seem unique. But the
dynamics of American politics tend to impose a cyclically recurring determinism on Presidential performance: Presidential personalities do not make Presidential politics but, on the contrary,
Presidential politics mold and remold Presidential personalities.

Thus, nearly fifty years after the Wilson tragedy, the disintegration of Johnson's Presidential personality from its brilliant
debut of 1964–5, in which he was unable to lose any fight on
Capitol Hill, into its bitter, paranoiac phase of 1967–8, in which
he seemed unable to win any fight there, reproduced the Wilsonian cycle in power terms. In policy terms, the swing of
Johnson's War Presidency away from his Reform Presidency
duplicated the experience of Franklin Roosevelt. Woodrow
Wilson had been there already. In the face of the deep-rooted
political determinism which changed Wilson's personality as it
changed his course, it is idle to speculate how different the course
of history might have been if the Wilson who guided the Federal
Reserve Act through a recalcitrant and divided Congress had
been the same Wilson who brought his plan for the League of
Nations home from the Peace Conference. The Wilson of 1913
was still fresh and flexible, ready to accept political compromise
as the catalyst of policy progress.

The Democratic convention of 1912 had adopted a platform
in the authentic tradition of Jacksonianism which denounced not
only the Aldrich plan but any scheme for a central bank. Radical
in posture, the platform was reactionary in calculation. It assumed that America, the only nineteenth-century participant in
the Industrial Revolution to grow and prosper without a central
banking system, could exercise the role of world leadership
thrust upon it (when England fell into crisis and London called
home its money) without improvising a banking system tailored
to its needs. From the moment Wilson took office, he left no
doubt of his sensitivity to the "do-nothing" record of the Democratic Congress in frustrating the program put forward by the
prior Republican administration; nor did he conceal his determination to free himself from the Jacksonian platform which the
Baltimore convention had embraced along with him.

Wilson took Bryan as his Secretary of State and sent for

Warburg as his legislative adviser on money—a flanking maneuver aimed simultaneously at both extremes which left him in firm control of the consensus in the center. The future Mr. Justice Brandeis was already in Wilson's close confidence; and, as Brandeis's biographer, Alpheus Mason, relates, "An apparently unbridgeable rift developed between more conservative advisors, headed by Representative Glass, and 'extremists,' headed by Secretary Bryan. They divided on the question: should the new system be controlled by the government or by the bankers? Bryan would never consent to any program which placed the money supply of the country under the thumb of Eastern financiers, and the loss of his powerful Midwestern support in Congress and in the nation would imperil Wilson politically. Glass, on the contrary, was adamant against subjecting 'the banking business of the country to political control.' Wilson's position was made even more difficult by warning signals from New York, that government tampering with the financial structure would produce a panic."

Under cover of the conflicting political slogans put forth by rival political factions, the fact quickly emerged that the spokesman of the reform establishment had carried into power the same intellectual preconceptions which had encumbered the conservative establishment in its loss of power. Senator Aldrich, until the day of his conversion to the cause of neo-European monetary modernism, had stood four-square on the principle of a rigid currency based on the bonded debt of the United States. Similarly, the opinion which Brandeis gave to Wilson as late as June, 1913, confused the morals of politics with the pragmatics of economics. Brandeis found legalistic grounds for urging the same anachronistic position on Wilson which Aldrich had originally urged on William Howard Taft: "The power to issue currency," Brandeis advised Wilson, "should be vested exclusively in government officials, even when the currency is issued against commercial paper. The American people will not be content to have the discretion necessarily involved vested in a Board composed wholly or in part of bankers; for their judgment may be biased by private interest or affiliation." Wilson, as adroitly as Franklin Roosevelt or Lyndon Johnson in their respective primes, proved himself flexible. He acted on Brandeis's political recommendation and on Warburg's financial recommendation.

Long before Lyndon Johnson conjured up the gimmick of a synthetic opinion consensus, the spectacle of Nelson Aldrich and Louis Brandeis in agreement showed that history in the raw sometimes anticipates the creations of political artistry. The normal presumption is that the middle way between conflicting extremes is, by definition, rational, moderate and constructive. But in the debate over the structure of the new banking system, the common ground taken jointly by Aldrich and Brandeis was legalistic, reactionary and impractical.

When Aldrich took his original stand on the right in favor of a currency based on the borrowing operations and the taxing power of the Treasury, and when Brandeis took the same stand on the left, their conservative-radical convergence expressed a shared American philosophy and experience. It also documented the characteristic American innocence of standard European operating practice. The European banking system had worked well enough to free excess liquidity for large-scale, sustained investment overseas, with America far and away the number-one beneficiary of its outflows. America's insulation from Europe's financial ways, therefore, reflected her more fundamental ignorance of how her own prodigious growth had been so largely financed.

Soon after Senator Aldrich approached the middle of the road from the right, Congressman Glass jumped across it from the left. Not too many years before, Aldrich had thundered against Glass as a scheming socialist and populist. Now Glass took over from Aldrich as the new spokesman of conservatism. It was not surprising when Glass, in his capacity as the House spokesman for the Wilson administration on money matters, denounced the know-nothingism typified by Bryan (who continued to meddle in petty banking reform politics, instead of turning his attention to the ominous tensions preceding Europe's explosion into war). But the spectacle of Glass attacking the flexible moderation of Warburg was news—especially after Warburg had made a convert of Aldrich.

These splits and feuds left no doubt how shaky the Wilson

coalition was, and how broad a spectrum it covered—even though Wilson scarcely commanded a consensus, having been elected as a minority President. Indeed, the instability of the Democratic coalition accounted for Wilson's decision to reach out for the expert who had influenced Aldrich. The standard defense against divisions within the "in" party is a counteroffensive to win allies among the "outs." Once Warburg won Aldrich over to his position, the smart move for Wilson was to join Warburg too; and in the end he did.

Wilson did not call Warburg in until other symptomatic rivalries and deep-seated divisions had shown how representative the issue of banking reform had become. Thus, Glass and Bryan were in agreement across the great ideological divide on the all-important issue of how the new banking system was to be structured, although they remained in violent disagreement on the fundamental question of what kind of money standard was to be adopted. On the question of banking system structure, Bryan as ever spun with reverse English under the impact of the hated money power. He was trapped in his own compulsive position as the ex officio opponent of anything and everything it advocated. Thus, because the "money trust" was all out for a central bank, he was for as many decentralized financial reserve points as the railroad system of the day had terminals. Glass, conservative and committed to gold though he was, nevertheless wound up on Bryan's side of the argument against centralization. He advocated local gold holdings, unaware that they are a standing invitation to hoarding, which demonetizes reserves into caches. So extreme was Glass's insistence on decentralization that his original proposal assumed that the only link between regional reserve banks would be not a new central bank but the Comptroller of the Currency (who, as critics were quick to point out, would then have enjoyed a greater concentration of personal power than any central bank board).

Although the radicals and the conservatives started out on opposite sides of the issue of paper versus gold, they wound up sharing the same position on the scarcely less controversial issue of the centralization of powers. Both groups of extremists agreed in their advocacy of a banking system compartmentalized into local pockets. But reform to achieve this end would have been no reform at all. No loosely knit association of local banking centers would have been equipped to meet even the peacetime pressures on it to function nationally, much less internationally: war would have brought chaos. Nevertheless, Glass was politician enough to rise above the restraints of modesty and claim credit for the contribution which the Federal Reserve Act made to financing and, therefore, to winning World War I.

By the time Glass published his memoirs of the period, he had been Secretary of the Treasury and was then in the Senate. He wrote: "If there was a trace of exaggeration in the estimate of that seasoned English economist who declared the federal reserve system 'worth to the commerce of America more than three Panama Canals,' nevertheless, it must be conceded that, in the crucial test of a world war, it was bound to be more indispensable to civilization than three times three Panama Canals. This merely means that I agree with the considered judgment of those eminent bankers of this and other lands who have said that the World War could not have been financed but for the Federal Reserve Act."

Even while the Federal Reserve was earning this accolade, its creator was being caught in the backlash of war hysteria. In the crisis of unpreparedness for the War Administration, the still unformed and untried Federal Reserve Board was in the midst of its first ordeal of emergency improvisation. It was a black day for America and her ideals when, on May 27, 1918, Paul Warburg wrote to President Wilson requesting that he not be considered for renomination to the Board on the expiration of his term.

"Certain persons," he wrote, "have started an agitation to the effect that a naturalized citizen of German birth, having near relatives prominent in German public life, should not be permitted to hold a position of great trust in the service of the United States. (I have two brothers in Germany who are bankers. They naturally now serve their country to the utmost of their ability, as I serve mine.)

"I believe that the number of men who urge this point of view is small at this time. They probably have not a proper appreciation of the sanctity of the oath of allegiance or of the oath of office. As for myself, I did not take them lightly. I waited ten years before determining upon my action, and I did not swear that 'I absolutely and entirely renounce and abjure all allegiance and fidelity to any foreign potentate, and particularly to Wilhelm II, Emperor of Germany,' etc. until I was quite certain that I was willing and anxious to cast my lot unqualifiedly and without reserve with the country of my adoption and to defend its aims and its ideals.

"These are sad times. For all of us they bring sad duties, doubly hard, indeed, for men of my extraction. But, though, as in the Civil War, brother must fight brother, each must follow the straight path of duty, and in this spirit I have endeavored to serve during the four years that it has been my privilege to be a member of the Federal Reserve Board.

"I have no doubt that all fair-minded and reasonable men would consider it nothing short of a national disgrace if this country, of all countries, should condone or endorse the attitude of those who would permit the American of German birth to give his all, but would not trust him as unreservedly and as wholeheartedly as he, for his part, serves the country of his adoption. Unfortunately, however, in times of war, we may not always count upon fair reasoning. It is only too natural that, as our casualty lists grow, bitterness and undiscriminating suspicion will assert themselves in the hearts of increasing numbers—even though these lists will continue to show their full proportion of German names."

Substitute Japanese or Negro for German, and the humiliating ordeal of this conservative banker in 1917 foretells that of the Nisei in 1942 or of Negroes in 1966 and 1967.

Wilson's reply took two and a half months to arrive, and it bore the telltale brand of appeasement. "Your retirement from the Board," Wilson wrote, shrinking from the political challenge to draft competence and integrity and to defy bigotry, "is a serious loss to the public service. I consent to it only because I read between the lines of your generous letter that you will yourself feel more at ease if you are free to serve in other ways."

Warburg's dismissal, coming at the height of America's effort "to make the world safe for democracy," demonstrated how far America had to go in order to live up to its own ideals, let alone to be in a position to export them. But Warburg's work, the creation of the Federal Reserve System, demonstrated America's distinctive ability to benefit in material terms from the import of ideas. In the half century since its founding, the Federal Reserve has become an integral part of both the structure of the economy and the structure of government. It was Warburg's achievement to make the two structures complementary to an unprecedented degree.

From the perspective of the chronic crises of the 1960's, it is possible to view the Federal Reserve as a mixed blessing. Unquestionably, the Federal Reserve System has been needed as the mechanism of monetary mobilization during total war, in World War II as much as in World War I. In peacetime, on the other hand, the Board's record of monetary management goes a good distance toward sustaining Professor Milton Friedman's argument that no management at all is better than the management that the Fed has actually provided. But Friedman's provocative "new laissez-faire" fails as prescription. No political authority can afford to forswear the use of the monetary lever. Moreover, there is no a priori case for holding that any monetary authority must prove incapable of implementing responsible, even though limited, influence over the economy—even if the Federal Reserve has proved so all too often in the past.

Aggressive monetary policy—above all, aggressive monetary restraint—does have a distinctive power to disrupt and dislocate the functioning of the economy. The domestic monetary crisis provoked by the need to finance the Vietnam War was striking evidence of the potential for disaster inherent in the management of the monetary mechanism. But the Vietnam money crisis was a testimonial to the destructive impact of *not* integrating monetary policy with defense policy, rather than proof that monetary policy must itself be destructive. The same institution which was responsible for provoking the money crisis was available for financing the war.

12 : WILSON'S FAILURE

THE BASIC PROBLEM of war finance is always the same: to eliminate the money constraint on the war effort. Governments adopt a variety of expedients to solve the problem. But whether coinage is debased, greenbacks are printed, bank credit is inflated or the money supply is expanded directly through the central bank, any government at war must, and somehow does, obtain the cash to pay its bills.

Any war, by definition, involves the diversion of resources from civilian to military employment. Even the primitive skirmishing of peasant economies involved the transfer of manpower from farming to killing. An economically developed nation fights its wars with its industrial base: the North in the Civil War showed the way. The more complex the economic system which goes to war, the more complex the problem of diverting resources becomes. Because the timetable of mobilization is so necessary, and because the premium on effective mobilization is so great, war again and again substitutes priorities and controls for the free workings of the marketplace. In total war, all governments must assert their unqualified right to first call on economic resources. No doubt it took an unregenerate speculator like

Bernard Baruch to lay it down, as he did during World War I and again during World War II, that governments which mean to make wars must be prepared to run markets. Because, in a modern economic system, money is the vehicle for transmitting real demands to suppliers, the first requirement of a wartime government is inescapably to take over the money market.

When war broke out in Europe in August, 1914, the money markets of the Old World, from London to St. Petersburg, were closed to outsiders. All money able to escape mobilization headed for New York. Thus, Europe's mobilization of money freed America to ignore the normal rule and to finance an all-out conversion to a war economy on a free money market basis. The need for controls was not felt, for the movement of money was entirely one way—into the U.S. Money had no place else to go. The result, inescapably, was virulent inflation without fear of balance-of-payments problems or of a recurrence of the pressures on the dollar which had forced it to a discount in the foreign exchange market during the Civil War. On March 30, 1915, Warburg wrote a far-sighted memorandum to his colleagues on the Board, warning against the rate of wartime inflation which, as he said, had already begun. The inflation that followed was so violent that, when Friedman took the financing of the Civil War as a yardstick, he found that, alongside the runaway of World War I prices, the Civil War provoked surprisingly little inflation—as he says, "thanks more to accident than to policy." After the initial financial setback caused by Europe's forced liquidation of overseas investments, the money supply and price level began to race each other upward from late 1914 through the end of 1918. By June, 1920, when prices peaked, the money supply was at more than double its level of November, 1914, the date at which the Federal Reserve Act had come into operation.

Nevertheless, long before American troops poured into Europe to turn the tide of battle against the Central Powers, the Federal Reserve System provided the defense-in-depth which saved America from panic and enabled America to finance the Western powers so that they could save themselves and stalemate the first phase of the war. But the Federal Reserve System was not envisioned or designed as an agency of war finance. All that it could have been expected to accomplish under the unexpected stresses of war was to prevent panic and to assure a continuous turnover of liquidity; and this, in fact, it did accomplish. Once inflation got ahead of provisions for financing the war, however, the damage was done; and it was cumulative.

Great lags are necessarily involved in identifying the need for war taxes, and for proposing, passing and collecting them. Meanwhile, the onset of war makes cash an immediate requirement. In the case of World War I, inflation had enjoyed a head start of fully three years before America became a belligerent, thanks to the sustained, large-scale impact of Allied purchases of munitions and supplies. As Warburg explained, the mobilization of real savings could not catch up with the emergency cash drain. "Each issue of Liberty or Victory Loan bonds had to be larger than the available savings of the nation," Warburg said. "Each issue forced the country to pledge its future savings and left a constantly growing amount of unplaced bonds."

The Wilson Administration's financing of World War I suffered not merely because its reliance on direct taxation followed the familiar pattern of "too little too late." Even more critically, it failed to control the money market while draining it dry of liquidity. America's successful financing of World War II and of the Korean War relegated its unsuccessful financing of World War I to an academic pigeonhole. But the fiasco of financing the Vietnam War revived memories of World War I and renewed its errors—in even more painful fashion because of a crucial dissimilarity in external circumstances. During World War I, money poured into the country, supporting the plausibility of reliance upon the free workings of the money market; during Vietnam, money was drained out. The crucial similarity between the two experiences was the omission of appropriate and necessary wartime controls. In each instance, business-as-usual war finance permitted an inflationary bank credit expansion. At the same time, it enforced a deflationary congestion in the long-term capital market. In each case, laissez-faire finance precipitated the paradoxical phenomenon of a deflationary money squeeze amidst an inflation of prices and costs. Like World War I, Vietnam subjected America to the worst of inflation on the cost side of the economy and to the worst of deflation on the money side.

The moment the American economy of 1914 started to boom under the impact of large-scale Allied purchases, common sense called for the Administration to be alert to the possibility of America's being drawn into the war. But neither the immediate deflation of values suffered as the direct result of the liquidation of European dollar assets nor the sustained price inflation which followed prodded the Administration into preparing for the obvious and the inevitable. Not until Wilson sacked Bryan and superseded him with Robert Lansing (the uncle of John Foster Dulles), an avowed and militant advocate of American entry on the Allied side, did realism intervene.

Early in 1916, Lansing wrote a confidential memorandum to the President in which he reported that Allied purchases had produced a favorable trade balance in 1915 of $2½ billion. But the purchase of American exports had exhausted the foreign exchange reserve of the Allies. They were threatened with a cutoff in supplies while we were threatened with depression. Lansing urged the President to retreat from the Bryan policy of neutrality and to lift the embargo against Allied borrowing which it had imposed. Wilson acquiesced, and the Allies immediately raised $2 billion. The strain on our overworked financial resources was considerable, but the dislocation to our financial apparatus was more serious. It had been structured to absorb capital from abroad. Now, while the war supply was overheating it, it was being called upon to create liquidity to send abroad.

Despite the omens and pressures originating in the marketplace, and despite the irresistible political pressures originating within the Cabinet, America's entry into the war found the Wilson Administration unprepared to face the problem of financing it. Only the newly established Federal Reserve saved the Wilson Administration from resorting to the printing press. "The Federal Reserve became to all intents and purposes the bond-selling window of the Treasury," Friedman writes, "using its monetary powers almost exclusively to that end. Although no 'greenbacks' were printed, the same result was achieved by more indirect methods using Federal Reserve notes and Federal Reserve deposits. At the beginning of U.S. participation in the war, Federal Reserve notes accounted for 7 per cent of high-powered money and bank deposits at Federal Reserve banks for 14 per cent; by the Armistice, Federal Reserve notes and deposits accounted for 38 and 21 per cent, respectively. The share of gold coin and certificates, on the other hand, fell from 41 per cent to 14 per cent, and the share of Treasury currency fell from 38 per cent to 27 per cent." Three-quarters of the Treasury's wartime expenditures were financed by borrowing and money creation.

Altogether, the fact of the Federal Reserve Board's existence made the difference between panic and mere disaster. If it had not existed to be drafted into the role for which it was not intended and not suited, the war could not have been financed at all. As it was, the unplanned financing of the war improvised the blueprint for economic disaster here and abroad for the generation which followed Wilson's. The runaway war boom set the pattern of postwar collapse and, more serious still, made the postwar collapse the formative cause of the financial maladjustments, dislocations and inadequacies which were to haunt the interwar years and, indeed, foredoom them to be interwar years.

The inflation suffered during World War I stands as a dividing-line in the history of American finance and in the history of American financial foreign relations as well. In the era between America's post-Civil-War return to the gold standard and the outbreak of World War I, America's primary problem had been its ability to maintain balance in its external financial relations. That is, America had to persuade Europe not to take home its gold too often and, when the squeeze was on, to send it back sooner rather than later. But as the result of the financial impact of World War I, "internal factors," as Friedman says, "mostly connected with the banking changes under the Federal Reserve

Act, began to have their main effects on the amount of change in the total stock of money, and indeed from some points of view can be regarded as the dominant factor in determining that change. In this respect, the situation was close to that during the greenback period."

America's financing of World War I catapulted the nation into a new era. The effect of the economic revolution precipitated by the accidents of wartime finance was to speed up the reversal of the historic process which had made American reactions dependent on European actions. In January, 1917, after the wartime inflation had already reached an advanced stage, the Federal Reserve Board agonized until it brought forth a statement which summed up not only the previous half-century of America's international financial relations, but also the next. It said: "When the Federal Reserve Act was drafted its principal object was to deal with national problems of banking and currency. Since its enactment financial and economic conditions in the United States have undergone far-reaching changes which were not foreseen three years ago. The United States has grown to be a world power in financial affairs and it seems necessary that the Act, which has proved of such great value in the treatment of our domestic problems, should now be amended in order to enable us to deal effectively with the new international problems which seem destined to play so important a part in our economic life. The banking system of the United States should be prepared to meet effectively two conditions of opposite character—one, the excessive and uncontrolled inflow of gold, the other the excessive and unregulated outflow of gold. The amendments proposed are designed to provide means of controlling an over-extension of loans based on new accretions to our gold stock and to provide for the mobilization and concentration of the gold holdings of the United States so that the flow of gold back into Europe, or to South America, or to the Orient, may be arranged without forcing any violent contraction of loans or causing undue disturbance to legitimate business."

The thrust of the amendments was to authorize the Federal Reserve System to issue its notes as legal tender based on gold reserves. The amendments fulfilled their intended purpose throughout the 1920's, enabling America to absorb billions of dollars of gold from Europe with virtually no price inflation. On the other side—and it was a side on which Keynes's potent pen was mobilized—the amendments freed America to violate in detail the rules of the gold standard game. Orthodoxy began and ended with the view that international equilibrium demanded that a gold inflow be reflected in price inflation and a gold outflow in deflation. Such national price adjustments, it was intended, would induce countervailing international flows of goods. A balance-of-payments deficit would become a surplus, and the result would be a beneficial reversal of the gold flow.

Instead, by the 1917 amendments, the U.S. exercised its unilateral power to break the rules and amass gold while insulating its economy from the normal inflationary consequences. At the same time, those who lost gold—and this was Keynes's complaint—would, once wartime controls were lifted, be forced into painful deflation or even more disastrous hyperinflation. The irony was that America's leap from international economic bondage to national economic freedom corresponded with the last gasp of American laissez-faire. In the 1920's, America—and no other nation—knew freedom of action. That freedom was dissipated in the years leading up to the world crisis of 1931–2. As a consequence, in 1933, Franklin Roosevelt took office under pressure to declare America's economic independence once again by taking the U.S. off the gold standard.

Even more ironically, forty years later, the escalation in Vietnam was not long in turning this originally liberating statute into a reactionary encumbrance. As fast as dollar deposits and gold losses agitated the fear that America might be overextending herself in Asia, they also excited speculation that relatively small gold losses to Europe would bring on a dollar crisis by running America out of her remaining quota of "free" gold. For wars and involvements in crisis created a de facto double standard for the dollar—one governing its domestic use, and the other its foreign exchangeability. The requirement that a high proportion of the country's gold holdings be frozen into an unneeded and unusable

reserve behind the domestic dollar left the international dollar
exposed to raids and harassment. Certainly, the gold reserve
clause accomplished no purpose domestically: it provided no
domestic security to offset the international insecurity it advertised. And, by the time of Vietnam, so long as America hesitated
to initiate the moves needed to demonetize gold and modernize
the international monetary system, the international dollar needed
all the gold that could be mobilized behind it.

During World War II, with Europe under siege, it had been
easy for Roosevelt to startle his always appreciative press conference audience with the word that "what I am trying to do is
eliminate the dollar sign. That is something brand new in the
thoughts of everybody in this room, I think—get rid of the silly,
foolish, old dollar sign." The dollar enjoyed an unchallenged
monopoly as premium merchandise no matter how inconsiderate
of the sensitivities of capital or of its own interests the American
government might be in exercising its Keynesian prerogative to
make the dollar worth what it said. But the Vietnam War took
form from the outset as a two-front war for America, as it had
been for France before her, which had to be fought against
currency raiders on the exchanges as well as against guerrilla
raiders in the jungle. Long after America was on notice that she
had to be prepared to dig into the jungle, she remained unprepared to defend herself on the dollar front.

Responsibility must lie with Lyndon Johnson for this embarrassment to his War Administration. At the crest of his popularity and the height of his power, in the week of his inauguration as President in his own right after his landslide victory over
Goldwater, he was urged to recommend to a Congress still
anxious to act on any and all of his recommendations the complete elimination of the gold cover for the domestic currency.
Even the Federal Reserve Board joined Johnson's liberal advisers
in this plan. But in January, 1965, neither Johnson's advisers nor
he himself were yet aware of the scale on which Vietnam was
fated to inflate the pressures on the dollar. In 1967, when it did,
this move became necessary as an emergency measure admitting
weakness instead of as a step toward modernization expressing
strength.

World War I destroyed an international equilibrium which had lasted a hundred years—one which had been resilient enough to survive the Industrial Revolution and the rise of European nationalism. The false equilibrium established at Versailles lasted barely long enough to disillusion the postwar generation with the ideals of internationalism. Woodrow Wilson's political failures led first to diplomatic defeat at the hands of his Allies at the Peace Conference, and then to political defeat at the hands of the Senate in the League of Nations fight. Emphasis on the diplomatic roots of the interwar tragedy is an understandable outgrowth of the primary emphasis which American studies put upon political history at the expense of economic and financial history. But while Wilson's failure on the international diplomatic front made his loss of leadership a political fact of life, the prior failure of his War Administration on the domestic financial front activated a ruinous wartime cycle of boom and bust—its culmination was the Depression whose child was Hitler and whose legacy was Hitler's war. The Wilson Administration's failure to stabilize and conserve the boom whipped up by World War I marked the spot at which the world was sentenced to fight World War II.

The end of the war presented the Federal Reserve Board with a challenge which changed the terms of its statutory assignment of responsibility without, however, again amending the Federal Reserve Act. The Federal Reserve Act had been passed to protect the country against failures in liquidity flow, especially from region to region, not to protect it against fluctuations in the business cycle. The explicit legislative purpose of the Act had been to commission the new Board to keep liquidity flowing during and despite the characteristic fluctuations in business activity at whose extreme limits on the upside as well as on the downside liquidity had invariably dried up in the past. But neither public opinion, nor Congress, nor, certainly, President Wilson, during his prewar period of concentration upon the problem, had regarded the Act as elevating the new Federal Reserve Board into either a high command over the economy empowered to regulate its fluctuations within an acceptable golden mean or into the economic equivalent of a supreme court empowered to judge when the economy had overstepped the guidelines of equilibrium.

The maladjustments which developed as the result of the Wilson Administration's overreliance upon free market methods to finance the heavy burden of wartime costs sent the Board adventuring on a new frontier in 1918. It began to act as if it had been entrusted with the positive management of the economy in order to stabilize cyclical fluctuations, instead of merely the negative responsibility for preventing stoppages in the flow of liquidity. During the critical and formative years from 1918 through 1920, the United States was without a functioning President directing its government: first because he was in Paris at the Peace Conference for a full year, then because he was stumping the country for his peace plan, and finally because he was isolated in paralysis. One of the major hidden costs of World War I, pyramided on top of its dollar costs, which were breathtaking by the dollar standards of those days, was incurred when the Federal Reserve Board was driven into the vacuum left by the default of leadership on the financial front. It reached out for and took over the role of monetary management which it has been expected to fill ever since, but which it was unqualified to fill then.

The strength of the European system, which Warburg Americanized in the form of the Federal Reserve, was its tying of paper to things, and, therefore, its provision of insurance against insolvency. But America also imported its weakness, which followed from the fact that creation of credit followed business activity. When the business pace accelerated, it produced more paper; when the business pace decelerated, it produced less paper. Consequently, the price of continuous banking insurance against insolvency was intensification of the swings of the business cycle. The system achieved elasticity only at the price of excess, raising the constant danger that changes in the money supply would follow changes in business activity, not lead them. Ever since Warburg, the Board has been whipsawed between the contradiction implicit in its original de jure responsibility of following the economy with injections of more liquidity or less (depending on whether activity was speeding up or slowing down) and its subsequent de facto assumption of responsibility for leading the economy.

This conflict between original statutory intent and subsequent operational habit came to a head conspicuously and violently when the inexperienced Board, following the boom, continued to supply the new liquidity which both fed the inflationary spiral and intensified it. The operations of the Board began to feed on the inflation in the economy as fast as the inflation in the economy began to feed on the operations of the Board. The annual report of the Board for 1919 admitted that "the purchasing power of the public growing out of high wages and large profits is greater than it has ever been before; and this purchasing power, competing with export demands arising out of the necessities of Europe, has raised prices to a point that takes no account of prudence. . . . There is practically unlimited demand for credit."

At the worst of its lapse of responsibility, the Board spoke with the voice of detachment that might have been expected from a historian, as if it were not itself the principal cause of the danger it was identifying. Once the Federal Reserve Board was seen to be manning an engine of inflation, controversy was bound to provoke division. It did so—not only between the Federal Reserve Board and the Treasury, but between the Board of Governors in Washington and the Federal Reserve Bank in New York. The New York Bank began to press for higher rates as a measure of restraint to slow the boom down before it crashed. The Treasury (although its Secretary was by this time the conservative Carter Glass and his Assistant Secretary was Russell C. Leffingwell, a Morgan partner) insisted that the Fed would do as well by simply falling back upon informal restrictions to limit credit applications deemed undesirable or lacking in priority. The Federal Reserve Board itself, without Treasury prodding, has again and again fallen back upon this same line of retreat with uniformly dismal results. The Treasury, as Friedman explains, had a double motivation. It worked to keep interest rates low in order to facilitate the funding of the floating debt as well as to protect the prices of the government bonds it had sold against lower market prices forced by higher interest rates. A related reason of equal sensitivity was that the banks held for their own accounts large amounts of recently floated government war loans whose market values provided the basis for their inflated loan portfolios. At the same time, they were also carrying customers who had borrowed against government bonds and were, therefore, vulnerable—as was the entire credit bubble—to any snapping of the string which a policy toward higher interest rates was bound to force.

The pattern of division between the Federal Reserve Board in Washington and the Federal Reserve Bank in New York and the System was prophetic. It anticipated the crisis in monetary policy ten years later in 1929. In the closing days of 1919, when the New York Bank was winning its fight for a policy of restraint, Governor Benjamin Strong of the New York Bank suddenly lost his nerve. Timing was his worst worry. He feared, quite rightly, that interest rates should have been put up long ago, but "to do it now would be to bring on a crisis." Then, however, the Treasury itself panicked. According to the diary of Board Governor Charles S. Hamlin (who had served as Assistant Secretary of the Treasury during the second Administration of Grover Cleveland, a sound-money President, and again at the outset of the Wilson Administration), it was at the Treasury's initiative that the discount rate was jumped early in 1920 by 1¼ percentage points to 6 per cent. This was a move of unusual violence providing prima facie evidence of policy failure and guaranteeing gyrations in the behavior of both the economy and the authorities. Over the opposition of the Board and of the New York Reserve Bank, Secretary Glass himself participated in the Board's fateful meeting and cast the tie-breaking vote, thereby precipitating a historic conflict over whether only the Board has the power to set its rates or whether in the end, the Treasury may invoke its own higher authority. Glass was painfully aware of the far-reaching implications of his impetuous intervention, and brooded articulately in a thoroughly uncharacteristic way over whether he had done the right thing.

But, well-considered or not, the deed was done; and Friedman notes that what resulted "was the sharpest single rise in the entire history of the System, before or since." As he says, "It produced an immediate retardation of the rate of rise in the money stock," and the deflationary panic was on. The decline in confidence and the rise in rates were sped by Assistant Secretary Leffingwell's official revelation that the postwar inflationary expansion, which coincided with the renewal of Europe's ability to absorb money, had drained gold out of the country at such a rate that "we were dangerously near leaving the gold standard . . . [and] that soon a new gold embargo would have to be put in." The moment Europe reopened as a market for money, the day of reckoning arrived for America's uncontrolled war-dislocated money market. The sharpest price decline in the history of the United States followed. Between May, 1920, and June, 1921, wholesale prices suffered a collapse of no less than 56 per cent. Inevitably, production and employment plummeted with prices.

In 1921, after the damage was done, Congress leveled the strongest and sternest possible criticism against the Board for having erred too long on the side of laxity and then too abruptly on the side of discipline. The Joint Congressional Commission of Agricultural Inquiry was feeling the heat and transmitting it to the Board, and with good reason; for the price collapse in America had triggered a deflationary chain reaction in America's crop export markets. The Federal Reserve Board tried to defend itself by retreating to the position that the corrective swing of the world economy, and not its mismanagement, had exaggerated the boom–bust whipsaw. But as Friedman says, "The United States had by that time become a substantial factor in the world at large and could no longer be regarded as dancing to the tune of the rest of the world."

In fact, by the end of the war, the causal relationship between America and Europe was reversed. When the bubble burst in America, it burst abroad. When it did, the dollar outflow to Europe stopped at precisely the time that the new system of reparations and war debts began to depend on a direct, sustained inflow of American dollars. From the moment the postwar bust deflated the bubble left over from the war, depression replaced goods and dollars as America's number-one export. The obsessive concern of every government in the world and the problem for the economy of the world became the revival of dollar capital outflows.

The artificial world boom of the 1920's was based on New York's short-term advances, at extortionate interest rates, to Central Europe. But before even this risk-laden operation got under way, the hyperinflations east of the Rhine had already fatally undermined whatever economic stability was left after defeat in war. Hitler's beer-hall *putsch* of 1923, although a fiasco, gave warning of the political implications of economic disruption in postwar Europe. From 1923 through 1929, the short-term dollar flow to Europe bolstered a semblance of economic prosperity and political stability. But in 1929, the speculative boom on Wall Street drew dollars back from Europe at a crisis rate; then the Great Crash liquidated those dollars. Hitler's farcical *putsch* had been the political price of the misdirection of American policy in 1919–21. Hitler's successful revolution in 1933 was the price of the continuing failure throughout the 1920's to get American policy on course.

13 : KEYNES'S REVOLUTION

THE GREAT DEPRESSION subjected the modern world to its one big crisis not directly or immediately connected with war. But the traumatic shock it inflicted simulated the psychological wounds of war. Moreover, the Great Depression marked the turning-point in history at which the effects of World War I began to assert themselves as causes of the disturbed behavior that was to bring on World War II. In fact, society developed a new response to depression which resembled its old response to war and which survived the Depression. In country after country, the new way of doing things called for governmental intervention in economic affairs on a scale hitherto seen only in time of war. Like modern total war, too, the Depression raised the clear and present danger of social revolution as the price of political failure to deal with it. Even Herbert Hoover recognized the similarity. In the spring of 1932, before Roosevelt forced him back into his position of defensive stand-patism, Hoover declared that America had to "fight the depression."

The political legacy of the Great Depression throughout the developed world was the recognition of government's continuous peacetime responsibility for the economic state of the nation. In American terms, this was the New Deal revolution. In the 1929–32 crisis of war within society, governments came to be held accountable for economic catastrophe, both at the polls and in the streets. Pleas of ignorance by political authority carried no weight against the misery, despair and chaos which the Depression brought. But the Depression yielded an intellectual legacy as well. For the Depression prompted a new analysis of the functioning of the economic system and a new rationale for government management of it. This was the revolution improvised simultaneously (but not collusively) by Keynes's pen and Roosevelt's politics.

The treatment for the Depression on which Keynes and the New Deal converged from their respective points of view came to be called "The Middle Way": Marquis Childs, in his report on the Swedish version of the welfare state, and the young Harold Macmillan, an up-and-coming establishment politician with a sensitive ear and a shrewd nose, hit on the same term at the same time. A middle way was certainly needed. Economic collapse had started a race for political power between totalitarians of the left and the right: both Fascism and Communism fed on social disintegration. The status quo was on trial to change enough to head off economic deterioration in time to avoid social disintegration. Nowhere was the challenge more direct than in Germany.

Germany's race against anarchy had begun as soon as the shooting stopped in 1918. But not until the hyperinflation of 1922–3 was brought under control did the forces with an interest in stability develop a fighting chance. Their progress was impressive until the Wall Street Crash of 1929 announced the cutoff in trans-Atlantic dollar flows. The pullback and liquidation of American short-term investments undermined the international economic foundations of the Weimar Republic and, simultaneously, unemployment destroyed its domestic political stability. Financial failure and industrial deflation produced a three-step chain reaction. It led from the money market to the productive apparatus to the streets, where the Nazi and Communist gangs developed a joint flanking operation against the Social Democratic-oriented moderates.

Kremlinologists have developed an absorbing literature of "whodunits" to explain Stalin's far-reaching miscalculation in working with Hitler. One line of reasoning has argued that Stalinism practiced good, orthodox Leninism in allying itself with the *lumpen-proletariat* in order to splinter the strategic alliance which the established order had forged with the labor aristocracy. Another view credited Stalin with the belief that the faster the Nazis took over, the faster their brand of terror would provoke a revolutionary reaction certain to entrench a satellite German Communism in power and to establish Berlin as Moscow's western outpost. Still another speculated that Stalin's seeming miscalculation masked a diabolical calculation: to insure Russian Communism against the centrifugal tug of polycentrism which, in fact, came into play with Mao in China and Tito in Yugoslavia after World War II, but which Stalin feared from Germany because of her industrial dominance more than from any other country deemed ripe for Sovietization. This last line of reasoning argued that Stalin had decided that he could do business with Hitler even before he discovered that he had no alternative but to try.

The course of history has enabled advocates of all three points of view to claim a measure of plausibility for their respective reconstructions of the crime. In any event, the payoff for German Communists made them the first tenants of Hitler's concentration camps. Stalin did do his fateful deal with Hitler. And Communism—specifically Russian Communism—became the beneficiary of the Nazi madness after it had destroyed first the old order and then its own new order, although not on any timetable the Communists had in mind before the fact and not before bringing the destruction of Soviet Russia within their reach. Polycentrism has grown into the specter haunting Communism. But, thanks to Communism's recurrent miscalculation about Germany, the source of the danger has turned out to be less economic (from Germany) than nationalistic (from Eastern Europe) and racial (as Moscow has come to see it, from China).

In Germany, the middle way unfolded as a rough and risky road at best. The postwar social order which had evolved out of Social Democracy's successive compromises with defeat, revolution, capitalism and reform rested on shaky foundations. The depth of Germany's depression had torn gaping holes in it. But even before the gangsters of both extremisms threatened to block it off altogether, the Social Democrats and their allies in search of the middle way foundered for lack of a road map. For although Germany was the most advanced country in Europe by Marxist standards of political development and by any standard of economic performance, it was the least advanced in terms of economic sophistication and political flexibility. In Germany, the political backers of moderation were prisoners of the impractical dogmas and unworkable shibboleths of orthodox economic thinking. In 1932, orthodoxy still proclaimed that deflation was the sole answer to depression—beginning with deliberate and purposive deflation of wages. At the very time when the mass of unemployed German workers was being intoxicated with demagogic appeals to nationalism, racism and class warfare, the government in Berlin had only one policy: cut the wages of those still employed.

Orthodox economic policy for dealing with unemployment began with an unresolvable contradiction. Orthodox economic thinking identified unemployment as nothing more serious than a short-term, transitory, self-correcting phenomenon. For 150 years, the mainstream of Western economic thinking had based its calculations upon an assertion, known to economists as Say's Law, which had been given its classic English form by John Stuart Mill: "Under ordinary conditions of industry, production and consumption move together: there is no consumption except that for which the way has been prepared by appropriate production: and all production is followed by the consumption for which it was designed."

A companion calculation supported the assumption that the normal functioning of an economic system produces equilibrium between supply and demand at the full-employment level of activity. It identified the meaningful timescale for considering economic conditions as "the long run." Domestic and international imbalances, temporary gluts and shortages, the movement of the business cycle—economic orthodoxy abstracted from all of these. Short-run events were considered to be merely the froth on the groundswell of national economic rise and decline.

The fact that short-run excesses continually disturb long-term trends was, of course, recognized and accepted. But the theoretical superstructure of laissez-faire insisted that any such disturbances were self-correcting. In the market for goods, excess supply forced down prices and was eventually absorbed by the greater demand that was forthcoming at the lower price level. An exactly analogous situation was held to exist in the market for labor. If, for any reason, men became unemployed, the answer for them was the same as for the sellers of any other commodity: to reduce the price at which they offered their product to buyers. In the case of the unemployed, this product was their labor, and their price was their rate of pay. Say's Law, reduced to the harsh realities of labor politics and economic policies, meant that the demand for labor would always assert itself if only the price was right. The fact that the process of reducing that price could be a long and arduous succession of strikes and lockouts, ending in widespread destitution and political revolt, was overlooked by those whose attention was concentrated on "the long run."

In the very book which accomplished the overthrow of the old orthodoxy, *The General Theory of Employment, Interest and Money*, Keynes identified the sources of orthodoxy's appeal. "That it reached conclusions quite different from what the ordinary uninstructed person would expect, added, I suppose, to its intellectual prestige. That its teaching, translated into practice, was austere and often unpalatable, lent it virtue. That it was adapted to carry a vast and consistent logical superstructure, gave it beauty. That it could explain much social injustice and apparent cruelty as an inevitable incident in the scheme of progress, and the attempt to change such things as likely on the whole to do more harm than good, commended it to authority. That it afforded a measure of justification to the free activities of the individual capitalist, attracted to it the support of the dominant social force behind authority."

World War I had declared a de facto moratorium on laissez-faire's hold over the political and economic leadership of the

West. The compulsions of total war required government intervention on an unprecedented scale with no nonsense about how
things could be trusted to work by themselves. War fever provided all the rationale that was needed to suspend the rules. But
Warren Harding, the hapless misfit in the White House, was not
alone in 1920 in greeting the end of the war as the signal for a
return to "Normalcy." His intellectual betters, who knew that
there was no such thing, were not aware that there was any better
way to move forward. And, in country after country, government
moved aggressively to turn the clock back into conformity with
the old theory. However, the difficulty of effecting the supposedly
necessary postwar transition to wage deflation provided a new
rationale for government intervention—and a peacetime rationale
at that. Not that the prescription of economic orthodoxy changed,
but laissez-faire was no longer plausible as the way to get it. On
the contrary, government had now come under increasing pressure to intervene on the side of the market forces pressing for
deflation—which were, at that point, the dominant ones. During
the abrupt slump of 1921, public authorities reinforced the deflationary pressures loose in the world economy with restrictive
monetary policy and direct pressure for wage cuts.

However imperfectly the old theory had been trusted to
work before 1914, the postwar world found it colliding with the
new fact presented by the Russian Revolution. Stalin laid down
the line that Soviet possession of one-sixth of the earth's surface
had constricted capitalism into a condition of general crisis. In
the geographical sense in which he meant this exercise in applied
Leninism, he was wrong, for capitalism did not need to expand
territorially in order to enjoy a stable prosperity. But in terms of
historical sociology, he was right. For the birth of the Soviet
system had imposed the death sentence on the orthodox theory
of laissez-faire capitalism, and it put capitalist societies on notice
that they would be executing their own death sentences if they
persisted in trying to cure unemployment with deflation. The
ability of the Soviet state to pass the positive test of competitive
performance was not yet in question. The mere existence of a
Soviet state in a major area put a greater burden on the old

order than the competitive challenge of coexistence was to put on the new capitalist order during the next postwar generation. The success of the Revolution in Russia provided an unmistakable alternative to capitalism once economic distress was allowed to pass the point of social peril.

The first response of the more imaginative of capitalism's defenders, notably Keynes, was to work out a technique of painless wage reduction. It had long been realized that there were two ways to reduce the real standard of living—the prerequisite, according to orthodoxy, for an end to unemployment. The more arduous method, increasingly unacceptable in the face of the Communist alternative, was by direct assault on money wages. The painless alternative was to cut the standard of living by raising the cost of living. Price inflation was an alternative to wage deflation.

In Britain as well as America, the advocacy of inflation as a shortcut to prosperity had a long history. The silver controversy had never reached the pitch in Britain that it had in America; on the other hand, "funny money" prophets or unrestricted credit creation held greater sway in Britain. Not until the 1920's did inflation become respectable as a deliberate policy for central banks and governments. But even then, the popular fear of rising prices was paradoxically compounded with the conservative fear that democratic government could not resist the temptation to fulfill its promises by debauching the currency. Every step of the way into the abyss of the Depression, governments and the opinion on which they rested embraced the deflation which was pursuing and destroying them, and built defenses against the reflation which they needed. The impractical and costly postwar decision to return to the gold standard had left no alternative, for the first requirement of adherence to the international gold standard was the subjugation of the domestic price level to outside forces. No single nation could stay on the gold standard while inflating unless all were doing so.

In the end, the totality of the climactic economic collapse and crisis tilted the scales in favor of inflation. By 1933, the disintegration of society loomed as the alternative threat to the

reflation of the economy. A balanced budget to restore prosperity was not Franklin Roosevelt's only campaign promise of
1932. He was also elected on an explicit promise to engineer
recovery by raising prices.

Inflation offered a way out of the dilemma of orthodoxy—
how to deal with an unemployment problem that had become
urgent although theoretically impossible. But the advocacy of
inflation was no more than a compromise expedient. In the form
it took at the bottom of the Depression, even in Keynes's *A
Treatise on Money* published in 1930, it did not attack the basic
flaw at the heart of laissez-faire orthodoxy. It did not recognize
that Say's Law is invalid: the production of "supply" does not
in fact create its own "demand," and it cannot. The advocates of
inflation were still operating within the assumptions of orthodoxy. They still looked on full employment equilibrium as the
"normal" situation. They still looked to the reduction of real
living standards as the one way to eliminate unemployment. All
that had changed was the attitude toward unemployment, for the
inflationists began with the fact of its existence and sought to
deal with it in the least painful way possible. But not all the
inflationists ended there. John Maynard Keynes did not.

Keynes's pilgrim's progress from the old orthodoxy to his
General Theory which superseded it led by way of Lloyd
George's 1929 pledge to end unemployment. The old scalawag,
whose demagoguery and deceit at Versailles he had excoriated
and exposed, became his companion in the wilderness. As early
as 1923, Keynes was making himself a name for radical theoretical writing to go with his journalistic controversiality. Almost
alone among academic economists, he urged Britain to retain
and take advantage of the freedom from the chains of the gold
standard which the necessities of war and postwar dislocation
had forced. He advised Britain to set about deliberately managing its money to produce prosperity, rather than tamely making
the foredoomed attempt to return to the mythical Golden Era
of prewar days. His sporadic journalizing was already reflecting
his deep and emotional response to the slump and stagnation
which would characterize Britain throughout the postwar years.

Most important, however, his intellect was becoming sensitized to the fundamental contradiction of pre-Keynesian capitalism.

Malthus and certain mercantilist writers (Keynes dug them out of the archives to provide a historical context for the *General Theory*) had seen the problem: effective demand may fall short of available supply at the level of production and income which corresponds to full employment. But Malthus had long since been damned and doomed for landing on the reactionary side of his friendly personal controversy with Ricardo because of his ideological commitment to defend the old landed aristocracy and their function, as he saw it, of providing the necessary extra margin of demand through their spending on luxuries. (Malthus got no credit from the twentieth-century liberal establishment for his prescience in identifying the progressive function which service products and service producers were destined to provide by the 1960's. On the democratized scale required by America's mass production economy, hair sprays and hairdressers, for example, do more to provide the last margin of consumption needed to balance production than Malthus ever expected from all the Duchesses of England combined.) The mercantilists could also be dismissed and forgotten once the free-trade dogma in all its pristine, if theoretical, purity had overthrown their basic theoretical and practical position. Only the occasional crank or heretic—such as John Hobson—remained to point out from time to time that the Emperor was wearing very few clothes.

When Keynes published *A Tract on Monetary Reform* in 1923, the main thrust of his argument was toward justifying a deliberate policy of monetary management. Incidentally, he tossed off a throwaway line which has since become a byword in the language on both sides of the ocean. Referring to the propensities of his academic colleagues to think and write in terms of long movements over time, Keynes accepted the probability that in the long run orthodoxy might apply. But, he added, "*In the long run* we are all dead." Far from simply scoring a point at the expense of ivory tower theorists, Keynes's quip presaged a revolution in economic thinking and as great a one in economic policy-making. For once attention was focused on the short run, once the supposedly transitory and frictional phenomenon of large-scale unemployment—supercharged with emotional concern and political necessity—came under the microscope, and once "normal" processes of adjustment were recognized as remediable states of equilibrium-plus-unemployment, then the road was open to the *General Theory* and beyond. A new managerial potential for control was put at the disposal of the ethical drives and political pressures responsible for the welfare state.

If the postwar slump in Britain provided the external stimulus to trigger Keynes's revolutionary pronunciamento, Lloyd George's political ambitions and frustrated condition provided the context in which insight became theory and theory became publicized. The elections of 1922 and 1923, the latter resulting in the first Labor government, demonstrated clearly that Labor had replaced the Liberals as Britain's official vehicle of opposition. Even the rout of the first Labor government in 1924, as the result of its failure to brand the Zinoviev letter the forgery it was subsequently admitted to be, left Ramsay MacDonald as Leader of the Opposition. The result on the Liberal side was a temporary remarriage of necessity between Lloyd George's cohorts, who had stuck with him through his early coalitions and subsequent wanderings in the wilderness, and Asquith's Liberal loyalists. Asquith went to the Lords and Lloyd George set out to find a program which he would sell with the fund—appropriately named for him and accumulated, Robin Hood style, from the notorious auctioning of honors and titles during his nearly six years as Premier.

A residual belief in free trade, a reliance on the Lloyd George fund, and a last fling at power—these were perhaps the only ties which bound the disparate groupings and solitary individuals whom Lloyd George mobilized under the banners which bore Keynes's theories in slogan form. But after a good deal of wandering, with Keynes often in the lead—in 1924, he went so far as to advocate that the Liberals should include birth control as part of their political platform—Lloyd George by 1927 had found a program. It was embodied in the Liberal Industrial Inquiry and elaborated in pamphlets, speeches and articles for the next three years. At its heart was a massive program of public works, aimed at putting Britain's million unemployed (an army in British terms) to work. Increasingly, however, the main purpose of the program was seen to be its use of the budget to pump money into an economy with excess resources—in men and machinery—ready to roll out new production without inflation if only the latent demand for goods and services could be made effective.

For a number of years, political and economic radicals had called for public works to deal with unemployment. (Two of them, Foster and Catchings, had great influence with the then progressive Republican Secretary of Commerce, Herbert Hoover, who was spearheading the drive to bigger and more responsible government from within the Coolidge Administration.) The reaction was commonsensical and as such, realistic. Nonetheless, no theoretical justification had been thoroughly worked out as to why public works *should* do the job. As late as 1938 in America, advocates of more public works had no understanding of the real nature of the remedy they were proposing, although this was two years after the *General Theory* was published. Consequently, they had no basis for anticipating the limitations to which their proposed remedy was subject.

What Keynes and his followers did was to spotlight the central nexus of savings and investment, and to explain the influence of monetary flows in determining the degree of imbalance in the economy. For the first time, national income and employment were viewed as variables whose equilibrium levels —along with those of interest rates—were determined by the balancing of savings and investment. And, what was crucial, he demonstrated that there was no reason to believe that the equilibrium level reached would be full employment.

Although public works have come to be identified with economic radicalism and, therefore, with Keynesianism, the fact is that Keynes downgraded government spending on public works as only one among several methods for raising the level of total investment. For, as he emphasized, investment, whether public or private, was the indispensable balancing item in the national economic account. Like his supposedly radical suggestion of price inflation as the way to meet the conservative requirement of real income reduction, government spending, which seemed radical, was actually conservative in its emphasis on investment, regardless of the source, as the *sine qua non* of national economic balance. Through the "multiplier" process— brilliantly worked out by Keynes's protégé Richard (later Lord) Kahn—investment spending was identified as a high-powered source of income generation. Savings out of this higher level of income were projected, in turn, as the source of balance for the new level of investment at a state of economic activity closer to full employment. What was true of the new investment in public works financed by borrowing was true of any net addition to spending not financed out of current income. Thus, Keynes added the government budget as a tool of economic management —budget deficits were indicated when it seemed desirable to raise the level of total investment and aggregate demand, and surpluses were indicated to lower them.

When the time came for Britain's 1929 election, Lloyd George made his pledge: to abolish unemployment within two years by priming the pump with government investment. And Keynes, in his pamphlet "Can Lloyd George Do It?" guaranteed performance. The result was two-fold. Both the Tories and Labor hastened to denounce Lloyd George's opportunism while declaring that each would do the job more effectively. At the same time, the Treasury provided a classic statement of the theoretical basis for do-nothingism. Even if the many practical difficulties that stood in the way of spending money could be overcome, the Treasury mobilized the full weight of officialdom behind the argument that such new spending could accomplish no more than the transfer of employment from some now at work to some now unemployed. This unflinching determination on the part of officialdom and orthodoxy to look at a million-plus unemployed—many by then out of work for nearly a decade —and to see only the mirage of full employment justified all of

Keynes's polemics, even those against close personal friends in the little world of Cambridge.

Nonetheless, orthodoxy triumphed, with historic irony, through the election of Britain's second Socialist government. Labour held office without a majority and, therefore, was stuck with responsibility for the dissolution of the relative prosperity of the 1920's without the power to do anything constructive. The schizophrenia of the period sent politics spinning leftward while economics still remained fastened to its moorings on the right. The hope of finding an opening through the middle rested on Lloyd George's last try for a comeback; and it failed miserably. In 1929, Lloyd George was the only political merchant desperate enough to put on display Keynes's first call for a new start. When he was remembered and rejected as the Pied Piper of radicalism, Keynes's old gibe at the "goat-footed bard" came back to haunt and humiliate him.

In the long run, of course, 1929 was the perfect time to be wrong politically for the right reason economically—provided that the investor in political futures could count on observing Keynes's own admonition to collect his winnings in the short run. Lloyd George no longer could. The Tories picked up the pieces in 1931 under the guise of an emergency "National Government"—just as they had done when Lloyd George and the war crisis broke Asquith in 1916. Meanwhile, Keynes was freed to devote six years of total effort to working out the theoretical basis for the policies toward which he and Lloyd George had improvised their way. Only in America, and there not until 1933, would Lloyd George's opportunism take practical shape as Franklin Roosevelt's opportunity.

Both Roosevelt's improvisations and the neo-orthodox innovations later adopted by advocates of inflation on both sides of the Atlantic obscured Keynes's central contribution. The political destruction of Herbert Hoover in America and of the second Labor government in Britain became milestones marking the political consequences of modern economic history. Up to that point, governments had from time to time been held responsible for bad times. But politicians had not suspected that remedies lay within easy reach and, accordingly, their normal recourse had been to play possum until the storm blew over or, with luck, to charge their opponents with the blame (as, for example, Andrew Jackson succeeded in doing in the money panic of 1832).

After the panic of 1932, the political "ins" began to operate on the clear understanding that winning politics assumed workable economics. The Keynesian revolution left governments responsible for achieving, administering and conserving prosperity. A full generation later, after the Keynesian approach had won general acceptance in America, it was one of the saddest ironies of the 1960's that war—the old original guarantor of American prosperity—intervened to cancel America's new commitment to the Keynesian revolution as a peacetime substitute for war.

14 : MORGENTHAU'S MISTAKES

AGAIN AND AGAIN, the coincidences of history have a way of introducing a rhythm into its processes which no dialectic imposed upon it can duplicate in dramatic effect or contain within a rigid formula. By one such coincidence, Franklin Roosevelt and Adolf Hitler took office and entered on their fateful collision courses within weeks of each other. Each represented a radical response, in terms of his distinctive national experience, to the impact of the Great Depression.

Hitler was the beneficiary of the Versailles system. When it crumbled, he took over. The Nazi movement began as an expression of rabid, vengeful nationalism rather than as the product of economic misery. But the extremist solution that Nazism represented—it was the same with Communism—fed on economic disorder and despair. The world depression of 1931–3 had hit hardest in Germany and the U.S. For Nazism, the devastation of 1932 presented the rarest of political opportunities: a second chance. Nazism had first sharpened its knife and tasted blood during the inflationary disaster which destroyed the mark in 1923. Hitler won control over Germany's future in 1933 primarily because the emotional unrest born of depression-fed extremism—expressed as nationalism, racism and militarism—preferred his brand of violence to the Communist alternative.

Roosevelt, like Hitler, was the beneficiary of the economics of the pocketbook rather than of the intangibles of politics. In fact, he owed his 1932 nomination to the widespread fear among Democratic politicians that only the emotional distraction of the Catholic issue, which would have been raised by another nomination for Al Smith, could jeopardize Democratic chances of cashing in on the "Hoover Depression." The main campaign problem for the "pleasant squire from the Hudson Valley" was to stay out of the way of the voters while they prepared to punish Hoover for their troubles. By virtue of being a Governor, Roosevelt was entitled to campaign in the stance of the challenger not privileged to have seen the coded cables from abroad. Accordingly, he held out adamantly against the most urgent Presidential pressures to involve himself in bipartisan excursions into the foreign field. The one controversial position he ended by taking was against prohibition—only the Depression itself was more of a provocation to the public. When Hoover held back for fear of offending church groups, Roosevelt quickly extended his advocacy of repeal to include the promise of jobs in the liquor and brewing industries.

History has been quick to credit depression with having thrust Franklin Roosevelt into the Presidency. But it has been slow to say which depression turned the trick—the one which laid Hoover low in 1929 or the one which resulted from the Wilson Administration's failure of financial management in and after World War I. If Roosevelt's candidacy was the child of the Great Depression brought on by the Versailles system, it was also the grandchild of the earlier formative depression after World War I. The challenge to American leadership during the postwar depression of the 1920's was international: to refinance Europe; to rebuild it; to make the peace work; to cement new trade and investment ties between America and Europe; to extend the orbit of solvent trade throughout Latin America; to face up to the ferment in the Far East by developing the commercial potential of China for the Western system; and, last but not least, to forestall any militarist Japanese threat to the Asiatic mainland.

But by the time of the fearsome Depression of 1929–32, the challenge to leadership had been whittled down everywhere along sharply nationalistic lines. Even England reverted to protectionism. Europe was still the center of the depression-torn world, even though World War I had left her dependent on America. The failure of the American system of financial support formalized the nationalistic consequences of depression on both sides of the Atlantic. With Europe and America insulated from one another by the stoppage of financial flows and the collapse of the international debt structure, the orbit of international commerce and finance suffered a sharp contraction. Latin America was no longer a factor and commanded no priorities. China was sealed off from the Western system, and Japan was attacking her. As Hoover floundered, and as Roosevelt prepared to swamp him, any promise which offered a plausible way to bootstrap any country out of depression was more than acceptable: it was ideal.

Roosevelt, therefore, took office as an economic nationalist. The failure of internationalism to stabilize a durable recovery after the depression of 1921 committed successful politicians in every country during the 1940's to nationalism as the price of success. (Even Stalin shocked the Marxist world by plumping for "socialism in one country.") In this broader sense, both Roosevelt and Hitler, taking office as they did simultaneously and on a resurgence of the tides of the depression of 1921, shared the same heritage. The politics of nationalism had become inescapable during the interwar years. But a political commitment to nationalism entailed a commitment to the economics of nationalism as well. Where nationalism ran in harness with militarism, as in Hitler's Germany and Stalin's Russia, the new slogans of full employment and full utilization of the capacity to produce were given a false ring of vigor by the simple expedient of establishing wartime economies. In Germany and Russia, and in Italy and Japan as well, the injunction, "In time of peace prepare for war," took on a new meaning. Not only did peace offer potential aggressors the chance to get the jump on their targeted victims, but stepped-up preparations for war enabled them to turn the corner into a militarized prosperity. No small part of the appeal of totalitarianism was the purposefulness with which first Mussolini, then Stalin and finally Hitler harnessed the energies of nationalism into the channels of militarism and put people to work: the fact of re-employment provided a disturbing contrast with the "wastefulness" of democracy and capitalism. The drift of democracy into the chaos of depression had awakened a hunger for action. Susceptibility to the appeal of action blacked out concern about its purpose and its ultimate end.

Communists have indicted capitalism for its supposed reliance on armaments for prosperity. In fact, during the 1930's, when capitalism was on the defensive everywhere—and especially in America—America took the lead in rejecting armaments as a shortcut to re-employment. Instead, America persisted in unpreparedness while suffering frustration in her pursuit of peacetime prosperity. The New Deal made its mark on the country without any operational recognition of the opportunity that Keynes offered or of the danger that Hitler threatened. Consequently, America's nationalism under Franklin Roosevelt took the form of a severely demilitarized isolationism as opposed to Hitler's offensive aggression and Stalin's defensive aggression.

The first phase of Roosevelt's Presidential career, from 1933 to 1940, was devoted primarily to domestic economic experiments, sometimes aimed at recovery, sometimes at reform, sometimes at both in a confused jumble, but always within a primarily national target area. These experiments of the New Deal between 1933 and 1940 were successful politically but unsuccessful economically. The New Deal was handicapped from its outset by the fact that American isolationism could not provide a framework broad enough to organize or support full recovery to prosperity. As a practical matter, by the time the limitations of isolationism became apparent, the normal workings of the New Deal economy were already being dislocated and hampered by preparations for war and political crises heralding the approach of war; and, before a verdict could be rendered on either Roosevelt's recovery or Roosevelt's reforms, war intervened. Because Roosevelt's final phase, in 1944 and 1945, was dedicated to peacemaking, and because he failed, he has gone down in history with Wilson as an unsuccessful and, therefore, an idealistic crusader for internationalism. But the fact is that he launched his Presidency as an essay in domestic economic nationalism.

America's first practicing Keynesian, Lauchlin Currie, was also the Administration's most talented economic technician (before he enmeshed himself in conspiratorial intrigues beyond his political capacities). He formed the conviction that the America of 1938 had completed all the recovery that could be hoped for in what he termed its "mature state." Currie expressed a prevalent pessimism which admitted and, indeed, assumed defeat in the New Deal's fight for the full peacetime utilization of resources, especially human resources, and, therefore, which invited concurrence in the Marxist prognosis. The most ebullient conversationalist among the New Deal intelligentsia was Jerome Frank, who startled and stimulated Washington with his renditions of Keynes's missionary efforts to explain public works as the economic equivalent of war. Nevertheless, while public works were tried on a scale which seemed excessive at the time (but which, in fact, erred on the side of modesty), neither these nor any other of the peacetime expedients adopted came close to engaging the capacities of the small-scale American economy of the interwar years. No economic equivalents of war, but only the real thing, would be able to put our economy to work and send it on an expansive course again.

In the light of Roosevelt's ultimate success in achieving the one objective he really planned—a stabilized postwar prosperity —it is ironic that his prewar record of economic experimentation should have been haunted by failure. But economic inconsistency often adds up to irrefutable political logic, and it did for Roosevelt. During most of his two peacetime terms, his Presidential performance was measured by how far the economy had recovered from its 1932 lows, not by how much more it would still have to improve in order to achieve full employment. While his political displays of pride over the economic progress achieved after 1932 won him reelection in 1936 and again in 1940, his campaign oratory told more about the conditions of which he was the beneficiary than of those of which he was the architect. Roosevelt's performance reduced itself to bad economics, but it added up to good politics: though it failed to achieve full recovery, it won elections.

Nevertheless, Roosevelt's grasp of the imperatives of history was immeasurably more imaginative than his ability to absorb theories of economics or to put them into operation. So far as economic ideas were concerned, he lived in what Catholic doctrine refers to as a "state of invincible ignorance." Moreover, he was innocent of any written or conversational familiarity with the Keynesian revolution. If he learned to translate his needs into the new language of the times, it was not because any tutor explained it to him, but because he picked up the language and its idiom from experience. As a matter of fact, the occasion of Keynes's coming to call on Roosevelt at the White House in 1934 produced a celebrated pair of wrong-headed guesses— Keynes sold Roosevelt short as superficial, and Roosevelt, irritated by Keynes's habit of invoking algebra as if it were black magic, reciprocated. FDR actually commented that he had been under the impression that Keynes was an economist and, therefore, was surprised and put off to find him talking like a mathematician. It was entirely on his own that Roosevelt stumbled onto the idea that politicians have an opportunity and government has a responsibility to manage the economy; that is, he discovered Keynesianism soon after he settled down to govern, and at almost the same time as Keynes himself did—certainly very little later. Roosevelt's failure to take full advantage of the opportunity opened up by the new Keynesian technique during his peacetime tenure of office has obscured the remarkable timing of his own independent discovery of its pragmatic equivalent and the political route by which he arrived at it. For Keynes's theory paralleled Roosevelt's practice.

Roosevelt's initial approach to the economic problem he inherited was deceptive because it was so simple. In fact, it was a compound of multiple simplistics. His economic and financial policies quickly bogged down in internal conflicts which burdened the straightforward aims of getting prices back up and putting men back to work with unfamiliar and frustrating complications. Through it all, Roosevelt dealt with economics at arms' length, as an amateur and a pragmatist. At least part of the failure of Roosevelt's prewar economic policies to achieve full peacetime recovery goes back to his lack of familiarity with economics. He had no way of knowing how practical his flash of political genius would turn out to be for the next generation; but he did not have enough faith in his own ideas to follow through on them; and his choice of advisers revealed his ignorance. Altogether, he performed like a tyro at economics but like a seasoned professional at politics.

The New Deal's one full-fledged attempt at economic innovation can be summed up in the slogan, "We need a Plan." The need for Planning—with a capital P—was taken to follow from the evidence that the free workings of the capitalist marketplace had demonstrably failed. Therefore, the new approach called for cooperation to impose a new discipline upon competition and assumed national quotas of planned expansion. The pressure for planning was backed up by widespread belief in Currie's Keynesian advocacy of the "stagnation thesis"—that America had outgrown growth and that its only hope lay in achieving a meticulous match of consumption with production. Finally, "Planning" symbolized a new spirit in Washington—a spirit of aggressive intervention by government in behalf of the "forgotten man."

The idea of planning had first been implemented in Soviet Russia, when Stalin launched his original Five Year Plan in 1929. Soviet planning achieved its main political goal, the creation of the heavy industrial base necessary for military power, but only at immense human cost. Moreover, the Russian economy had not recovered by the late 1960's from the exploitation of agriculture and the geometric compounding of imbalances which the Stalinist forced-draft industrialization had engineered into the structure of the Russian economy. But America's planning in the New Deal era did not achieve even its political objectives.

The National Recovery Administration was the main vehicle of FDR's plan, and it was supplemented by the Agri-

cultural Adjustment Administration. Their joint purpose was
to avoid a repetition of the disastrous market gluts and price
breaks of the Depression. Therefore, both emergency operations set out to prevent production from getting ahead of
consumption. The New Deal's original approach to the recovery
problem revealed its total disorientation from Keynes's contemporary position. He had identified the basic need—"the means
to prosperity," in his phrase—as a sustained increase in the
money-good demand for goods and services. A higher price level,
by contrast, was the popular nostrum. But, properly understood
in Keynesian perspective, higher prices would be a consequence
and not a cause of recovery, although their impact would speed
and solidify the process. Thus, a paradoxical state of affairs
resulted: production was restricted, despite its already depressed
level—in order to promote recovery! The confusion is simple to
explain, once the priority given to higher prices is recognized:
the effect of reductions in supply, with demand remaining constant, is to push prices up. Clearly, the New Deal began by
putting the price cart before the production horse. But its political luck saved it from its economic folly.

The cult of planning had expressed a popular revolt against
the blight of poverty in the midst of plenty. The spectacle of
Washington clamping ceilings on production closed off the
avenue to "abundance," another catch-word of the years before
it was taken for granted. As the country watched "little pigs"
slaughtered in the cause of higher pork prices while thousands
upon thousands of Americans subsisted in malnutrition, it took
a new look at the muscular thinking which had made such a big
splash in Washington during Roosevelt's frenetic first hundred
days. FDR's initiatives had snapped the economy out of the
Depression and into a limited recovery. But the contradictory
impact of those expedients brought their effectiveness into question early in the game, even while he himself was still a winner.
Consequently, he had a chance to fall back and take a new
look too.

A new look was certainly needed. Roosevelt had let the
NRA blunder into an administrative trap as politically deadly
as its upside-down economics threatened to be costly. For the

NRA gave real power over production and prices to employer groups as groups, and it balanced this grant of power politically by the legal recognition it gave to labor unions. If the NRA's intellectual roots were socialist, the economic blueprint it was following had been originally devised for the Fascist corporate state. In fact, however, the threat the NRA presented to market-place liabilities was more than offset by its inability to mobilize the potentially immense and politically irresponsible power that it possessed. To settle the matter, the "old" Supreme Court bestowed a political windfall on FDR by declaring the NRA and the other New Deal planning instruments unconstitutional in 1935. Once the issue was switched from Administration achievements to Presidential purposes, FDR was home free. He transformed his first economic detour into his second political landslide in the 1936 election.

The New Deal's infatuation with planning diverted it from the effective use of what Keynes identified as the main engines of prosperity—monetary and fiscal policy. FDR's misdirected efforts reflected a perverse choice of economic advisers. Certainly, to avail himself of the most modern thinking on monetary policy at least, FDR would not have had to come to terms with Keynes's formidable personality. Much closer to home was Professor Irving Fisher of Yale. Fisher, the first authentic American innovator in the field of economics, was ahead of even the most sophisticated Europeans. Anticipating the other economists of the day, including even Keynes, he had proposed the remedy of the hour: he had pioneered the concept of the commodity dollar. By this Fisher meant a domestic monetary standard tied to no specific commodity, like gold or silver, but one that measured the composite of domestic commodity price movements and, therefore, of business activity and of liquidity requirements.

Fisher led the way to the idea of discretionary monetary policy as a means of managing the domestic economy, as opposed to the rigid orthodoxy which subjugated the money side of the economy to the arbitrary and uncontrolled price fluctuations of precious metals. In fairness to Keynes, he was the one who integrated the idea of monetary management into a general theory of how the economy functions. And when, in the 1960's, the effort finally began to modernize the international monetary system along those lines, by then considered routine in the domestic sphere, the foundation already existed in the program which Keynes had conceived and fought for unsuccessfully against the Roosevelt Administration at Bretton Woods in 1944. Fisher, however, was the seminal, creative and altogether practical American economic pioneer of those transitional years of ferment, who formulated concepts later to be recognized as Keynesian before Keynes formulated them himself. But he lacked the political backing and acceptance which is indispensable to recognition for an economist, and he completed his creative labors in the wilderness of academia. In the spirit of creative cameraderie, Fisher dedicated his key book, *The Purchasing Power of Money* (its title was prophetic of inquiry and experience to come), to Simon Newcomb, whom he described as a "pioneer in the study of 'societary circulation.' "

Instead of listening to Keynes or Fisher, Roosevelt allowed himself to be influenced by Henry Morgenthau, Jr., his intellectual *valet de chambre* in matters involving the application of intellect to finance (neither of which area of activity had the slightest interest for FDR except as means to ends or as necessary evils). Each and every idea that Morgenthau promoted through his special relationship with Roosevelt turned out to be a mistake: his final scheme for the de-industrialization of Germany was merely the best-known because the most conspicuously and authentically his own creation. But to the extent that the various "spend–lend" experiments of the New Deal proved to have come too late and to have done too little, the chief engineer of the roadblock against them was invariably the stubborn, suspicious, loyal and devoted lieutenant who divided his time between command of the Treasury and attendance at the bedside. And, to the extent that the novel monetary and economic experiments of the New Deal were neutralized, their innocent but ignorant saboteur was invariably this familiar of Roosevelt's. His inability to understand or accept new ideas prevented the fiscal follow-through from the Treasury which is the precondition of success for any monetary or economic experimentation. (At the same time, his total personal devotion led FDR in 1939 to take the unusual step of vesting authority over the lend–lease phase of mobilization for war—political dynamite in that pre-election year—in the Treasury, as a way of keeping secret the extent of America's preliminary involvement in the fortunes of the Allies.)

In his opening gambit as a senior member of the Roosevelt team, Morgenthau brought a professor he knew to Roosevelt in much the same manner as a patient brings his doctor to a friend. Sadly enough, the professor whom Morgenthau brought to Roosevelt happened to be a quack, and a famous quack at that: George F. Warren, who practiced "funny-money" alchemy at the New York State College of Agriculture at Cornell. Irving Fisher was ready for his time, and the times were ready for him: he was the historical figure evolved by American economic thinking; Roosevelt was the emergent political practitioner of the period who needed him and who in any intellectually mature society would have insisted on having him. Instead, Roosevelt had Morgenthau, and Morgenthau saddled him with Warren.

Moreover, the times were ready for the old gold standard to be scrapped. In fact, the times were ready for any initiative that America resolved to take, and any American initiative was bound to work with dramatic effect. When a depressed economy reaches the limit of social endurance, it either disintegrates into social anarchy and political revolution or it bounces back up into a sharp recovery which generates its own momentum. This is how the "Roosevelt recovery" developed. The best proof that Roosevelt's domestic initiatives worked is that the world staggered back to work despite the actual international initiatives that America took. Professor Warren stuck Roosevelt with a nonsensical "funny-money" gold policy and a new gold exchange standard with which Roosevelt, in turn, stuck the world. How wrong-headed this remedy was at the time is made crystal clear by Marriner Eccles, the eminently practical and wholly frustrated Chairman of the Federal Reserve Board during the Roosevelt Administration. Eccles's recollection, in his *Beckoning Frontiers,* of the mumbo-jumbo which was sold to Roosevelt is irrefutable:

"Administration leaders in these early weeks [of 1933] were

not unaware of the pressing need to restore national purchasing power. They aimed to do so by raising commodity prices through a devaluation of the dollar in terms of gold. Viewed in a reverse image, they meant to raise commodity prices by increasing the price of gold in terms of dollars. . . .

"As a result of the banking measures taken earlier, the very few Americans who held any gold were required to surrender it. The millions of destitute and unemployed had neither dollars nor gold. How, then, could an increase in the price of gold that might be exchanged for more dollars reflect itself in an increase in effective purchasing power? How could this action create more effective consumer demand? So far as increasing domestic purchasing power was concerned, the results would be nil.

"What dollar devaluation succeeded in doing was to attract the gold of the world to American shores, in exchange for which foreigners received more dollars. A substantial increase in our exports resulted as the new supply of dollars was spent on the purchase of American goods. But ultimately the policy brought us more than three fourths of the gold of the world, for which we had no use.

"This could have been foreseen long before . . . there was no need to devalue the dollar in terms of gold, or increase the price of gold in order to raise commodity prices. Devaluation by itself would not bring about any increases in prices. Prices could be raised only if the government created effective purchasing power by a spending–lending program based on deficit financing. If this was done, there was no need to resort to the devaluation program. With the existing supply of gold and without any change in its price the banking system could expand its operations to meet all monetary and credit needs."

A generation later, the fiscal and monetary crisis brought on by the Vietnam War confronted America and the world with the tragic consequences of Morgenthau's amateurishness, Warren's quackery and Roosevelt's susceptibility. The fatal flaw in America's financial defenses during the Vietnam battle of the dollar had been put there more than thirty years before. It was Warren who had resolved the suspense in the guessing-game over the price of gold by recommending that it be fixed at $35 an ounce. Not that the particular price at the time of the last fixing had mattered. All that did matter then and continued to matter in the 1960's was the holdover link of the dollar to gold, a link which defined America's obligations as de facto manager of the world's money. The obligations saddled her with voluntary responsibilities to maintain a gold reserve which did her no good domestically, and which gained her no reciprocal international consideration or advantage, but which exposed her to scrutiny and sanctions from foreigners who were not obligated to observe the same rules and who had obvious incentives to put the dollar at a disadvantage. America's first unilateral opportunity to take the world, as well as itself, off gold, and thereby to substitute conscious management for mysticism and habit as the guiding spirit of the world's money system came in 1933. The 1944 Bretton Woods Conference was the second. In the late 1960's, America paid the price for her failures of imagination and literacy twenty-five and thirty-five years before.

Roosevelt's response to failure on the economic front was to seize the initiative on the political front. By 1935, businessmen had recovered sufficient confidence in themselves to take the counteroffensive against FDR: the Liberty League was their vehicle. As the 1936 campaign drew close, FDR responded by thundering against the "economic royalists." When, at the Democratic Convention in 1936, he warned the "forces of selfishness and of lust for power" that, having met their match in his first Administration, they would meet their "master" in his second, he alarmed even Keynes. The era's leading economic revolutionary hurried off a confidential plea to his political counterpart. Keynes warned FDR that public works alone could not bring recovery and that the role of private investment was critical. In almost as many words, he expressed alarm lest the New Deal kill the goose that laid the golden egg.

Keynes urged Roosevelt instead to tame businessmen to his purpose because, his letter explained, they are "much milder than politicians, at the same time allured and terrified by the glare of publicity, easily persuaded to be 'patriots,' perplexed,

bemused, indeed terrified, yet only too anxious to take a cheerful
view, vain perhaps but very unsure of themselves, pathetically
responsive to a kind word. You could do anything you liked
with them, if you would treat them (even the big ones), not as
wolves and tigers, but as domestic animals by nature, even
though they have been badly brought up and not trained as
you would wish. It is a mistake," continued this remarkable
document, "to think that they are more *immoral* than politicians.
If you work them into the surly, obstinate, terrified mood, of
which domestic animals, wrongly handled, are so capable, the
nation's burdens will not get carried to market; and in the end
public opinion will veer their way."

But New Deal tax policy implemented the rhetoric of
FDR's move to the left. The Depression had made money a
giveaway in the capital markets: the only activity left to the
harassed investment banking community was to refund the high-
coupon bonds left over from before the Depression into low-
coupon bonds, which turned no wheels and found no work for
new money or unwanted men. Nevertheless, Roosevelt's Treasury was forcing corporations to pour new dividend disbursements into the idle reservoir of capital unwanted on any terms,
adding to the uneconomic surplus in the reservoir and freezing
the underemployment of capital which corresponded to the underemployment of other resources—especially manpower. Because money was so cheap during the prewar years of
post-Depression stagnation, tax devices calculated to increase
dividend yields created no incentives to bid up stock prices and
thus to reopen the equity avenue to capital investment. So long
as interest rates remained low, add-ons to dividend disbursements forced by tax gimmicks scattered capital without strengthening markets or quickening commitments. And so long as
private investment continued to be depressed and government
investment failed to take up the slack, cheap money alone could
not produce recovery.

The 1938 recession eliminated any possibility that America could achieve full peacetime recovery. As an example of
the intellectual confusion of which Morgenthau was capable and

to which Roosevelt was susceptible, the Treasury policy which produced the recession was as worthy of the dunce-cap as was its gold policy at the outset of the New Deal. Again, Eccles's account is definitive:

"The 1937–8 recession . . . was due principally to a rapid and speculative building up of business inventories at a time when government spending was drastically curtailed and when consumer income was further reduced by the inauguration of the Social Security law. With swollen inventories on the one hand, and with sharply curtailed consumer purchasing power on the other, a disconnection was formed in the economy that made a deflation inevitable. . . .

"There was a general desire in all quarters to convert money into things in the belief that costs of goods were going to rise higher. Many business interests feared they might have difficulty in getting deliveries, so they placed orders not only for current needs but for future ones. This accentuated further the rise in prices, and the speculation in inventories grew to a volume of over $4 billion in 1937.

"While this was taking place in the business world, the government in 1937 was *reducing* consumer disposable income by almost $4 billion. This was in contrast with an increase of such income by $4 billion in 1936. The reduction was largely due to two factors. First, the new Social Security law that went into effect in 1937 resulted in a collection of $2 billion in social-security taxes; no part of this was disbursed in benefits. Moreover, the tax pulled potential buying power out of the pockets of the very people most likely to spend the money if it had not been taxed away from them. Second, no soldier's bonus of $1.7 billion was paid in 1937 as it had been in 1936. These combined factors resulted in a $66 million federal cash surplus for the first nine months of 1937 in contrast with a huge deficit in the previous year. Most significant of all, *the consumer disposable income in 1937 contracted by an amount roughly equal to the inventory that had been accumulating.*"

The crowning example of Morgenthau's inspired fiscal and monetary mismanagement took the form of a proposal at the worst of the 1938 recession to impose a Federal sales tax on all retail purchases above ten dollars—as a recovery measure! It took all the king's men to give this brainstorm a decent burial and to get on with the compromise "spend–lend" program which brought the economy back to a state of imperfect recovery. Meanwhile, upwards of ten million men were still unemployed, and the abiding problem of the interwar years, how to stimulate expansion, was still unsolved and largely unfaced.

But not even the recession of 1938 canceled the political credit balances that Roosevelt had created with the country by the impetuous confidence he had demonstrated when he took over in 1933. Then, one simple act—substantively meaningless, but psychologically cathartic—had established FDR as "the champ": he closed the banks in order to open them again and, thus, exorcised the Depression. No difficulties developed for the credit structure with the 1938 recession, for the simple reason that the recovery was still too young to have had a chance to build a new pyramid of debt on the wreckage of the old. Consequently, Roosevelt was able to ride out the storm stirred up by the aggravation of his problem of seemingly permanent unemployment. And he was able to hold his own politically despite the obvious inadequacy of his 1938 recovery measures. In the end, Roosevelt managed to avoid responsibility for the economic drag and the psychological cloud which, at more fundamental levels, deepened doubts over the ability of capitalism in America —and, therefore, anywhere—to achieve a full utilization of resources without war. By the time Wendell Willkie started to develop it into a serious issue during the 1940 campaign, the politics of war had become a hotter issue than the economics of peace. Roosevelt seized on the former as his vehicle for staying one jump ahead of Willkie.

Nevertheless, the 1938 recession had thrown Roosevelt onto the defensive. His resistance to remedies big and bold enough to get the economy moving kept him there when the slump in steel operations to under 20 per cent of capacity provoked the Keynes-oriented faction of his Administration to push for a $10-billion package of "spend–lend" projects. FDR characteristically cut his New Dealers back to $4.8 billion and, also characteristically, his fear of even this commitment was that it was too much, not too little. While, as he said, he aimed his promises a little to the left of center, he was careful to steer his performance a little to the right of center.

Then, abruptly, the war changed the terms of debate and responsibility. The resistance which developed to Roosevelt's 1940 candidacy on the issue of the third term confirmed his own judgment that only the war justified another try at the White House. In fact, the war not only justified Roosevelt's third-term candidacy, but made it inescapable. It also distracted him from the argument, suddenly irrelevant in operational terms but fundamental in its implications, over the failure of the New Deal to have nurtured the tired and faltering baby recovery of the 1930's. Paradoxically, however, Roosevelt developed a keen and practical new interest in economic operations as the war distracted his attention from the economy.

Roosevelt was a competitor and, as a competitor, he was a showman. It was second nature for him to shoot at the targets in his sights and to claim credit for the kill. As a politician, between elections as well as during campaigns, Roosevelt had run like a race horse—against the nearest horse he could see. He had not only outrun Hoover, but had driven him out of the Presidential arena—as even Hoover, for all his political obtuseness, realized by 1936. In the process, Roosevelt beat the immediate issue of depression-and-recovery. Consequently, the fundamental issue of full utilization of resources was allowed to fade into an abstraction to be given lip service only.

When Willkie started to turn recovery into an issue, the war erupted into a bigger issue. The moment it did, it raised the ghost of FDR's political youth and sent him running against Woodrow Wilson's wartime record, determined to beat it. He did. Once the war freed him from worry about full employment and economic expansion, stability superseded recovery as the problem, and Roosevelt solved it. He did not live to see his success. But by the time he died, it was assured. His wartime strategy of economic mobilization secured the foundations of postwar prosperity. Only his plan for peace failed.

15 : ROOSEVELT'S SUCCESS

ROOSEVELT'S RISE coincided with the advent of the radio age; and his mastery of the airwaves anticipated Kennedy's later success in exploiting the strategic weaponry of the TV studio. These new techniques of political communications effected a revolution in political campaigning which did not stop on election day. The layering of the new politics of public relations onto the conventional politics of power and policy imposed a corresponding set of TV-oriented priority claims on the time and energy of each new Administration. Since Roosevelt's time, no Administration has found itself free to concentrate from week to week on problems not at the top of the list on current public-interest questionnaires. What Santayana deplored as the "solipsism of the present" has come increasingly to dictate the terms of contemporary American debate and decision-making. But where Santayana referred to pathological cases of the individual mind held incommunicado in its own private world, the new communications media have induced an obsessive governmental concern with short and necessarily erratic swings in mass sentiment.

Public officials, being candidates, have eagerly cooperated

with the popular living-room news media in cutting peepholes in the veil of government operations. Thanks to the power of the mass media, today's voters—in their capacity as viewers—have shown themselves able to make the government switch its priorities as easily and as capriciously as they themselves switch stations; and the political merchants with survival expectations have learned to stage the kind of shows most likely to attract audience attention. But, politics being politics and the public being the public, the result has necessarily been an optical illusion. What the public has seen when the TV screen showed the Cabinet Room in the White House and the War Room in the Pentagon and the Open Market Committee Room in the Federal Reserve Board has been exactly what Alice saw in her looking glass—first a cloud of mist and then an entrance into a looking-glass world where everything works backwards.

By the mid-1960's, the public's illusion that watching the powerful meant sharing the responsibilities of power had proved self-defeating. Johnson resented the public's interest at the same time that he manipulated it for his own needs; and his manipulations operated by reversing the "realities" which appeared on the television screen. The public reciprocated his dislike and resentment and yet responded to his rough treatment, which it confused with omens and promises of early victory in Vietnam. By the same reverse logic, Vietnam was undeniably unpopular, and yet each new round of escalation ordered by LBJ won him more popularity at the time, as even his critics admitted. But Johnson's popularity was not the kind accorded the magnetic aristocrat, the ordinary but determined county judge, the genial ex-general or the model, book-carrying college graduate—all of whom had preceded him in office. It was the grudging acceptance granted a clumsy but powerful spirit, part ogre and part lout, who paid a bitter price in public affection and creditability for his old-fashioned orientation toward operations at the expense of image.

It is scarcely an exaggeration to say that Roosevelt's radio voice was the rudder that steered him and the country through the storm over the war issue at the climax of the crisis election of 1940. Willkie performed impressively when he had a crowd within earshot, but he stumbled miserably before the radio audience. His campaign style was a throwback to the era of Bryan. Again and again he whipped up his crowds by pulling out all the stops as he went off the air instead of as he went on. He hurled the ultimate political weapon of the year—the last year of the old, provincial American isolationism—when he charged that the boys were on the transports. But Roosevelt's voice was his antimissile missile. Less than a week before election day in 1940, FDR induced the country's most vociferous and politically flamboyant America Firster, Joseph P. Kennedy, to go bail for the *bona fides* of his isolationism. To a Boston audience, FDR said he had been pleased to "welcome back to the shores of America that Boston boy, beloved by all of Boston and a lot of other places, my Ambassador to the Court of St. James's, Joe Kennedy."

The actual promise to avoid war which Roosevelt was heard to make meant less than his unforgettable reference to *"my* Ambassador," if only because its flamboyance conveyed the meaning Roosevelt needed to register with the antiwar vote. The difference between having been heard to start to say "our Ambassador," and seeming to stumble into saying *"my* Ambassador," was the difference between good taste and good politics, and the choice was a very easy one for FDR. The country wanted peace. Roosevelt's voice played the politics of peace, and played it as winning politics. But the crisis demanded America's participation in the war, and Roosevelt knew it. He knew also, as he steered into the crisis, that he would need a new crew to man his new War Administration. His manipulation of the airwaves brought him the freedom to maneuver that he needed in order to feel his way toward the manipulation of the levers of power. And he knew enough about war to know that the critical levers he needed to manipulate were those controlling the war economy. The secret of Roosevelt's success in leading the war economy to a happy postwar landing is that he approached the problems as a challenge of war leadership and not of economic management.

The military economics of World War II present a study in paradox. America's economic mobilization to hold the line first for England and then for Russia boomed the economy. But Hitler could have brought both Russia and England to their knees, as he did Western Europe, and America would still not have gone to war. It took the monumental irrationality of Pearl Harbor to free America to bring the power of her economy to bear in the military contest across the Atlantic. The provocation offered by Japan's naval blunder sent America to war and, fiercely and effectively though America's troops fought, it was not with her troops that she won the war: it was with her economy. And it was not by plan or efficiency of organization but by the sheer momentum of production that the American economy overran first Europe and then Asia. In *The Struggle for Survival*, published in 1951 when memories of Roosevelt's War Presidency were more vivid than Korea and Vietnam have left them, I described the tortuous stratagems to which Roosevelt resorted before his home-front high command developed a plan which mobilized America's productive potential to swing the tide of battle; and I explained how Roosevelt relied on the momentum of American mobilization to overrun the enemy. It was a wise exercise of judgment on his part and, in its skepticism toward the practicalities of organization, it was a practical one.

So long as America needed a plan to insure preparedness before war came, America was foredoomed to unpreparedness. Pearl Harbor freed America from dependence on planning and allowed her to mobilize her enormous momentum behind the war effort. Once America concentrated her attention on the war, the American economy began to generate the wherewithal of victory at a stupendous rate. Making allowance for the start-up time needed to organize the mass production of war items, it was only a matter of months before all the materiel required, from landing craft to cartridge cases, began pouring out in quantities that other belligerents regarded as wasteful. Our armies did not hit the Normandy beaches until June, 1944, but cutbacks signaled the filling up of the production pipeline as early as 1943.

In the closing phase of the war, the wartime director of the Bureau of Mines, James Boyd, who was doing double duty as

Chief of the Metals Branch of the Army–Navy Munitions Board, revealed the naïveté born of America's economic strength in his analysis of the German copper situation. Copper provides a fine illustration of the contrast at the time between American and European scales of operation and standards of comfort and austerity. What the normal American scale of operations took for granted as a minimum requirement, the most advanced foreign calculations regarded as lavish. America's by-product wastes were Europe's basic minima. With copper, as with other strategic materials, America first ran herself into shortages to meet her minimum requirements and lost a few months' tooling and shipping time. But she won the war by swamping the enemy with the sheer bulk of her armament and supporting production, and thus she was spared the ordeal of having to fight on equal terms in the war of bodies and bomb shelters.

Within this framework, it was Boyd's expert judgment (based on what Washington knew about the flow of new production available to the German war machine, and on its per-man calculations of military requirements) that Germany would run out of copper in six months. Because copper is always a scarce item in military operations, this was a crucial judgment, carefully arrived at. But to the surprise of Boyd and the entire American planning operation, when the time came to assess the German situation after V-E Day, Germany was found to be swimming in copper. Her ingenuity and austerity in substitution and reclamation of battle scrap had more than offset her deficit in production and her lack of resources.

Until Pearl Harbor, the burden was on the government to justify further cutbacks in civilian production in order to raise quotas for war production. Pearl Harbor reversed the priorities. The question of how much industry would be able to produce for the military buildup was turned into the question of how far the rationed home-front operation could be cut back. So far as the automobile and other mass-production industries were concerned, once the permissible ration of auto production was cut back below a minimum annual rate, the compulsions of public relations and cost accounting combined to argue for a complete termination of business-as-usual and an all-out conversion to war production. But before too long, the authorities in charge of regulating production and directing resources into approved uses found themselves under pressure to use their rationing powers to limit the military "take" from the economy. The emergency Administration in Washington soon discovered that the last ton of steel needed to produce the hundred-millionth high-explosive bomb made a more direct and effective contribution to the war effort if, instead, it was tagged for reallocation into the first ton of steel needed to produce a freight car to carry bombs already manufactured to a port of embarkation. More than incidentally, it also discovered that the only way to make sure that bombs once produced would find freight cars to carry them to the front was to guarantee the civilian economy an irreducible ration of resources which the military could not preempt.

In the race to organize and ship war production, the performance of the economy during World War II far surpassed all the old World War I records—not least because, especially toward the end, it evolved an incomparably more sophisticated and effective system for analyzing requirements and scheduling production. The Controlled Materials Plan, formulated by Ferdinand Eberstadt, put the availability of steel, aluminum and copper back-to-back with the requirements for all three basic materials created by the military end–use of products bearing them. When, for example, the military programmers pulled numbers out of the air for production schedules which, if budgeted, would have called for the use of four times more copper than the entire supply available to the economy, schedules were deflated into balance with availabilities before the military could run hog wild. Consequently, Roosevelt's War Administration, by bringing programmed demand into alignment with supply, succeeded in holding back the wartime inflation of basic commodity prices as Wilson's War Administration had not.

To be sure, inflation was inevitable. War always makes it so. But the question of whether the cost of a wartime inflation proves intolerably pernicious or benignly self-curative depends on its timing. If it takes its toll while the war is still on, the productivity of the civilian economy and the availability of manpower cannot possibly saturate markets with the new supply which is the only ultimately effective offset to price and wage inflation. But when the price–wage push is deferred until the war is over, the supply side of the market is given an opportunity to catch up with the price–wage push and to contain and reverse it. Indeed, a postwar price breakout can serve a highly constructive purpose, for it puts a profit premium on rapid transition back to civilian production. After World War I, the inflationary catch-up proved too explosive to be corrective. It had run out of control before the Armistice and continued to spiral upward in the "flash" boom of 1919. By the time production could be redirected to meet civilian demands, the self-reinforcing process of hyperinflation was under way. Consequently, it took the collapse of 1920–21 to put an end to the inflationary madness. Fortunately for the U.S., the economic structure which came out of World War I was sound enough to absorb the breakneck run-up and run-down of prices. Other countries, from Germany eastward to Russia, faced social collapse as wartime inflation escaped correction and ended in complete debauchery of the currency and disintegration of the social system.

America's experience after World War II stood in sharp contrast to the loss of control which produced the speculative disaster of 1919–21. Wartime inflation had been effectively limited and, consequently, postwar inflation was contained within reach of operable economic reality. The inflation in prices that took place between 1939 and 1948—from the beginning of the transition to war until the completion of the transition to peace —was milder than the comparable price explosion of the World War I period. Wholesale prices rose 147 per cent during the 71 months from June, 1914, to May, 1920, but only 118 per cent over the 108 months from August, 1939, to August, 1948. Moreover, the more gradual progression in the World War II era—an average inflation of 9 per cent per year versus 15 per cent per year in the Wilson period—obviated the need, as well as the opportunity, for a drastic downward postwar price adjustment. Other economic variables had time to adjust to the higher level of prices, so that the stable, secular postwar boom which got under way in 1946–7 began from a level of prices and money wages substantially above that of the prewar period.

Because Roosevelt managed to defer his problem of wartime inflation, he avoided one of the more serious errors of omission of the Wilson War Administration, while affording himself the satisfaction of matching a definitive success of his own against a glaring failure of Wilson's. Because the Controlled Materials Plan imposed a civilian control over the normal military impulse to inflate requirements, enough progress was registered in balancing military demand against civilian supply to hold back price inflation. The Roosevelt War Administration also succeeded in scoring another first: it held back wage inflation, limiting wage increases within the scope of the Little Steel Formula to 15 per cent. Ironically, the Roosevelt War Administration maintained and strengthened its formidable ties of support with labor by limiting wage increases. The Wilson War Administration had jeopardized its immeasurably weaker claims on the loyalty of labor even though it permitted wage rates to go sky high because it let prices head even higher. But the Roosevelt War Administration restrained prices through its system of direct war controls, as the Wilson Administration failed to do. Real earnings rose throughout World War II.

The totality of the conversion to war production after Pearl Harbor helped to explain why both price and wage inflation were deferred for the duration and why they were made inescapable afterwards. With construction and consumer durable–goods production shut off; with capital goods and metal-working activity subject to stringent rationing; with transportation limited; with fuel, rubber, food and even shoe consumption cut back to subsistence rates; with upward of 12 million men in uniform; and with prices and wages subject to ceilings—there was no place for money to go but into the reservoir of excess liquidity. At the same time, innovation on the fiscal front contributed in a pattern-making way to both the short-term deferral of inflation and the long-term buildup of deferred demand.

Roosevelt's wartime announcement that he had mothballed Dr. New Deal and commissioned Dr. Win-the-War to take over revealed the limitations of his own view of the situation over which he was presiding. If there was any one article of faith which the advocates of more reform held in common with the advocates of American intervention against the Axis, it was that war would indeed mothball the New Deal. Paradoxically, however, the more sincerely and systematically Roosevelt recommitted his new War Administration to war, the more far-reaching in subsequent effect the reforms it designed for the financial engines of the war economy turned out to be. The official dichotomy between reform and war was more apparent than real. The new wartime tax structure was confirming the pragmatic intuition of James Forrestal, then Secretary of the Navy and later Secretary of Defense. For the tax structure was built directly from the Keynesian blueprint: America's wartime tax forms read like an appendix to Keynes's *How to Pay for the War*. The fact that this lucid and eminently practical tract for the times became the blueprint for America's wartime tax structure, which in turn became the model for its permanent tax structure, easily makes this the most effective of all Keynes's many effective essays in persuasion. Unlike his dissents, his polemics and his theories, *How to Pay for the War* has become too influential still to be read. Experience—of peace as well as of war—has long since familiarized everyone with everything it says.

Pay-as-you-go was the keynote of the emergency system of wartime taxation. Given record wartime income flows and the forced backup of all normal discretionary uses for money, it made sense. Economically speaking, no better use for excess cash existed than to pay taxes out of the increment left over after "voluntary set-asides" for savings. This would have been true even if the only economic function of high wartime income taxes, withheld at the source, had been to buttress the emergency system of price controls by holding down cash demand and prices, thereby protecting the real value of savings and maintaining the incentive to save. Wartime stabilization was doubly assured by the simple ingenuity of the insurance for the economy which the new tax system provided. For losses and lapses of income during the postwar years were treated as refundable out of taxes paid in the war years. As late as 1945, the conservative management of the War Administration underestimated the effectiveness of this built-in fiscal stabilizer which the emergency tax system engineered into the postwar structure.

In the closing months of the war, a representatively influential misreader of the omens was Assistant President James F. Byrnes, once Roosevelt's manager in the Senate, later his balance-wheel appointee to the Supreme Court, best-known as his frustrated stalking horse for the payoff Vice-Presidential nomination of 1944, and, subsequently, Truman's Secretary of State at the outset of the Cold War. Byrnes, sensitive to conservative financial projections, put primary emphasis on the emergency schedules of unemployment compensation to stave off a postwar slump. He noted with nervous satisfaction that they had been extended to cover twenty-six weeks of joblessness.

In fact, this supposedly primary system of postwar depression insurance was never tapped, and Byrnes's fears proved over-conservative. The instant reversibility of the war-emergency tax system sufficed by itself to prevent any postwar emergency. Even more, the universal confidence born of the knowledge that tax payments made would be refundable as instant income—and tax-free income at that—enabled expectations to supplement actual refunds. By contrast with World War I, the four-ply system of war taxes, price controls, civilian rationing and, above all, money controls had made money cheap during and despite the buildup of emergency demands for it. The savings reservoir was filled up instead of drained dry during the emergency years —a meaningful contrast with the drift of war finance during the Vietnam crisis and with the drought condition to which it reduced the money markets.

This quick and continuous drainage of excess cash out of the economy and into the Treasury had the effect of holding back prices during years of maximum cash pressure on prices and wages. For the duration, it protected the equity in cash of everyone who had cash and, therefore, provided at least temporary term insurance for the purchasing power of the cash holdings of everybody who was accumulating cash—and everybody was. The system, by virtue of being instantly reversible into refund flows, served the additional purpose of giving everyone with an exposure to losses or to lapses of income a free and quick claim on instant credit without regard to money conditions or to future creditworthiness. The new system turned the Treasury into a bank and enabled the Treasury to turn the economy into a bank.

Thus, cash paid—or more precisely, advanced—to the government as taxes created a trustworthy, usable, money-good backlog of capital. The tax dollar, withheld and collected at the source but instantly refundable on claim of need, was immeasurably more useful as the strategic instrument of war finance and positive prosperity than the dollar supposedly "invested" in war savings bonds. The dollar that was supposedly taken away turned out to be usable, where the dollar that was clearly lent provided no liquidity in time of need and was exposed to eroding inflation before it could be used.

Economics and ethics apart, in terms of the new managerial and analytical challenge to anticipate and to limit short-term fluctuations in the postwar economy, the new tax system of instant withholding and instant reversibility established the two-way flow of the tax dollar as a major factor determining the direction, the pace and the predictability of the emergent postwar economy. The tax dollar began to evolve as the "swing" variable to offset changes in volume of the business inventorying dollar or the capital investment dollar or the consumer spending dollar which all lie beyond the direct control of government. The innovations of war finance during World War II changed the chemistry as well as the structure of the American economy.

The fact that the wartime reins on the economy were held tight during a period of maximal savings flows and forced underconsumption was enough to guarantee a catch-up "by the wild horses of inflation" (to use a favorite phrase of Lyndon Johnson in his Senate days) once the restraints came off and the money that had been banked became free to chase goods again. Harry Truman's caretaker Administration did not find itself forced to dismantle the apparatus of price controls until 1946, a delay which was bad for the Administration and for the country. Truman's miscalculation in overstaying the welcome of price control raised so much political fuss that it grew into one of the principal causes of the landslide which gave the Republicans control of the Eightieth Congress. People in the food-growing states could not understand and would not tolerate a situation in which, with the war over, it paid them to hold animals back on the land instead of shipping them to market. People in the meat-consuming states could not understand and would not tolerate a situation in which, with their pocketbooks full and their wage rates inflated as well, their diets could not at least go back to normalcy too.

Rationing in one form or another held back consumption and hampered free money in its chase after goods until the end of 1946. Moreover, demobilization and reconversion did not really take effect until the beginning of 1946. But the war boom had started up in 1940, and 1941 had been a banner year in which earnings, capital formation and savings had largely got the jump on controls and taxes. Altogether, therefore, the liquidity reservoir enjoyed the benefit of the better part of five rich years devoted mainly to input with very little drainage. Taking the Biblical rule of thumb of seven lean years and seven rich years, and making due allowance for technological acceleration since the time of the Scriptures, the 1941–6 period of high savings, low consumption and record accumulation of backlogs of money-good demand guaranteed equal time to the postwar period of money use and consumption catch-up. A postwar "catch-up" boom was all the more certain because World War II, more than any war in history up to that point, had created limitless new technological openings for capital investment.

The war had provided the money to finance what was needed, and demobilization made people and facilities available to do the work. On top of all this, the war ended not in the mirage of a false peace but in the reality of the Cold War, which limited demobilization and guaranteed a continuing if erratic cycle of "stop–go" for the new defense cycle which the Cold War activated. Before the five emergency years of forced oversaving and underconsumption could be averaged out by five Cold War years of catch-up in consumption and investment and use-up in savings, the Korean War had broken out. Thus, America avoided the postwar test she had expected and feared: how successfully would she put her enlarged economic capacities to peacetime use without the intervening corrective shakeout of a postwar depression?

FDR used the economic side-effects of World War II to activate the postwar potential for prosperity. But his success on the domestic economic front was offset by failure on the international financial front. The dangers of war boom and postwar bust to which Roosevelt responded so creatively were no doubt far closer to home—in terms of geography, politics and time. But the opportunity and the need for providing a suitable international framework for the postwar world appear, in retrospect, to have been no less compelling. Long after American opinion had come to take for granted FDR's achievement in planning the successful prevention of a postwar depression, it could view with justifiable harshness his failure to balance this breakthrough with comparable vision on the international side. In fact, the same economic theorist whose program FDR followed in molding his wartime fiscal policy was rejected by FDR in formulating a plan for a postwar monetary system.

The 1944 Bretton Woods Conference was the occasion of postwar monetary planning. The key protagonists were Britain's Keynes, on the side of modernization, and America's Harry Dexter White, ironically enough on the side of reactionary standpatism. (The extent to which White's Marxist political convictions influenced his judgment as a Treasury expert must remain an open question. It is, nonetheless, relevant in that his strong stand in favor of retaining the link to gold and against financial modernization reflected a view of the nature of money no less conservative than Marx's own intellectual acceptance of "metallism.")

Keynes envisioned—and proposed in hard practical terms— the international equivalent of what each and every nation had evolved for itself, sooner or later, as part of the process of growing up. His plan was a central bank of central banks, an international clearing house on whose books the reserve assets of national central banks would count as deposits. His aim was the flexibility and liquidity, which well-managed central banking can (and at times actually does) bring to the national banking system.

By contrast, White's plan simply recreated the discredited gold exchange system of the 1920's. The International Monetary Fund was to be added as a hedge against the short-term recurrence of any whipsawing financial crisis and as an "iffy" long-term compromise with the more far-sighted followers of Keynes. In fact, White's proposals—endorsed by the U.S. government —carried the day against Keynes's bitter dissent. The irony lay in the fact that White's institutional structure would do the job that Keynes had conclusively demonstrated needed doing only as long as the U.S. stood willing and able to perform the role which, as Keynes had foreseen, only an international institution could over the long run fulfill. Only a few voices in the wilderness could be heard, most notably that of Professor Robert Triffin of Yale, whose "Triffin Plan" constituted an updating of Keynes's original proposal.

During the first fifteen years after Bretton Woods, the need for Keynes's super-central bank went neglected as the U.S. proved capable of providing an acceptable medium of exchange for international transactions and a desired store of value for international reserves. But in the 1960's, Keynes's conservative misgivings were justified as forty-year-old doubts recurred. The most intelligent French statesman of his day, Pierre Mendes-France, a former Governor of the Bank of France, put the problem to a sophisticated Cambridge University audience in 1966: "The system can only work when the U.S. supplies liquidity by running international deficits and every dollar of deficit that the U.S. runs injures confidence in the system."

By 1967, it was evident that the price to be paid for the expediency of the U.S. government nearly twenty-five years before was a high one. At Bretton Woods, the U.S. could have written Keynes's vision into operating reality. But by the time the need to do so was recognized, the unilateral opportunity to do so had long since been lost. The failure of American imagination at Bretton Woods carries a double sting—the adoption of Keynes's plan would have placed the U.S., as the number-one creditor in the world, in an immensely strong long-term position. America's international assets, largely invested at long term, would have continued to expand and to accrue ever-growing returns. But the short-term debts, which by 1967 far exceeded any summation of realizable short-term U.S. assets, would, under Keynes's plan, have been switched to the account of the International Clearing House, to be the collective responsibility of all who participated in the real wealth which the debt creation reflected. It is rare for a nation to have the unilateral freedom to construct an international environment of its own choosing; it is far rarer for a nation in such a position deliberately to ignore its own self-interest, not even in the interest of others, but rather out of a compound of prejudice, ignorance and perverse idealism. At Bretton Woods, the U.S. had this rare freedom. But at Bretton Woods, the U.S. rejected the opportunity which that freedom allowed.

The American failure at international monetary planning for the postwar world contrasted sharply with FDR's success on the wartime home front. But as an exercise in deliberate model-building, in contrast to FDR's inspired improvisation, it set the pattern for American postwar performance. In the arena of strategic programming—economic and military—America's success was unquestioned. But she proved incapable of learning from it. In fact, World War II taught Russia more about America's role in the world than it taught America.

The lesson which Russia learned from America's success in bringing the weight of behind-the-lines economic power to bear on the fighting front was that it pays to function as an arsenal with allies fighting at the front, instead of being a belligerent at the front with an ally as an arsenal behind the lines. America did not seek or plan her role as the anti-Axis arsenal in World War II, and Russia could very largely blame her own opportunism and Stalin's paranoid incompetence for the monumental losses she suffered. America could not have planned the successive strokes of luck which delayed her entry into the shooting war until she could mobilize her economy to provide the cover it did for her Allies as well as her own troops. But after America wound up playing the providential role of arsenal to the anti-Axis alliance, and as if she had planned it that way as a plot designed to bleed and sacrifice Russia, Russia resolved to reverse the roles: to force America to commit her more skilled, more scarce and therefore more economically valuable manpower against Soviet satellites. Russia stood behind those satellites, arming them but not manning their lines. By definition, these satellites were on the Communist side of the Iron Curtain, and they were remote from American centers of strength. Once America committed military manpower to such fronts, Russia was able to turn them into situations of American weakness by the simple expedient of sending arms.

It is difficult to say which spectacle was more unlikely—that of American military power tied up and bogged down by a fifth-rate Communist satellite or that of Russia's pitifully inadequate and mismanaged economy taking advantage of exposures created by America's strategic unpreparedness. Yet both have become familiar facts of life.

In 1965, the Johnson Administration escalated the war in Vietnam on the assumption that Russia's good offices, motivated by her fear of China and by her hope of doing business with America, would guarantee an escape hatch for Washington under favorable circumstances. In 1967, too, the fact of America's stalemate in Vietnam invited Russia to experiment with the second front in the Mediterranean—obviously a high risk area in the very center of the world economy, by contrast with Vietnam and Korea before it. Given Russia's commitment to the long view and to the strategy of position, the fact that she had positioned herself to activate a second front was at least as meaningful for the Cold War as the outcome of any preliminary skirmish on it. No doubt the Kremlin felt amply justified in its commitment to Sinophobia. But on the second front, which it took advantage of America's immobilization in Vietnam to open in the Middle East, Russia could not justify chauvinism as a defense mechanism against aggression. Her arsenal-like stance behind Nasser encouraged her to turn the Middle East from a seething volcano into an erupting one, stoked by the fires of racism which the politicos in the Kremlin found as congenial as had their Czarist predecessors.

America has persisted in regarding her strategic and military problems abroad as nothing more than a series of local outbreaks in the various Koreas and Vietnams and Egypts which have become the fronts supplied by Russia in her post-1945 stance as the arsenal of anti-Americanism: hence America's failure to concentrate on developing direct leverage upon Russia, so that our general interest in peace-keeping can be insured, our exposed strategic outposts guaranteed, and our economy relieved from strain. World War II had spurred America to the greatest peace-time boom in history. But it had also spurred Russia to the strategic operation which, by 1967, would frustrate and divert America's unique economic potential.

16 : FORRESTAL'S DILEMMA

AMERICA'S COMMITMENT to worldwide involvement as a national way of life began with the decision to back Britain in 1940. Our first expression of that commitment was economic: lend–lease aid. And during the peace that followed the war as well as during the war itself, the economic implications of worldwide commitment became as significant as the political and military implications.

During 1945, defense spending had peaked above $81 billion. Because civilian activity was so severely rationed while war production enjoyed every conceivable priority, defense at the end of the war accounted for nearly 40 per cent of the Gross National Product. Meanwhile, the controls which held civilian activity back were also deferring inflation. Consequently, increases in the GNP as well as in the cost of living during the last three war years were surprisingly nominal in view of the circumstances. Then, during the interval between demobilization in 1945 and remobilization in 1950, while the economy was making up for lost time and using up its newly stored liquidity, defense spending was cut back sharply. What was surprising about the cutbacks, however, was not that they were so large but that they were so limited. For the first time in our history, postwar demobilization did not go to the extreme of total disarmament.

America's earlier wars had left no aftermath of danger creating a permanent requirement to keep a portion of the country's resources mobilized. The occupation of the South during Reconstruction stirred up political violence and retarded the modernization of the South, but it created no fiscal or economic changes arising from the need to maintain a peacetime defense establishment. After 1918, America dreamed of peace and deceived herself into believing that she had bought it for Europe by the dispatch of money. To prove that she was isolated from danger, she could point to her display of dreadnoughts, although the naval spectacular which continued all through the 1920's only distracted attention from the need for a strategic plan and an overall defense program to implement it. But the Armistice had ended the stimulus of armaments spending as abruptly as Sarajevo had activated it.

After World War II, the Cold War changed the historic pattern of economic fluctuation between war and peace. It forced America to limit demobilization to the dismantling of the superstructure of emergency, and to commit herself for the first time to a permanent peacetime minimum of defense programming. America's head start in the atomic arms race helped to harden the lines in the Cold War and forced the decision to form a permanent peacetime base. Although America's temporary monopoly over the new atomic weaponry argued for cutbacks in conventional forces, it made full disarmament impossible. The billions needed to support the new peacetime defense base seemed to involve a great deal of money; but, in the end, the cost proved nominal because of the expansion of the economy. Politically, however, the resolve to retain a permanent peacetime defense operation set counterforces in motion.

Five years after World War II ended, the Korean war provided an ex post facto rationale for the unprecedented peacetime defense effort, while at the same time demonstrating how costly were the international commitments that made this effort necessary. The fact that the war took America by surprise testified both to the purity of her intentions and to the amateurishness of her operations. For her intentions, America had no need to make excuses. For her operational amateurishness, she could have no excuse to offer, for she had been warned. A man of extraordinary perception and devotion had, literally, died in the effort to insure that America would not have to pay a price in blood for unpreparedness in the strategic arena. The man was James V. Forrestal.

Forrestal was the most creative of the new crew Roosevelt had recruited during the transition to his War Presidency. He was the least conventional and the best read. He looked the part of the sophisticated tough; he had boxed with Gene Tunney (who was twice his size), and his broken nose only added to his air of being a hero out of a Scott Fitzgerald novel.

Roosevelt had a respectful feel for the place and the potential of the Irish in American politics. He owed his own political advancement to the progress of the Irish and to the problems their progress brought them. Al Smith, when he mounted his difficult Presidential candidacy in 1928, had wanted to make sure that, in the likely event of his defeat, he carried his home state of New York. Smith had taken the precaution of balancing his own Catholic candidacy for the Presidency with the selection of Roosevelt as a gubernatorial running mate on the calculation that the great name FDR bore would bring assets to the ticket balancing his own; Roosevelt's presumed dilettantism marked him an unlikely rival the next time around.

By 1932, however, times had changed for the Democratic Party. The Irish candidate's need to find a Protestant balance wheel had been replaced by an incentive for Irish political leaders, with a vested interest in victory, to find a Protestant candidate. From the outset of his Presidency, Roosevelt had seen that the various Irish political allies which had backed his nomination over Al Smith's were in their turn going to exact a claim on a future nomination. If only because he was annoyed by the eager ambitions of James Farley and Joseph Kennedy, he decided, in 1940, to create still another Irish possibility who would be more amenable to his own interests and less stridently clannish. Forrestal's characteristics suited Roosevelt's purposes.

Forrestal was a Duchess County-bred Irish-American. His

family, like Jim Farley's, had its roots in the building trades. But his own social evolution had anticipated the Kennedy story. His career included Princeton and Wall Street, where he had been a negotiator and broker plenipotentiary for Clarence Dillon, the remote, elusive, cold, rich and powerful "Wolf of Wall Street." Forrestal was not a professional Catholic like Kennedy or Farley, but had strayed from the faith; thus, he could display the assets of his Irish background without risking the liabilities which at that stage of the game still faced any Catholic candidate. Moreover, Forrestal would not be the only lapsed Catholic to be offered an option on availability for the Presidential succession. Senator Jimmy Byrnes of South Carolina had emerged behind the weak Senatorial leadership Roosevelt preferred to work through as his principal broker with the Congressional establishment, and Roosevelt was soon to encourage his ambitions for national office by designating him as his wartime Assistant President. Roosevelt liked to balance his favorites as well as his opponents against one another; and, thus, the rise of Byrnes not only opened the way for the development of a political potential in Forrestal's administrative role, but indeed invited it. The talents he brought to the White House staff were supplemented by the credentials of an Ambassador. For once the Depression brought Wall Street into disrepute and broke Morgan's half-century hold on the levers of political finance, dollar incentives superseded hierarchic disciplines and thrust Dillon, Read into intimate contact with the New Deal. Even the Wilson Administration had not been as closely involved with the House of Morgan during World War I, when Morgan was acting for England and France and when the Wilson Administration was moving first to finance the war for the Allies and then to win it for them.

Roosevelt was the second young man to have turned a wartime mission as Assistant Secretary of the Navy into a Presidential career: his envied and hated cousin Theodore had been the first. When FDR offered Forrestal the same stepping-stone job, he told him what he told so many others, including young Congressman Johnson: "You remind me of what I might have been like if I had not suffered the disadvantages of being born a Roosevelt and having a Harvard education." The words he added, to the effect that a successful wartime Assistant Secretary of the Navy need not be a Roosevelt in order to develop an outside chance at the Presidency, were heady wine even for an intellectual sophisticate whose instinct was to shun the crowd and to despise efforts aimed at currying popular favor.

Although Forrestal had forged his axis with Roosevelt's Washington from a Wall Street base, his connection with it had developed through the New Deal stalwarts with whom he had dealt at the Securities and Exchange Commission, notably its strongly liberal Chairman (later Supreme Court Justice), William O. Douglas, who was Forrestal's main sponsor at the White House. And Forrestal's approach to the dynamics of crisis reflected this sponsorship. More than anyone else close to Roosevelt, or in the intermediate circle around the inner circle, Forrestal saw that the war crisis in Europe offered a Bismarckian solution to Roosevelt's problem of how to develop an acceptable mix of recovery and reform. Perhaps Forrestal's remoteness from the electioneering side of politics sharpened his sense of practicality about the managerial side. At any rate, he guessed that the approaching war was going to assure Roosevelt a release from the frustrations which had for eight years disrupted his economic and social programs. While less practical thinkers worried whether more money for guns meant less money for butter, Forrestal understood that money for guns meant new jobs and a rising standard of living. As he put it, "The people in the South who haven't been getting enough to eat are going to get more grub now, and get their teeth fixed too."

From the time of his appointment as Undersecretary, Forrestal had been the real power in the Navy Department behind the bipartisan public-relations operation of Secretary Knox. He moved up to the number-one spot in 1944. This promotion was something of an innovation on FDR's part. Roosevelt always liked to separate the man who possessed the real power to make decisions from the man responsible to the public and to Congress for the use of that power. It was Roosevelt's way of insuring himself against both the liability of failure and the competition of success. A man who failed at the use of power could be quietly liquidated, while one who succeeded too publicly was denied the opportunity to make political capital at the President's expense out of his achievements.

Forrestal emerged from the ordeal of war as Washington's most impressive administrator of America's strategic involvement. His understanding of the forces at work in the postwar world was as outstanding as his administrative competence. Two vivid recollections of Forrestal in 1945 have remained with me over the years. The first dates back to his return from Germany after Hitler's suicide—Forrestal had been the first American to fly into Berlin on V-E Day. With an artist's grasp of meaningful symbol, he volunteered: "The first thing I saw as I looked out the plane window when we taxied in was a pile of rubble and a woman lying on top of it having a baby." Several weeks later, I recall having asked him whether it was his judgment that Russia would declare war against Japan before our forces closed in for the kill. "How in hell are you going to stop them?" was his reply (at a time when Russian maneuvers for the spoils of victory were still seen by nearly everyone as a sincere contribution to victory by a friendly ally).

Forrestal foresaw a fateful dilemma of national purpose. What drove him to suicide in 1949 was the sense of fear and frustration he developed because he saw so early and so realistically the price America would pay for having seized the head start in the atomic arms race. His own dilemma arose from his sense of America's dilemma. How could America use the unique and enormous power which possession of atomic weaponry gave her? How could she translate into real political advantage the military might which could not be unleashed? How could she negotiate and compete with the emergent power of the Soviets at the level of ordinary political competition when the deterrent she held was too big to be employed—so big that she could wipe out the opponent with whom she needed to bargain? And this unique position of power could not last, for nothing was going to stop Russia from joining the atomic arms competition and turning it into a stalemate. The moment Russia did, America's monopoly would end. Meanwhile, she was torn by a bitter debate between the Hawks and the Doves of the period over whether her new atomic power represented a safeguard for the security of America or a threat to the peace of the world. It was a war of words: the only calculation more certain than that America's advantage would be a source of self-deceptive smugness while it lasted was the companion calculation that it would not last very long.

In fact, Russia took very little time to turn America's meaningless atomic arms head start into a meaningful stalemate. For Russia, the achievement of atomic stalemate represented as positive a breakthrough as building the bomb had for America. Although atomic weaponry conjured up visions of the end of the world, the confrontation returned to the political arena. And the stalemate over unusable atomic power soon cleared the way for Stalin to score another breakthrough: with nuclear weapons immobilized, the manpower at hand on his side regained its value.

The world had taken many revolutions of military technology in stride before Hiroshima, but atomic weaponry produced instantaneous shock and universal recoil. In the past, destructive innovations had been local, and their impact gradual. By the time any generation of possible victims faced danger from the latest addition to the arsenal of attack, the defense was at work on a creation of its own: the castle wall, armorplate, the gas mask, the anti-aircraft gun and the air-raid shelter each, in its turn, seemed formidable enough to bring reassurance, if not security. But against the atomic bomb, defensive therapy could offer no modern equivalent. Until an automated and automatic missile defense could be proved more than a theory, the only deterrent to atomic threat could be still more atomic bombs. In fact, the generation after Hiroshima witnessed still another reversal of experience. Whereas in the past an arms race which involved weapons of relatively limited destructiveness led to war, the atomic arms race escalated the chances of destruction toward annihilation. It thus put a premium on reopening the channels of political negotiation as fast as failures of political negotiation threatened to precipitate world war.

The illusions bred by America's monopoly over atomic

weaponry lasted longer than the monopoly. One of them was that the bomb would police the world and guarantee the peace. Since America alone possessed the bomb, this misconception was taken to mean that command of the ultimate weapon equipped us to be the world's policeman and peacekeeper. America persisted in wearing her policeman's badge until long after she lost the club that went with it. A related illusion welcomed the atomic deterrent as insurance against a postwar recurrence of arms burdens and arms race.

Instead, the atomic arms race grew into a fixed and irreducible burden on the resources of every country with a vested interest in power or a stake in survival. By the late 1960's, for example, the suspicion that even Israel had a rudimentary atomic capability strengthened her hand in her confrontation with the Arab world. Nor did the atomic bomb buy insurance against shooting wars. On the contrary, it licensed local wars by guaranteeing that they would remain local. First Korea and then Vietnam, accordingly, created add-ons to the basic atomic overhead which the aftermath of World War II had already riveted onto the budget. As Russia responded to the incentive to build her own deterrent, the Cold War spread its strange new normalcy to war-in-peace. Before the police power of the atomic threat made its appearance as a factor in world politics, the powers had been on notice that any local conflict might escalate toward total war. It took the atomic arms race to make the world safe once more for imperialistic adventures.

The local wars which broke out in the 1950's under the umbrella of peace-through-fear-of-atomic-war showed how well Russia had learned from America's function in World War II as the arsenal of her allies. America reacted with fear and anger to revelations that Soviet agents had filched her atomic secrets a few months before Soviet scientists would no doubt have duplicated them anyway. But American opinion would have been better advised to take alarm over Stalin's appropriation of her formula for organizing military victories through the lend–lease of military assistance to front-line allies who absorbed the casualties. The unplanned pattern of events which enabled America to do so well out of the two world wars provided the prototype for the plan which has enabled Russia to do so well out of Korea and Vietnam. Stalin and his successors clearly saw the profits to be gained by involving their chief rival in indefinitely prolonged stalemates against minor opponents on remote frontiers, where she would not suffer military defeat but could not achieve political victory. The insurance against military defeat enticed America to move into each front. The elusiveness of political victory froze her there.

Since the unlimited nuclear punch which America alone possessed after World War II was unusable, her dependence on it left her vulnerable to any limited conventional provocation. This was the strategic dilemma which Forrestal, almost alone, saw clearly from the outset of the Cold War. The insight into danger which could not be avoided, and the responsibility for action which could not be taken, combined to destroy the balance of his reason. He was the custodian of an omnipotent force, but one which would retain its omnipotence for only a short while. He could not order the use of the ultimate weapon while it was still America's monopoly. And he also saw clearly that the moment it ceased to be America's monopoly, the choice of weapons and of when and where to use them would no longer be his or America's. The strain of the double responsibility for a wasting present and exposure to a vulnerable future was too much for him. America's brief spell of atomic security had been a snare and a delusion. Worse still, it had been a treacherous waste of time.

Forrestal failed to resolve the strategic dilemma with which America had to grapple in the postwar world. But his failure was offset by a characteristically pragmatic response to the fact that America would have to live with that dilemma, even if he could not. As one of the few who realized that the lessons of World War II would have to be institutionalized if they were to be learned, Forrestal set out to give America the institutional framework she would need in order to live in an age of permanent crisis. His achievement—and it was more his than anyone else's —was the National Security Act of 1947. His authorship was recognized when Truman appointed him under the Act to be the first Secretary of Defense.

The National Security Act has not really unified the armed services or subjected them to the discipline of civilian policy guidance. But it has set up a ring within which the running military–civilian fight can be contained. Further, it has promulgated rules by which the President, the Congress, the press and interested pressure groups can judge round-by-round results. In Secretary McNamara's heyday, the compromise built into the National Security Act invited him to draw tight lines of centralized command and to send generals off saluting like privates. But the structure of power provided for in the Act is apt to prove self-correcting. For McNamara became the victim and the prisoner of his early arrogations of responsibility. The military chiefs whom he subordinated to his commands made records against him while they followed his orders. No unified structure of military command can ever interrupt two-way communications between the military and the Congress: it can only drive those relationships underground while subordinates are on trial to make or break their commander. In McNamara's case, the underground resistance provoked by his administrative absolutism did not save the country from the consequences of his mistakes. But his administrative power turned into a political liability—not only for him, but for Johnson as well—when his opposition within the Armed Forces took advantage of his mistakes to make itself known.

The ambivalence of power in the structure of military–civilian relationships within the Pentagon power-structure was balanced, as Forrestal recommended and as Congress decided, by a fundamental resolution centralizing responsibility at the policy level. The center of responsibility was intended to be the National Security Council. Its mission, as created by the Act of 1947, was to insure against any divergence between strategic commitments and the military and industrial muscle required to back them up. Forrestal went a step further than the letter of the Act. Foreseeing as he did that any effective implementation of strategic commitments with defense support would involve the economy in general and the fiscal ties between the government and the money markets in particular, he suggested that the President invite the Secretary of the Treasury to participate in the proceedings of the Council.

The problems seen and raised by Forrestal in the debate over defense unification have never been resolved; therefore, his recommendations remained as relevant at the height of the Vietnam crisis as they were three years before the outbreak of the Korean War. On March 18, 1947, his comprehensive testimony before the Senate Armed Services Committee described the National Security Act and the philosophy behind it as providing "an organization which will allow us to apply the full punitive power of the United States against any future enemy. It provides for the coordination of the three armed services, but what is to me even more important than that, it provides for the integration of foreign policy with national policy, of our civilian economy with military requirements; it provides continuing review of our raw material needs and for continued advance in the field of research and applied science.

"It is clear to me," Forrestal said, "that the experience of the past war made necessary certain changes in our government system for national security. Both World Wars showed . . . that modern total warfare requires more than an army and a navy. It requires the use of agencies of Government other than the military departments, and in fact every department of Government had a part in the last war. Military strength today is not merely military power but it is economic and industrial strength. I might also say that it is fiscal strength. It is technological resourcefulness, and it touches every field of knowledge. . . .

"Above all, modern war is economic and it is worldwide. Prior to World War II this was not fully appreciated. It was appreciated very little by us in World War I because until the end or toward the end of the war we were not confronted by the manifold problems of the shortage of materials, of transportation, of supply, and of manpower that we faced in this one very shortly after the onset of it. The shortage of manpower, the necessity for the evaluation of priorities, the balancing of our productive capacity against military requirements—all these pressures made some form of civilian–military coordination essential. Agencies were created to coordinate the economic life of the Nation with the requirements of the military establishments. On the whole they worked well. . . .

"We have incorporated lessons of the past into this bill. Provision is made for coordination of our military and economic requirements on a continuing basis by the establishment of agencies such as the Munitions Board and the National Security Resources Board."

In answer to a not very precise question from Chairman Gurney, then the Senior Republican Senator from South Dakota, Forrestal summarized his statement of the problem with a pithy formulation of the interdependence of strategic purpose, its defense implementation and the financial support needed to mobilize the sinews of war: "Our national strength is economic, industrial, and fiscal . . . whatever contributes to our being able to retain all of those elements, including our financial strength, keeps us fit and competent to wage war."

Jiu jitsu is the art of using an adversary's strength as a decisive weapon against him. In the history of the Cold War, after Russia broke America's original monopoly on atomic weaponry, the Soviets proved that jiu jitsu is no Japanese monopoly. As Forrestal had foreseen and feared, Russia extended the stalemate from the global front, where atomic missiles were loaded and aimed but not fired, to the local fronts on which it was safe to shoot out local wars. The moment the stalemate was extended beyond the atomic level, on which it was not safe to shoot, to the local level on which it paid Russia to have her satellites shot at, her new style of jiu jitsu came into play against America. For, as Forrestal said in his reply to Chairman Gurney, wars call for the mobilization of economic and financial resources; and, therefore, they inescapably involve the economy and burden the economy with the cost of financing their requirements.

When Forrestal committed suicide in 1949, he left America stranded somewhere between a nonshooting Cold War and a shooting local war. But he also left his country with the administrative equipment and a strategic view which prepared it for the local shooting wars that were to come. Forrestal's memory has been badly served by superpatriots on the fringe of the political mainstream, who have confused his vision of America's crucial dilemma with their own paranoid nightmares, as well as by their opposite numbers at the other end of the political spectrum, who have lost sight of his sense of national priorities in their own propensity to practice a McCarthyism of the left. McCarthyism, whether of the right or of the left, attempts to demonstrate guilt by association; but the most conclusive refutation of the charge that Forrestal was guilty of atomic imperialism is offered by his continuing association with Justice Douglas. Douglas made no bones, while Truman was President and Forrestal was serving in his Cabinet, about asserting that Truman had no understanding of foreign affairs and that Hiroshima had been a crime and a blunder. During Forrestal's final tragedy of psychiatric disintegration, when he was fair game for attacks from the left, Douglas was one of those who remained loyal to him.

All through the 1960's Douglas had been the Ambassador to the liberal power structure of both Johnson and the Kennedys; and Senator Robert Kennedy had regarded Douglas as his principal senior adviser during his rise to prominence and power, despite Douglas's strong support of Johnson as the best man in 1960. In 1967, Douglas committed his enormous prestige with liberal opinion to the assertion that it was Truman who bore primary responsibility for the Hiroshima decision. Meanwhile, the legend of Forrestal's atomic imperialism had caused its advocates to adopt him as a martyr to their cause. But Forrestal's suicide stands as the conclusive repudiation to those who would turn him into a proto-Bircher with a simplistic set of answers. It was the unanswerable questions that killed him.

The period between Forrestal's death and the Korean War saw a painful reenactment of the dramatic preliminaries to World War II. The villain of the piece was Louis Johnson, who took over from Forrestal as Secretary of Defense. Sometimes ambition whipsaws a man. This happened to Louis Johnson. During the false peace after Munich when Roosevelt was refusing to face up to the war crisis it had made inescapable, Johnson had been the militant Assistant Secretary of War in charge of industrial mobilization, serving under a quiescent Secretary of War, Harry H. Woodring, who wanted no part of it. It was Louis Johnson whom Roosevelt had repudiated when he gave the country his famous assurance that he had no plans for the mobilization which he was, in fact, already manipulating inside the Treasury. It was this same Johnson whose ambitions for elevation to a wartime Secretaryship were again frustrated when Roosevelt made his radical move to neutralize Willkie's business candidacy by reaching out for two ranking Republicans, Henry Stimson and Frank Knox, to man his War Cabinet—Stimson as Secretary of the Army and Knox as Secretary of the Navy. When Dr. Win-the-War rose above the politics of party to play the politics of principle, no controversial Democratic stalwarts ascended with him.

It was scant solace to Louis Johnson that Dunkirk and Pearl Harbor found his critics guilty on the familiar charge of "too little too late." For he had committed the fatal political error of pushing for too much too soon. In 1950, with Forrestal gone and a Democratic President who was calling on the party faithful to close ranks and giving recognition to those who heeded the call, Johnson resolved to avoid the error which had proven so costly for him during his tenure as Assistant Secretary of War a decade earlier. Elevated at last to command over the entire defense establishment which Forrestal had knit together, Johnson did not risk his second chance by advocating levels of defense spending which overshot the mark of public acceptance. This time he undershot the mark. He set out to accommodate the demand for economy in defense spending, and he succeeded better than he knew. Korea found him busily dismantling the apparatus which needed to be reactivated instead.

Louis Johnson's appointment to preside over the power center in the Pentagon was a commitment to the future. The liberal groups, which were suspicious of Truman and whose support he needed, were downright hostile to Johnson, with his World War II reputation for hawkishness at the Pentagon. Adding to the President's embarrassment and to his new Defense Secretary's vulnerability, his new Secretary of State, Dean Acheson, was committing the Administration to a hard line against Russia. A prudent defense backup of Acheson's foreign policy would have called for expansion of the defense budget and the defense establishment. It certainly would have given strategic support requirements an overriding priority over the temporary public relations of pleading guilty to past budgetary deficits in the hope of claiming credit for future budget balancing. At the very least, it would have outlawed any further defense cutbacks.

Truman paid for the loyalty for which he was known, and Johnson paid for the image with which he was stuck. Louis Johnson was only a politician and not at all a crusader; and it was the irony of his fate that twice he deliberately walked the political plank for a principle. The first time it reflected his military foresight; the second time, his fiscal imprudence. The first time, the President suffered for sacrificing him; the second time, the President benefited. For Truman's primary loyalty was to Acheson: where Acheson led, he followed. And, if history judges his Presidency in a favorable light, it will be because he did. But the hard line to which Acheson committed the Administration turned Louis Johnson into an expendable commodity the moment his political compulsion to remake his image surfaced.

Louis Johnson's about-face from Hawk to Dove proved fatal, not so much because it invited suspicions of opportunism as because it sent defense policy into reverse when foreign policy called for it to go forward. The defense budget for the fiscal year in which the Korean War began called for expenditures of $14 billion and committed the Administration to a further cut to $12 billion in the following fiscal year. In the world of the atomic bomb, of big bombers to carry it, and of occupation troops to concentrate the responsibility for and share the wealth in the defeated countries, a defense budget of $14 billion, with a commitment to cut it to $12 billion, approximated operational zero, even in the absence of a shooting war. It was as if Forrestal had never lived, the National Security Act had never been written, and the National Security Council did not exist. Such a total lack of awareness of the crucial link between foreign policy and fiscal planning foreshadowed the Vietnam fiasco of the 1960's.

17 : TRUMAN'S TRAP

HARRY TRUMAN was the third Democratic President of the century. His tenure in office—after Roosevelt died, the bomb fell (by his order!) and the war ended—followed the Wilsonian–Rooseveltian pattern of division into a Reform Presidency and a War Presidency. Unlike the Reform Presidencies of his Democratic predecessors, Truman's was ineffective: instead of performance in the present, it offered promises for the future.

Truman was bailed out of the failure of his Reform Presidency by the onset of his War Presidency—and his escape surprised him no less than it surprised everyone else. But both Wilson and Roosevelt had won the wars that ended their essays in reform. Wilson's effort to make the peace which victory in war made possible destroyed him physically as well as politically. By the time Roosevelt died, victory was merely a matter of time, although the pattern of postwar conflict was already set. Truman, by contrast, having been saved from his failure at reform, was destroyed by his inability to win the war which followed.

The Korean conflict was the last of the long line of America's wars to prove an unquestionable plus for the economy. But it was also the first of America's wars that was not needed as an excuse for economic management. By the time of Korea, the New Deal and the Keynesian revolution had made economic management conceivable and even respectable. Thus, the Korean War stands as a "swing" event in the history of America's political economy.

Korea started a new cycle of war boom and postwar expansion. But several other interrelated political developments were already combining to give the post-World-War-II boom a new lease on life. In 1948, Governor Dewey's amateurish and ineffective campaign had helped Truman win reelection. The drama of this upset momentarily distracted attention from the fact that Truman, in his hour of greatest triumph, had won by a vote of no-confidence in Dewey rather than by a vote of confidence in himself. Nevertheless, Truman's repudiation of the "do-nothing, good-for-nothing Eightieth Congress" created a temporary party consensus uniting the reelected President and the newly elected Eighty-First Congress.

More than the political cycle swings with fluctuations in the relationship between the President and Congress. The psychological cycle of investment confidence does too. Although amateur speculative opinion expects the stock market to rise and fall with the business indices, it is more likely to follow the political returns. Again and again, the outbreak of political fisticuffs between the President and Congress has knocked the stock market down. And, just as regularly, the return of harmony in the fundamental political relationship has set the stock market on its feet again and generated confidence up and down the economy. The stock market, anticipating the crossfire between a Democratic President and a Republican Congress in which business was about to be caught, had collapsed in the fall of 1946. The election of 1948 produced a renewed vote of confidence in the benevolent leadership which a new activist consensus might be expected to offer an expectant and grateful economy.

This confidence was justified by three political moves which were to be translated into irresistibly expansive arithmetic. The first was the Marshall Plan, whose main architects were Dean

Acheson, then still Undersecretary of State, and George Kennan, then on his way up from the State Department Policy Planning Staff. By guaranteeing the Western alliance that America would not only lead and protect it, but would also finance it, the Marshall Plan added a new dimension to the economy of the free world. In addition, it avoided the burdensome structure of postwar debt which had doomed the prosperity of the 1920's to the crash of 1929. The Marshall Plan provided for Europe's reconstruction to be not so much financed as endowed. Contrary to Lenin's theory of imperialism, the hallmark of capitalist prosperity has been the free expansion of interdependent markets and the liberalization of capital flows between them. The Marshall Plan assured a full generation of solvent expansion for the trans-Atlantic community, not least because it set the valves which controlled money flows to carry capital in one direction—from America, where the wartime supply had accumulated, to Europe, where the postwar demand had been created.

The two other political moves by the Truman Administration which reinforced the pattern of postwar expansion were an assumption of leadership over the emergent civil rights movement, and an espousal of the full employment philosophy. At the time, the impact of each stance was more symbolic than quantitative. But, as a symbolic stance, each added authority to the rapidly growing influence of the governmental factor on decision-making and on the psychological atmosphere surrounding decision-making. This impact was seen in investment decisions to buy common stocks, and in corporate decisions that anticipated higher levels of construction and installation costs and a steadier rate of demand growth. The result was a potent addition to what Keynes called "inducements to invest." During the Depression, government intervention had been viewed as a threat by business, and it had further depressed investment calculations. Now it changed into a bull point. Truman's commitment of Presidential support to the civil rights movement promised to add an extra domestic push to the expansive course of the economy over the long term. The institutionalization of the full-employment philosophy in the Employment Act of 1946 provided a new prop under prosperity in the private sector.

The political and social changes generated by World War II had built a new security into the lives of people who were discovering that their labor was no longer a commodity subject to the vagaries and hazards of the marketplace. Real national income, deflated for price increases, rose by some 60 per cent from 1940 through 1950. During the same years, while consumer prices rose by nearly 70 per cent, real wages in manufacturing more than doubled. The mere arithmetic chalked up by the upward spiral of postwar incomes and wage rates told only part of the story and not the most important part at that. The immediate and inescapable aftermath of the war forced a renegotiation of labor–management relationships. Symptomatically, the pattern-making renegotiation was bargained out on the picketline. The pattern was set when the United Auto Workers strike against General Motors turned into a maverick revolt by Walter Reuther against the hierarchs of his own union. The Washington Labor establishment sided compulsively with the established leaders of the UAW, and the Truman Administration sided, just as compulsively, with the "House of Labor" (as John L. Lewis called it) against its residents. Reuther's strike against General Motors lasted from Thanksgiving of 1945, to Easter of 1946, and he won a record dollar-and-cents settlement. But the issue—not readily reducible to arithmetic but expressive of the changed postwar balance of power in labor–management relations—was that "hunger must no longer be an issue at the bargaining table." Reuther won on this one, too.

On the economic side of the new political economy, the growing governmental factor was fostering one major source of demand which had been accelerated by the war. This, in turn, accelerated two major sources of demand which had been retarded by it. The war years had produced a bumper crop of babies. Now the postwar expansion was upgrading income levels and stabilizing income expectations. The result was that more than normally expansive leverage was acting on a more than normally expansive combination of phenomena. Meanwhile, wartime rationing—especially in construction and public services—had deferred spending and accelerated savings. Even if the years of war and demobilization had not upped the birth rate and increased the size of the average family, a major wave of catch-up building was certain to start the moment war controls were abandoned; so was a significant expansion of state and local government activities, which had been curtailed sharply for the duration of the war. Both expectations materialized. The building boom and the large-scale reactivation of local government programs augmented and maximized the growth of demand generated by the bumper baby crops.

The housing boom developed extra impetus from the easy money policies which facilitated access to the overflowing savings reservoir. At the same time, the rising level and steady flow of incomes supported the use by state and local governments of their taxing powers. Inescapably, the baby boom plus the housing boom plus the new sense of security about savings and incomes called for more public services from state and local governments. The adoption by local governments of the "tax–spend–lend" philosophy and practices that had been popularized by Harry Hopkins during the New Deal solidified optimistic psychology. Business activities aimed at marketing products for young families and serving residential and public construction strengthened the consumption side of the fundamental market equation. Sustained net gains in consumption and construction secured the economy against the danger that inventory recessions, which tend to develop when production levels run ahead of consumption, would get out of control.

The formal commitment of government to maintain full employment in peacetime meant that now the need for war as an economic stimulus was over and done with for good—not just for a generation, as before. It would take Vietnam to show that war, by diverting money flows from uses that had developed with growth, had been transformed from a spur for the economy into a drag on it. Americans still carried a highly personal sense of guilt over the failure of the League of Nations, and America's leading role in the United Nations raised hopes that lasting peace had been won. The terror of atomic war not only made war unthinkable as an expedient but, by a kind of reverse English, bolstered the hope for peace. Consequently, when war came in 1950, it found the economy buttressed with solid new defenses in depth against a slump that could not start.

Unemployment would not have remained the overriding fear that it was, and remedies for unemployment would not have commanded the top priority that they did, if anyone had suspected that another conventional war lurked just around the corner—even though war no longer had any positive function as a temporary remedy for unemployment. But although America was evolving peacetime economic stimulants, the outside world was by no means clear that she was outgrowing her dependence on war. Above all, Stalin kept Soviet orthodoxy wedded to the Marxist–Leninist thesis that the "contradictions" within the capitalist bloc would provoke the wars that, as he charged, the capitalist economies needed in order to prosper.

Eugene Varga, dean of Soviet economists, had been demoted as a heretic in 1947 for expressing the realistic appraisal that America would neither have a postwar depression nor be drawn into capitalist wars. By 1952, Varga was again toeing the party line. In *The Changing World of Soviet Russia,* David Dallin quotes the official Russian economic journal: "Varga admitted that he was mistaken in assuming that under the present conditions, in connection with the extreme aggravation of the contradictions between imperialism and Socialism and the extreme preponderance of the U.S.A. over other capitalist countries, Lenin's thesis of the inevitable wars between capitalist countries becomes obsolete. 'I admit,' stated Academician Varga, 'that I was wrong in this question. Comrade Stalin gave sufficiently exhaustive proofs of the inevitability of wars between capitalist countries at the present stage.' "

While Stalin was "proving" that all war is inevitable, but that wars between capitalist nations are more inevitable than wars between capitalist and socialist nations, he himself was planning to reverse his own dialectical success. Convinced that America needed a war and that the war America would get would be against another capitalist country, Stalin gave us a war we did not need—against his North Korean Communist satellite.

Korea seemed a limited war to America because it was a

local war. So, in its turn, did Vietnam—and for the same reason. But Russia fought each war as a new kind of two-front war
—not as Hitler had, by dispersing and dissipating resources,
but by concentrating and conserving them. On the first front,
Russia caused America to be engaged where she was bound to
be weakest—on the Asiatic land mass—in body-to-body combat.
On the second front, Russia caused America to be engaged
where she was admittedly strongest—in her own economy.
America's involvement on the first front automatically involved
her on the second front. Because the Asiatic land mass was so
remote and so difficult of access for a modern American expe-
ditionary force, the most effective access to it that America could
find led through her own domestic economy. America's only
way to mount even a small military operation in Korea was to
support it with a big supply operation in her economy at home.

An old-fashioned essay in Yankee imperialism, armed with
bayonets and shielded from the economy, such as the one which
had sent the Marines into Nicaragua in 1927, might have been
fought out in 1950 on the cheap. In fact, as late as 1954, the
CIA launched a Bay of Pigs operation in Guatemala that
worked, and it mounted this operation in a professional, strong-
arm atmosphere austerely independent of the economy. But the
Korean War was not conceived by military intelligence in an
ivory tower: it developed as a full-blooded reflex action to political provocation and, accordingly, it was not and could not be
insulated from the economy. Officially, it was designated a police
action, undertaken by the U.N. Actually, for the U.S. it was a
war. Over and above the political terminology, however, there
may be value in drawing the fine line between the police action
which is too small to trigger chain reactions in the economy and
the real war, however small, which does. Legally speaking, the
historians of international relations will disagree about Korea.
Economically speaking, however, historians have nothing to
argue about: it was a war.

The loading of the decade's second war boom on top of
the postwar structure of prosperity was bound to make the war
more costly and its aftermath more dislocative than if the crisis

and its imminence had been anticipated in the Truman Administration's economic policies. The price of the unemployment-and-slump insurance which the Korean War soon made unnecessary was reckoned in the Korean inflation. This small war, which lasted less than half as long as World War II, which was limited to one minor front, and which was based on an economy much larger and more productive than the economy of 1940, forced a disproportionately high degree of inflation. In three years, the consumer price index rose 12 per cent, with more than half of the rise occurring in the first year of the war. In that same year, wholesale prices rose by a full ten per cent.

The moment the Korean War front was activated, so were the subterranean reserves of power in the American economy. In short order, Louis Johnson's miserly defense budget of the pre-Korean lull was seen to be wholly inadequate. From a budgeted expenditure of $14 billion, the promised cutback to $12 billion projected a 14 per cent surgery. But though the planned deflation in the defense budget which Korea interrupted was considerable, the actual inflation in military spending which Korea provoked was spectacular. In September, 1950, the President asked Congress for his first wartime supplemental appropriation of $17 billion and, in November, he followed this up with a request for an additional $19 billion. The first five months of the war, therefore, produced something like a 250 per cent add-on to the defense budget—almost before we had begun to fight.

The politics of the military appropriations game during the Korean War roused the ghosts laid to rest after the Mexican War. Although the U.N. (with Russia absent) had voted for the Korean "police action," Truman had neglected to ask Congress for its constitutional prerogative: a declaration of war. Senator Robert Taft, still smarting over his rejection by his party in 1948, staked out his claim to a 1952 nomination when he declared support for the purpose of the war, but opposed the way the President had taken it on himself to launch it without Congressional leave. Clay's fight against Polk was reenacted in modern dress. And Lincoln's counterclaim in defense of his opposition to Polk's "unconstitutional" war—that he had voted full support for everything the troops needed and more—came to be widely echoed in Congress. The more Congress questioned Truman's purposes and methods, and the more it resented his tactic of bypassing the prerogative it could neither forget nor forfeit, the more it took refuge in the Lincolnian stance. Congress pointed to its support of the troops at the same time that it explained its resistance to the President.

Truman's tactic worked well enough to leave a lasting impression on one of the younger tacticians in Congress. When Lyndon Johnson found himself, fifteen years later, inviting attack as Polk and Truman had, he practiced one of his by-then-famous slow-motion maneuvers of deception against Congress. Not only did he not ask Congress to declare war; but he did not say how much he was spending, or intended to spend, on Vietnam. Nevertheless, his Congressional critics, in traditional fashion, invoked support of the troops as political insurance against the risk they ran in offering resistance to Presidential overreaching in time of war.

The politics of the Korean War both repeated and anticipated history, but its economics were unique. The increase in procurement dollars made its economic impact on America qualitatively greater than its military impact on power relationships in Asia or between America and the Soviet bloc. An American policy decision of far-reaching strategic implications increased this economic impact by expanding the scope of the war operation on the home front. This decision came into being as the Defense Support Program.

Again and again, the conundrums of an earlier generation crystallize into the marching orders of the next generation. "Guns or butter" took on a pejorative meaning during World War II, at a time when the War Administration threatened to brand as a Quisling anyone who disagreed with its decision to black out Broadway in order to remind the country that there was a war on—as if anyone could forget. But the Korean War reversed the pressures and revitalized the resolve to demonstrate that the American economy could simultaneously support high and rising civilian standards of living and high and rising military costs.

The purpose and the function of the Defense Support Program, formulated on the civilian side of the Truman Administration to supplement the requirements and the requests of the military authorities, were simple enough. It aimed to broaden the base of the American economy sufficiently to make room in it for a military operation of Korean War dimensions, or even two such at once, while still keeping the civilian economy free to churn the economic and social equivalent of butter at a prosperity clip. I vividly recall a conversation with Henry Fowler, then administrator of the Defense Production Authority, when I jokingly put to him the possibility that the Defense Support Program might work so well that it could create an economy big enough to support a future Korea, or even two at the same time, and still leave room for a recession. By the time the Korean defense administrator was presiding over the Treasury at the climax of the Vietnam crisis, which coincided with the worst of the Vietnam recession in business, this joke of fifteen years earlier had ceased to be a laughing matter.

The Defense Support Program was not involved with the direct procurement of planes, ships, tanks, guns or even medical supplies—nor with the direct labor costs required to produce and maintain the material of war or to man the front lines. Instead its immediate aim was to expand industrial capacities at the base of the economy. The Defense Support Program took up where the Controlled Materials Plan had left off in World War II —with steel, aluminum and copper. It embraced transportation and communications equipment, power plants and components of production: machine tools, valves, bearings and the like. Its aim was expansion and its tempo was quick.

The Defense Support Program was one of the most effective operations ever planned and executed by this or any other government. It was also both confused and confusing—as might be expected of a preparedness plan developed in the middle of a war whose outbreak had already caught us unprepared. Launched as a crash program to catch up with and compensate for past peacetime failures of preparedness, its ultimate purpose was to insure the economy against squeeze and shortage in future emergencies. The immediate effect was to overload our economy with the cost of buying preparedness for the next war at the same time that we were financing the war at hand.

The ideal time for any country to buy preparedness insurance against future emergencies is during a period of slack, before an alarm sounds. But if a country is caught unprepared by a war alert, the most favorable economic situation for emergency catch-up operations is that following a series of slack years, when mobilization is able to draw on idle reserves of capacity and manpower. Roosevelt, in this respect, was lucky. The failure of the New Deal to find a peacetime solution for unemployment simplified the economic side of the problem of war mobilization as much as the traumatic shock of Pearl Harbor had simplified the political side. Exploiting his luck, Roosevelt had moved incisively to limit the inflationary impact of mobilization. Of course, his administration of World War II did not prevent the inflation which followed. But it did defer inflation, which is about all that any War Administration can do. And because Roosevelt managed to keep the price curve flat, he was able to encourage the production curve to soar.

The Korean War provided a double contrast to World War II—first, because it was smaller and then, because of the absence of a Pearl Harbor to force immediate wartime controls. Because World War II was so terrifyingly big, all attention was riveted on the problem of winning. Korea was small enough to provoke frustrated second-guessing over the failures of planning which had left America exposed on its Far Eastern flank. Policy-makers, therefore, made complicated plans for controlling the future before coping with the present. Our Korean War effort to achieve a greater measure of planning coordination than had been necessary during World War II began by duplicating the pattern-making failure of the management of World War I. It invited a pernicious start-up price inflation which got ahead both of operations in the private sector and of planning in the public sector, neither of which ever caught up.

In an article in *The Yale Review* at the outset of the Korean emergency, I wrote: "Undeniably, the process which is priming our new 'Preparedness–Prosperity' pump with $50 billions of 1950–51 money in order to get back $10 billions of World War II production, is sending prosperity upward faster than it is pushing preparedness forward. In World War II, Henry Kaiser explained his operating extravagances on the practical grounds that he was buying time with money. Today, money is much cheaper and time is much more costly. We seem to have devised a technique for wasting money to everyone's profit. But our squandering of time can profit no one.

"Roosevelt's application of Baruch's theory [of price control] suggests the remedy: control inflation first, and then determine to what extent the crisis permits mobilization to be uncoördinated. Instead, we appear to be committed to an earlier Rooseveltian experiment. On the grounds that prices do not have to be controlled, higher taxes are about to be loaded onto our inflationary sellers' markets—as though all sellers, corporate and individual, sellers of labor as well as of goods and services were not free to pass all tax increases on to their customers and employers. The experiment will be painful but popular. Our three-cycle, price-wage-and-profit inflation will become a four-cycle price-wage-profit-and-tax inflation. But tax inflation is not inflation control. And, therefore, the inflationary taxes in prospect cannot buy even the beginning of coördinated mobilization."

Ironically, the Korean War inflation got under way just as the Keynesian doctrine of peacetime monetary management first reached Washington on the policy-determining level. By one of the oddest quirks of economic fashion, orthodox conservative opinion carried its opposition to statism to the point of swallowing Keynesianism hook, line and sinker. The conservatives, who for years had railed at Keynes as a radical, discovered at first hand to what conservative uses the apostle of painless—or credit—regulation really could be. Mistaking the formality of inflation-control for the reality of crisis-control and mistaking monetary-control for inflation-control, they rushed into heedless dissent from Baruch's authentic and practical conservatism, deeding the proprietary rights to the gospel he had preached since the fiasco of World War I to the emergency administrators who took over the control of production and prices.

Despite the stimulus of the war, there was slack in the civilian economy at the outset of the war and it continued to grow, thanks to the neo-Keynesian credit controllers. Materials conservation is clearly the responsibility of production planners. Nevertheless, credit controllers, having begun by trying to stop inflation, began to curtail production.

World War I and World War II had conclusively shown that the proper function of the Federal Reserve in wartime is to be the financial agent of the Treasury. In fact, the Federal Reserve wartime policy of pegging interest rates at minimum levels in order to facilitate Treasury financing operations had been continued after the war ended in 1945. At the outset of the Korean War, the Federal Reserve remained committed, as it had been since 1941, to supporting government security prices in the open market. Its first response to wartime inflationary pressures was to impose selective controls on consumer credit. Shortly, however, pressure began to build up to free the Federal Reserve Board from its subordination to the Treasury and to turn it loose to mobilize the weapons of peacetime monetary management against the war-generated inflation.

The principals in the Fed–Treasury conflict were Treasury Secretary John Snyder, Truman's political intimate, and Federal Reserve Chairman Thomas McCabe, a conventional Philadelphia business leader. The broker who mediated the settlement and who also emerged as its beneficiary was Assistant Secretary of the Treasury William McChesney Martin. As Assistant Secretary, Martin negotiated the compromise which, in March, 1951, gave the Fed the substance of its demand. Then he became Truman's appointee as Chairman of the newly independent Federal Reserve. The *New York Times* reported at the time: "On its face the switch appeared to indicate a victory for the Treasury—with its man in charge of the opposition. But most observers said Mr. Martin would stand up for the Reserve's independence. . . ."

Over the next two decades, "most observers" were not to be disappointed. Martin began his tenure at the Fed by using a war crisis to arrest the Treasury's future freedom to exercise peacetime economic management—at a time when, purely by chance, the proper wartime relationship of Treasury to Fed had been in effect. Fifteen years later, Vietnam offered Martin a second chance at wartime monetary management. His first response was to exercise the Fed's long-cherished independence in order to throw the nation's economy into one of the worst money squeezes in history, a "first" in monetary miscalculation which demonstrated that a slump is not impossible when a war boom seems certain. His second response was to join the Treasury in the reenactment of the disastrous financial policy of World War I. In response to the pressures of incipient panic late in 1966, monetary policy was reversed from crisis restraint to ease without the offsetting introduction of selective wartime controls. A peacetime Federal Reserve, free to make its contribution to economic management, could be a useful asset—even though the managerial record of Martin's Fed between the Korean and Vietnam emergencies was far from confidence-inspiring. But a Federal Reserve Board free to perpetrate in wartime the peacetime irresponsibilities to which the nation became conditioned from 1953 to 1963 abused its license to err. The Fed–Treasury Accord of March, 1951, proved in practice to be a long-term managerial liability which offset the long-term operational asset embodied in the Defense Support Program.

Before the Korean War was many months old, Washington had reactivated all the standard measures of emergency control mothballed after V-J Day: price and wage control; the Controlled Materials Plan, limiting the right of industry to receive steel, aluminum and copper; and rations on sugar, meat, tires, gasoline and other common consumer items. Tax collections were accelerated and the excess profits tax was reimposed. As fast as incomes inflated, possible and authorized uses for money disappeared. The rationing of materials and manpower, for example, deferred construction activity until the next postwar boom. As at the outset of World War II, money in circulation multiplied; and, as throughout World War II, it had no place to go but into the common reservoir of accumulated liquidity. Draft calls went up, and state and local governments found themselves short of employees all over again and forced by the new emergency controls to cut back on even fully financed spending programs. Business buyers and housewives raced each other to load up on supplies of everything in sight as if the drawing of the line along the 38th parallel, which no one in America could see or identify, had sounded the call for the country to dig in to a state of siege along every Main Street from Oregon to Florida.

Although the war was accelerated, it was not the immediate pressure of direct military requirements which sent prices and wages spiraling and labor shuttling from job to job at a record rate of turnover; which triggered the inflationary wartime behavior requiring recontrol; and which caused the hastily improvised apparatus of recontrol to spur inflationary psychology instead of to soothe it. The reason for recontrol was the Defense Support Program, which played no direct or immediate part in the conduct of the war, and whose backlash was the inflation which had provoked the controls and was making them ineffective. It was the Defense Support Program which pegged business demands for money, materials, machinery and men at record levels entirely unrelated to current or even prospective sales expectations. The moment anyone had a right to receive controlled materials, or to retain draftable men, or to raise pay scales in exemption of the wage freeze, or to claim priority in the production scheduling of suppliers, everybody else wanted as much and more. The restraint of controls spurred the emergency demand which required controls, so that for the duration of the game, the system of emergency controls became a kind of administrative and psychological equivalent of a servo-mechanism, creating its own momentum and therefore justifying its own existence.

The launching of the Defense Support Program put industry on notice either to shut down or to expand along lines qualifying businesses for the right to use materials, to claim priorities and to retain manpower—as well as to claim accelerated depreciation and thus to defer taxes at the new emergency rates. It was a very easy choice. Money was no problem once the credit controllers were themselves controlled. Credit was rationed to the consuming and borrowing public and, consequently, it became freely available to any business with an appropriate defense rating, which every business had or could get. Overnight the enforced deflation of consumption triggered an unprecedented and seemingly limitless inflation of production, which it financed.

So feverish, for example, was the rush of the steel industry to avoid the penalties of failing to expand, and to take advantage of the incentives to expand along the guidelines laid down by the Defense Support Program, that the steel mills themselves soon accounted for a volume of current business equal to 20 per cent of their capacity. And this was loaded onto top priority ratings enjoyed by bona fide military suppliers. The steel industry provided a telling measure of how marginal the bite of direct military demand was relative to the overload of priorities-inflated defense-support demand. Direct military demand on the mills accounted for no more than 10 per cent of capacity—roughly half the capacities the mills were preempting for their own expansion. By the time every other industry had lined up to process its ration tickets in Washington and to present them to the mills, the war economy had been infected with an acute case of "all-at-once-itis."

The peculiar nature of government planning was not the only reason for the inflation which greeted the war. A major structural contrast with World War II and, for that matter, with World War I, set inflation going before government policies accelerated it. World War II had suspended all market fluctuations in Europe. But the Korean War turned every market in Europe into a seller's paradise. Europe's economy is import-based. The normal effect of any jump in the prices of the basic materials which it imports is to put a squeeze on its earnings. When the American economy of 1950 went to war in Asia, it inflated every world commodity market, and it guaranteed prosperity to every raw material and crop exporting country. But America was still the most important industrial exporter to the primary producing countries—that is, until the war and its "priorities inflation" saddled industry with more business than it could handle at home and turned its energies inward. Europe suddenly found the inflation of its import costs profitable. The commodity exporting countries not only needed industrial exports but, for the first time, could afford to pay for them—and in a seller's export market from which America had eliminated herself and which Europe dominated by default.

The fact that Korea, by contrast with World War II, found Europe free and profiting from inflation defeated any chance the Truman Administration might have had of nipping inflation in the bud. The framework within which Roosevelt's War Administration was called upon to administer mobilization was relatively simple because the problem was purely domestic. But the worldwide scope of the Korean inflation made it impossible to control from Washington. The Truman Administration of the Korean War never did come to grips with the problem of how to manage the domestic economy in a limited war whose opening gun unleashes international economic forces beyond its control. Neither did the Johnson Administration in the Vietnam War. But America's failure guaranteed Europe's success.

Until the outbreak of the Korean War, efforts to promote world recovery had been impeded by the "dollar gap." The end of the war had not only left America the world's banker, but it had left all the world's money in the bank, with not enough of it circulating in the outside world. To be sure, the Marshall Plan made a beginning at circulating dollars, but it took the Korean War to do the job. In 1949, America's trade surplus came to a whopping $6.7 billion. In 1950, it fell abruptly to a mere $2.3 billion. The difference was accounted for by the scale on which America stepped up her imports of just about everything at just about any price. Dollars paid to the commodity exporting countries turned them into solvent customers for industrial products from Europe and Japan. But America's shortages opened the door for an upsurge in direct imports too.

Meanwhile, America put on a demonstration of economic and financial strength which no War Administration in history had ever dared contemplate, much less implement. Despite her own inflationary boom, she maintained her peacetime flow of government grant and loan aid overseas at the high level begun at the end of the war. Moreover, throughout the Korean War, private U.S. investment continued to flow abroad at an average annual rate of nearly a billion dollars a year. Not only were no foreign exchange controls needed: on the contrary, liquidity poured into America all during these years, reflecting the fact that the world was sharing in the war, and America was getting its full share of the dividends of war prosperity. In 1951 and 1952, America actually gained gold. Although gold was a much less significant psychological factor during the Korean War than it came to be during our involvement in Vietnam, America's foreign short-term creditors demonstrated their confidence in the wartime dollar by choosing it over gold and every other investment medium as the place to put their liquidity.

Korea was perhaps the only conflict in history which moved the world economy closer to international financial equilibrium. The war inflation which hampered America's management of her own emergency, when exported, benefited the rest of the world's economy. The prosperity exported by America's inflation was to exert momentous influence on the world balance of power long after the Korean War was over. It freed Europe to develop her strategy of peace and prosperity into a balance-of-power position between America and Russia.

The crest of the wartime boom was passed before the war itself was over. While the military were still pressing for allotments of men and materiel big enough to guarantee victory, industries whose distribution was subject to priorities began to report that capacity reserved for rated customers was not being spoken for. Before Eisenhower was called upon to weigh the fateful decision whether to head north or to head toward the conference table, a consensus among business buyers had crystallized. They were pulling back from new commitments—just as the military buyer had already cut back during World War II before Eisenhower's armies crossed the Channel. Before the actual fighting in Korea ground to its predestined stalemate in

1953, the war on the economic front was won, and the impetus
as well as the scope of the subsequent expansion was foreshadowed by the fact that wartime investment in expansion had
been completed.

The Defense Support Program, which overloaded the economy and subjected it to the dislocation of wartime controls,
generated the drives which made the postwar expansion remark-
ably vigorous after a short and mild transitional interlude of
readjustment. Lead times had been lengthened during the wartime period of delivery congestion, so that plant and equipment
on the drawing boards in 1951 did not go to work until 1954 or
thereabouts. When it did, quickened production cycles combined
with head starts in automation and upgradings in quality, as
well as in the newer arts of process control, to give the new facilities a competitive market advantage at the very time when
pent-up demands on the civilian economy were pouring back to
market. As fast as credit was decontrolled, tax advances to the
government were refunded. Without plan or leadership, and
without need for plan or leadership, a repeat performance of the
economic miracle which followed World War II occurred. The
facilities and the equipment which had been rushed out to keep
up with competition, when the normal channels of commercial
sales were shut down by *force majeure,* found customers anxious
and able to catch up with the consumer demand that had backed
up during the war. No sooner was the new equipment installed
and endowed with customers than it generated the incentives
and the means for its own expansion. Incredible though it
seemed and unprecedented though it was—even by comparison
with the favorable performance of the economy after World
War II—the wartime investment in expansion generated a new
postwar investment in expansion as fast as it came on stream.
The recovery from the brief transitional recession of 1954 accelerated into the investment boom of 1955–6.

Eisenhower was the beneficiary of the Korean War on its
political side at the time, and on its economic side afterwards.
Its victim was Harry Truman. By the time Truman discovered
that he could not end the war, it was too late for him to stop it.

All he had time to do was decide not to avail himself of his right to run for reelection against the man whom everyone credited with the ability to win wars.

By campaign time in 1952, the country had decided that only a change of Administration could end the war. Consequently, no Democrat could win the Presidency and no Republican could lose it. Eisenhower had the good fortune not only to be nominated in a "can't lose" year, but also, once elected, to be endowed with the favorable economic consequences of the war whose political consequences had made him President.

Truman's entrapment in the political backlash of Korea had consequences that went far beyond the 1952 election. There was no closer observer of the process by which McCarthyism took hold in the nation and by which Truman lost control of his own future than freshman Senator Lyndon Johnson. In 1952, Democrats were whipsawed by the triple charge of being soft on Communism, getting into wars, and being unable or unwilling to end the wars they got into. A dozen years later, when he had the option of expanding or getting out of his limited war in Vietnam, Johnson's decision to escalate reflected his sensitivity to Truman's fate. Having run and won as the peace-and-prosperity candidate, Johnson moved to outflank any potential neo-McCarthyite sentiment. His derision of the "cussers and doubters" was his attempt to avoid Truman's trap.

18 : EISENHOWER'S ESCAPE

THE DEMOCRATIC Presidents of the twentieth century have been "action" Presidents. As such, their terms in office can all be divided into phases identified by the direction their actions took: at home, reform; abroad, war. Wilson, Roosevelt, Truman and Johnson each presided over first a Reform Administration and then a War Administration. By contrast, at least since Harding's term, Republicans have been tagged as "do-nothing" Presidents. Eisenhower's Presidency confirms this diagnosis.

Eisenhower's essential contribution to America's well-being took place during his first months in office. He ended the war in Korea, and he satisfied critics both on the right and the left that he would not attempt to repeal the New Deal. Thereafter, he was free *not* to use the opportunities which peace abroad gave him to deal with problems at home. His freedom from having to act was the measure of his political accomplishment.

The Eisenhower success story chronicles the triumph of an engaging public *persona* over policy or organization. What worked for him were his personality, his grasp of personal politics and his delegations of responsibility—for the Cold War to Secretary of State John Foster Dulles and for the economy to Secretary of the Treasury George Humphrey.

Eisenhower's political career began with the prestige he derived from having won the war and the reputation he brought back from Europe as the engineer of victory. Supporting his public personality were his private political relationships. The country which elected Eisenhower had long since become a preponderantly Democratic country. In fact, Eisenhower himself had recognized this in 1948 during his brief sabbatical in the intellectual world as President of Columbia University when, as Herbert Hoover had done in 1920, he angled for the Presidential nomination on the Democratic ticket. More particularly, despite Eisenhower's impressive victory in 1952, the Congressional machinery continued under the control of the interlocking membership of small blocs of Democrats whose leaders made up a club of their own. Their manning of the legislative levers and their supervision of the flow of budgetary funds were as thoroughly professional in orientation toward power as the gestures of the Republican leadership were amateurish.

All Eisenhower had to do in order to do well personally was retain his public reputation as America's leading expert on war and peace. But to do well politically, Eisenhower had to do well with Congress. This meant that he was under pressure to turn the liability represented by his apparent dependence on the Republican leaders, many of whom mistrusted and resented him as an interloper and a poor "party man," into a new asset based on his ability to develop working relationships with the Democratic leaders. He quickly found them as anxious to cooperate with him as he was dependent on working with them.

In 1953, three interrelated motivations figured prominently in the calculations of the Rayburn leadership of the House and the new Johnson leadership of the Senate. The first reflected a sensitivity to the widespread, if underground, feeling which had been strengthened by the Korean War—that if prosperity is apt to run out under the Republicans, war tends to come in with the Democrats. The Congressional leadership had a healthy respect for the public's carryover acceptance of Eisenhower as the man who had been trusted to win the war and who therefore could be trusted to keep the peace. The second consideration was prompted by the excesses being perpetrated by Joe McCarthy: McCarthyism challenged the Democrats to establish continuity with the new Administration. McCarthy's charge of "twenty years of treason" would become as preposterous as it was offensive once the programs and orientation of the old Democratic regime were followed up and made respectable by the new Republican Administration.

The third angle which Johnson and Rayburn played looked to the future. As a Presidential hopeful—one whose hopes had been ratified by FDR himself—Johnson fell into the category of a professional Congressional politician. Though in the past this would have counted against him (as it did so obviously against Clay and, as late as Wilson's day, against Champ Clark), it did not necessarily eliminate him from consideration. In the twentieth century, Truman and Harding had served their apprenticeship in the Senate too. Johnson's interest lay in positioning himself as the legitimate middle-of-the-road successor to both Roosevelt's radicalism and Eisenhower's moderation. Johnson's chance of maneuvering his Presidential ambitions into the range and reach of political lightning depended on his ability to deny a power base to any new national figure, like Stevenson. Moreover, Johnson had a positive political motive for doing business with Eisenhower. He had to "go national"; and his one way of doing it was as the responsible and cooperative partner of the nonpartisan President (who, as Johnson never tired of pointing out, was a Texan too). And so Eisenhower's charmed life was protected by Johnson's ambition.

Eisenhower's projection of his public personality above the party conflict and his private politicking with the Democratic leaders across party lines were two of his techniques for dealing with the problems of the Presidency. His conduct of the Cold War required a third technique—and a fourth was necessary to fulfill the responsibility which devolved on any President, now that the Keynesian and New Deal revolutions required governmental intervention in the operation of the economy. Personality and personal politics had been Eisenhower's forte all through his career in the Army. The care and cultivation of his image and of his strategic relationships had been the secret weapon he had used to catapult himself up through the ranks. These two preoccupations he continued to manage himself. The conduct of the Cold War he delegated to John Foster Dulles; and the responsibility for the economy, to George Humphrey.

These delegations of authority in effect made Dulles Assistant President for Foreign Affairs and Humphrey Assistant President for Domestic Affairs. Both men took over with great zeal, Dulles confident that he knew how to stem the tide of Red power and Humphrey confident that he could manage to staunch the flow of red ink. Dulles quickly developed a shrewd and effective defense for staying one jump ahead of problems which he could see but not solve. Leaving his department to take care of itself, he assumed a whirlwind peripatetic role, contriving always to be conferring on a continent other than the one under the immediate scrutiny of Congress and the commentators. Humphrey decided early in the game that prudence was the better part of valor, and his performance in office observed a discreet distinction between his orthodox financial convictions and his practical gift for camaraderie. He developed warm personal relationships with Congressional leaders, who paid no attention to his views and with whom he readily agreed as to their practical irrelevance.

Truman had been an easy target for criticism in his time; so was Eisenhower. But just as Eisenhower's retreat into nonperformance made Truman look better as each year passed, so Johnson's advances into overperformance in Vietnam began to make Eisenhower look better. Whatever criticism Eisenhower may have deserved, however inadequate he was made to seem by his passion for golf and his penchant for muddled expression, the fact is that he knew better than to let himself be euchred into a public commitment of troops to the Asiatic bog.

The world never knew how close America came to taking over from the French in Vietnam the moment they pulled out;

and the fact that we did take over afterward has obscured the closeness of the war at the time. The acceptance of stalemate in Korea on the northern Asiatic anti-Communist front invited a speedy test on the southern front. When it came, in October, 1954, Dulles pressed the President for a decision to intervene. Eisenhower sent Dulles to the Senate to confer with his two friends in command there, Chairman Russell of the Senate Armed Services Committee and his trusted protégé Lyndon Johnson, upon whom Russell had conferred the Chairmanship of its key Preparedness Investigating Subcommittee. Between them, Senators Russell and Johnson made the most powerful partnership on Capitol Hill in the earmarking of military appropriations.

Dulles requested authority to send technicians to Vietnam. Russell and Johnson refused it, and Congress promptly adjourned. A few weeks later, Assistant Secretary of State (later Senator) Thruston Morton called Russell in Georgia and said that the Secretary had asked him to convey a message. He told Russell that the Secretary wanted him to know that the President had nevertheless sent the men. Russell recognized that the decision was a prerogative of the Commander-in-Chief. He also expressed his disapproval of the wisdom of the decision, adding, "Before you know it, we're likely to have 20,000 men there." Recalling this incident in the years when Johnson was rationalizing his own entrapment in Vietnam by invoking the precedent set by Eisenhower, Russell punctuated his reminiscence with the ready admission of how woefully his projection had erred on the low side.

But the commitment of technicians to Vietnam really did remain limited. Further, from Eisenhower's standpoint, it had the advantage of being more or less secret and, therefore, marginal in terms of politics and the budget. Overall, in fact, Eisenhower's policy was a policy of noncommitment and noninvolvement. Its practical effect was to let Dulles express his passion for positive thinking but not to let him do anything in a positive way. Where Theodore Roosevelt had admonished America to walk softly and carry a big stick, Eisenhower encouraged

Dulles to make all the noise he wanted but to brandish no weapons.

Eisenhower's intervention in the Suez war prevented the Franco–British–Israeli alliance from demolishing Nasser before Russia had committed her equipment and advisers to his survivial. But any error of judgment on his part was mitigated by the more conspicuous blunders of the British and French governments whose gratuitous interference prevented Israel from fighting and winning her own war and who ignored their own susceptibility to an American veto. Eisenhower exercised this veto, characteristically, to preserve the status quo. The scene of Eisenhower's crowning achievement in the conduct of the Cold War was Lebanon, where, in 1958, he contrived to land the Marines and to get them out again without a shot being fired.

Two years before, the Hungarian Revolt had offered Eisenhower his one opportunity to gamble on what the Kennedys later popularized in their show business jargon as an eyeball-to-eyeball confrontation with the Russians, and he would have none of it. Eisenhower was determined to sit on the lid, and he did. Even while the famous Bay of Pigs affair was being cooked up by the CIA, Eisenhower, upon leaving office, went so far as to warn Kennedy that cancellation of a project so explosively risky would be preferable to failure. The warning punctuated the contrast between his eight years of peacekeeping in office and the Asiatic wars of the Democratic reformers who preceded and followed him. The reformers sneered at the General for his political apathy, but the General was entitled to the last laugh when history showed that the peace kept in his time conserved the gains of reform more securely than the wars the reformers started after he retired.

Altogether, Eisenhower's commitment on the Cold War side of his Presidential problem was to "peaceful coexistence," constructed in its most passive sense. No new international commitments undertaken by the Eisenhower Administration pyramided additional security burdens onto the budget or significantly altered the relationship of the defense establishment to the economy. It was an interlude of quiescence in the emergency cycle.

It was, however, a period of turbulence and transition for the economy. The 1952 decision of the Republican establishment to "win with Ike" rather than to gamble on following Taft into a contest over principles had involved much soul-searching and had left many scars. Taft had been entitled to large commitments from Eisenhower, assuring him consideration in matters of both patronage and policy. These were given. Ezra Taft Benson, for example, received the Secretaryship of Agriculture. The arrangement between Eisenhower and Taft encouraged speculation by wishful Republicans and wishful Democrats alike that Eisenhower had acquiesced in an ultimatum from Taft to scrap the New Deal. But such a demand would have been out of character for Taft. He was too self-consciously sardonic in his acceptance of the times, and in his recognition that he was out of step with them, to have made it. Such a resolve would have been even more out of character for Eisenhower as altogether too activist for his complacent approach to his ceremonial position.

Moreover, any commitment by Eisenhower to repeal of the basic Roosevelt reforms would have jeopardized his relationship with such powers as Speaker Rayburn. Though he was Eisenhower's smuggest and most reliable Democratic accessory, Rayburn would have fought like an enraged tiger to protect the Roosevelt legislative heritage of bank deposit insurance, the SEC, the FHA, and other once radical reforms which he himself had helped legislate into the normal operations of the social structure.

Actually, Rayburn was closer to Eisenhower than Johnson was, and it was through Rayburn that Eisenhower again and again neutralized Johnson. In the recession year of 1958, for example, I was one of those who led Johnson to accept the argument for a cut in tax rates as a remedial measure. But the project proved premature when Johnson failed to persuade Rayburn to go along with any such novel idea in a year of budget deficit. Nevertheless, a reactionary activism hostile to the Democratic Congressional leadership in domestic affairs would have cost Eisenhower the strategic hidden asset which provided protective cover for his passivity during quiet years and secured his flanks during troubled ones. If Paris was worth a mass to Henry IV, a nonaggression pact with the Democrats in domestic affairs was worth their commitment of bipartisan support to the Republicans on the conduct of foreign affairs, especially when such a commitment brought the Republican President a windfall of Democratic support for preserving the status quo on sensitive issues of economic policy.

Eisenhower's decision to take sanctuary in do-nothingism was, therefore, progressive by default. Its effect was all the greater because it came after Truman had launched his decidedly more radical Fair Deal and failed to get it adopted. The subsequent history of American politics would have been entirely different if Eisenhower had thrown the immense personal prestige he commanded when he took office behind an activist drive to dismantle the New Deal at a time when the country was war-weary; when it was susceptible to red herrings packaged and brandished by Joe McCarthy; and when times were good and resistance was low. If Eisenhower had led or even fronted for a drive to turn the clock back, the Democratic Administration which followed his—and, in that case, a Democratic Administration surely would have followed his—could have won a "doer" reputation for seeming to fulfill its promise to get the country moving again by the simple expedient of reinstating a suspended New Deal.

As things worked out, instead, when Kennedy took over, the emotional pendulum had swung back from complacence to activism. His Administration's record of performance hinged on its ability to legislate its platform. If only the reinstatement of the New Deal had been involved, this would have been child's play. Instead, a resistant Congress in 1961 found it easy to block any real advance beyond the New Deal. Eisenhower's passive stand-patism toward the New Deal in the 1950's made Kennedy look bad when his effort to implement Truman's efforts and Stevenson's idealism failed. And it made Johnson look good when he took over in 1963 and, as Senator Eugene McCarthy put it, "recorded progress by legislating the Truman platform of 1948."

Although Eisenhower refused to contemplate an attack on

the established New Deal reforms, he was anxious to shrink the permanent peacetime defense establishment. He made no bones about his sensitivity to the political burden he carried as a military man. He would have helped himself if he had been free to reverse his field and disabuse critics and skeptics of their suspicion that he had a vested interest in his former profession. The obvious way for him to have turned the liability of his military past into the asset of a reputation for political independence would have been by imposing a discipline on the defense establishment. If successful, such a stand would have lowered defense budgets, and Ike was anxious to take it. The one topic on which he belied his reputation for dislike of "heavy" subjects was the inflation and waste built into the defense budget. His criticism of the budgets over which he presided was as fierce, and his resentment was as deep, as that of any member of the gallery to which Barry Goldwater subsequently played (though Goldwater himself was not against the defense budget and Eisenhower really was).

As a practical matter, Eisenhower's preference for a return to pre-Korean War budget levels could be supported on the grounds that America retained a wide lead in advanced weaponry. And so long as Eisenhower allowed Dulles to talk but not to back up his threats with troops, new money to expand America's arsenal would not be needed. The determination to hold the line against Communism relied on the atomic potential which, once established, was relatively inexpensive to maintain. Furthermore, no compelling economic argument supported the continuing commitment to a defense budget approaching $50 billion as indispensable to prosperity. On the contrary, Eisenhowever agreed with Secretary of the Treasury Humphrey that the high rate of government spending, of which defense was far and away the largest item, was more likely to run the economy into a depression.

George Humphrey had come down to Washington with a prospectus as simple as that of the young Congressman-elect in *Mr. Smith Goes to Washington.* He took one look at what he found and invited condemnation as a traitor to his class by deciding to prolong the provocative excess profits tax beyond the statutory expiration date which the Democratic Congress had set. He took another look—this time at the inflated mountain of short-term debt piled up in the Treasury that needed to be rolled over week after week—and made another decision: this one earned him salvos of applause as the saviour of his class. He decided, like Alexander Hamilton before him, to launch a long-term government bond issue in order to start funding the debt.

The difference between the problem Humphrey had inherited and the problem Hamilton had identified was that Humphrey's had got too far ahead of the country to be brought under control by any isolated token act. The result of Humphrey's valiant effort to sell bonds on appeal to principle recalled the question Al Smith had asked the morning after election day in 1928: "Where were all those people who clapped for me during the campaign?" Humphrey's token bond offering attracted a great deal of applause but very few buyers. The money market put him on notice to follow where his Democratic predecessors had led; for the only alternative to Democratic easy money was a Republican money squeeze. Humphrey complied.

Five years later, before Humphrey's education had been entirely completed, he staged a repeat performance of Salmon P. Chase's somersault on the greenback issue. In January, 1957, Humphrey did his duty in presenting the budget for fiscal year 1958 and then spoke his mind by denouncing it as inflationary and wasteful. But Eisenhower's acceptance of the fiscal realities led Humphrey to retire while he still had some laurels to rest on. Eisenhower's acceptance of the political realities caused him to replace Humphrey with Robert Anderson, a long-time associate of the Texas Congressional establishment.

Anderson's appointment revealed a generally unsuspected wiliness on Eisenhower's part. He seemed to be learning to play the Washington game as shrewdly as he had played the Army game. The patronage he bestowed on the Democratic leadership put it on notice to demonstrate its fiscal responsibility. The Democratic leadership had been making capital of its bipartisan dedication to defending the flag. Now Eisenhower made capital for himself by demonstrating his bipartisan dedication to the defense of the dollar. Because this strategy anticipated the period of his record deficits, the restraint he imposed on the Democratic Congressional leadership was all the more effective.

Eisenhower was surprised and frustrated to discover that, despite his conviction and despite the merits, the post-Korean defense budget was uncuttable. The arguments for a $40–$50 billion defense budget as a permanent fact of life were elusive, complicated and sophisticated, but they were unanswerable. First came the administrative and technical arguments for "inside" consumption, which were better unstated so far as the public was concerned: continuing commitments were unfunded; new commitments in the next generation of weaponry (also unavoidably unfunded) were overdue; cash payouts to retirees and accruing obligations to prospective retirees exceeded budgeted allotments. Above all, the cost of cancelling many activities of dubious security value would have invoked disturbingly large cash drains —nonrecurrent, to be sure, but enormous while they lasted.

Beyond the inside technical arguments existed an overriding inside political fact too explosive to be divulged and too complicated to be controlled. The requirement which justified an extraordinary level of sustained defense spending in the absence of emergency was the danger of another Korea. But the extraordinary and admittedly unintelligible fact was that the nearly $50 billion a year that America was committing to defense was not buying her any immediate combat capability. In fact, it was doubtful whether the swollen defense apparatus of 1954 could still be mobilized to meet a localized overseas emergency as readily as the skeleton forces on hand at the time of the Berlin airlift in 1948 had been. Notwithstanding all the slogans about "more bang for the buck" and "cutting fat but not bone and muscle," and notwithstanding the billions pouring into advanced systems and abstruse projects, America found herself losing her ability to field a single division on a hot front in time to cool it down.

The public arguments against a sharp offensive aimed at

cutting the defense budget were even more compelling than the inside ones. The frustrating nonfunctional waste in the post-Korean level of peacetime defense spending had taken on the proportions of a classified secret. But the fact that so much money was running into so many military channels in a steady yearly flow had become critically important for both Eisenhower's domestic political position and America's international strategic position. After Eisenhower had put his enormous international prestige behind his personal decision to accept an armed stalemate in Korea, and after he had permitted Dulles to launch a war of words against Red power, a decision on his part to cut the defense budget would have been universally interpreted as "scuttle and run." Such a disclosure would have invited the world to conclude that America was either turning toward appeasement or committing herself to atomic confrontation.

The decisive pressure to muddle along with the status quo came from the Congressional establishment. A decision to liquidate spending commitments was bound to suggest the same disturbing dilemmas of appeasement or nuclear confrontation to voters at home as to governments abroad. Congress always has a vested interest in logrolling programs close to home, and a big program committed to stay big and get bigger is less controversial than one which is first overdeflated and then reflated. In terms of fiscal sensitivities, the Democrats took comfort in the spectacle of high peacetime spending by Republician guardians of the public purse strings in the absence of an emergency and for no readily intelligible purpose. But they had no intention of taking any heat for inflating appropriations for cash expenditures in order to pay the cost of widespread cancellations of programs.

The Democratic hierarchy in Congress took protective cover behind the familiar slogans of bipartisanship. Was not the President the greatest living authority in military matters? Were not his decisions providing bipartisan continuity with those made by the preceding Democratic Administration? Was not the Democratic Congress giving the Republican President everything he asked for? It was a plausible position enabling Congress to claim that it was guarding both the interests of the taxpayer and the nation's security. This last calculation particularly suited the interests of the up-and-coming Senator who held the franchise for preparedness investigation, Lyndon Johnson, for it was based on the fact that neither the public nor the President was sensitive to the distinction between the process of Congressional appropriations and the process of Executive disbursements. In one typical Eisenhower year, for example, the Democratic committee hierarchs took credit for cutting nearly $5 billion of wasteful appropriations out of Eisenhower's budget. In the process, they took over the issue of economy. But the dollar drain out of the Treasury continued undisturbed, and so did the strategic status quo.

For the first time in history, major military expenditures exerted almost no stimulating influence on the economy. During the Eisenhower years, the economy became so big that even a $40–50 billion item could get lost—especially when so much of it was dissipated on overhead whose start-up investment had long since been spent, and so little of it represented real investment in industrial expansion. The economy had outgrown its dependence on the defense-spending status quo. Liquidation or substantial retrenchment would not have brought on a slump. On the contrary, elusive though the point was to diehard critics of the "industrial–military complex," the liquidation of programs would have duplicated the short-term inflationary impact of 1945 by accelerating tremendous cash flows into the economy to meet contractual obligations to settle canceled contracts. Over the long term, the dynamism of the private sector would have been able to feed on resources set free by a stagnant public sector.

19 : MARTIN'S
       : MYSTIQUE

THE POST-KOREAN WAR boom did not reach its crest until the
end of 1956. In fact, the Defense Support Program adopted
during the Korean War had planned it that way. The plan had
pretty well insulated the broadened base of the civilian economy
from the political volatility inherent in the defense cycle. The
industrial base of the economy had become big enough to absorb
emergency defense escalation without developing shortages, and
too big to have to depend on any erratic external stimulus for
its lift. In fact, as Vietnam was to show within a decade, it had
become so big that it could support an expanding overseas military operation and a domestic business sag at the same time.

The net effect of the changes set in motion by the Korean
War was that the defense budget lost its traditional trend-making
role. In fact, the inflationary postwar trend built into the civilian
economy began to exert a more direct influence on military
dollars available for disbursement than the traditional factor of
military inflation exerted on the economy. The military procurement dollar was buying less firepower because the economy was
paying more for labor.

The post-Korean wave of investment spending took a great

deal of money. Predictably, the money came first from tax refunds, and secondly from the immediate corrective adjustment in business activity which freed considerable excess liquidity. But as the postwar boom asserted its underlying vigor, still greater demands for money appeared. Then, as the boom accelerated into the superboom of 1955–6, money began to tighten. The capacities projected during the war were coming on stream at the same time as catch-up demand from the consumer economy, with its inevitable backwash of credit demand, was gathering momentum. Consumers and producers were competing for credit.

By this time, the expansive impetus of the Korean War had added a new dimension to the overall economy. Its aggregate scale in GNP terms was 25 per cent larger in 1956 than it had been at the outset of the Korean War (when, in turn, it was more than half again as big as at the outbreak of World War II). The production of electric power can be taken as the lowest common denominator of industrial capacity. From its 1950 level of 388,674 million kilowatt hours, it soared to 684,-804 million kilowatt hours—a jump of more than 75 per cent within six years. The production of aluminum, a prototype growth industry, more than doubled between 1950 and 1955, rising from 962,000 tons to 1,902,000 tons. The production of steel, a typical work-horse industry which was lagging behind the growth parade, rose from 86,461 million tons in 1950 to 102,872 million tons in 1956. This was a more moderate rate of improvement, but still formidable—especially in view of both the competitive inroads of newer products with greater growth potential and the new competition producers were facing in world markets and, indeed, in the American home market.

The private sector's rising demand for money was layered onto rising demands for financial accommodation from the public sector. Thanks to Eisenhower's twin decisions to dismantle neither the New Deal nor the defense establishment which had grown up during the Democratic years, and thanks also to the post-Korean boom, both the fiscal and monetary authorities found themselves on a new frontier at least half a decade before

John Kennedy popularized the concept. Before the mid-1950's, no period of boom or superboom had coincided with a high level of government spending on social welfare, plus a high and irreducible burden of tax rates, plus a large permanent peacetime defense budget. A booming cyclical demand for money by the private sector had never before had to compete with a massive and continuous governmental requirement for short-term finance. A booming peacetime demand for capital by the private sector had never before had to bear a high burden of tax accruals as a carryover from past wars and as insurance against future ones.

"All-at-once-itis" had come to be accepted as a fact of wartime life when money was chasing goods during World War II and, more particularly, when the Korean War boomed defense-support investment at an even greater rate than it stimulated normal wartime expenditure. In the past, each successive adjustment to all-at-once-itis had been facilitated and disciplined by war controls. But the post-Korean forward move into a new "normalcy" of stabilized defense, coinciding as it did with expansive investment by big government and big business, was producing a return of all-at-once-itis without the familiar spur of war and without the familiar protection of war controls. William McChesney Martin's management of the Federal Reserve Board, which the Eisenhower Administration had found in Washington along with the Democratic management of Congress, took alarm. It reached for the money control levers which Keynes had identified and which he had recommended that monetary managers use as economic accelerators or decelerators. And the Fed threw them into reverse.

By the mid-1950's, a simplistic Keynesianism had come to enjoy considerable nonpartisan recognition in America. When Keynesianism won official acceptance at the Federal Reserve Board, in fact, it was because of its adaptability to conservative implementation. For what the monetary authorities, led by Chairman Martin, took from Keynes was his rationale for monetary management. Not that the idea of the monetary regulator or its application by the central banking authorities had originated with Keynes. Since the 1870's, when Walter Bagehot had attempted to educate the Bank of England to know what it was doing when it raised or lowered interest rates, monetary ease and restraint had become the accepted tools of control by banks the world over. But Bagehot's concern had been the adjustment of a mercantile economy which was critically dependent on international money flows to counteract payments problems, currency dislocations and trade disadvantages. The Depression decade had exposed severe limitations in the American monetary mechanism: an abundance of cheap money had not been used to put men and machines to work. More generally, tight money, when pushed far enough, has a restraining effect on those sectors which are sensitive to the cost and availability of outside finance, while monetary ease is less likely to have an expansive impact— it is easier to pull with a length of string than to push with it.

Keynes had gone beyond the traditional pragmatics of monetary policy in order to integrate a theory of money into a general theory of how the economy functions. Martin's Federal Reserve reversed the process in the mid-1950's. Its administrators abstracted monetary policy—with all its power, when used as a check, to dislocate and disrupt—from the context of the economy to which they sought to apply it. The facts of life in the new era of big government—with its permanent structure of high tax rates, with big business locked into long-term investment programs and with a growing shortage of skilled labor— all seemed to be ignored. In fact, the Federal Reserve Board went at the job of managing the nation's money as if it were the Bank of England inducing London merchants to increase or decrease their small and liquid inventories of foreign trade staples in the days when Britain still ruled the waves.

As things stood in America after Korea, the Board's "corrective" measures had a disproportionate impact on that part of the private sector sensitive to short-term monetary conditions. In order to have an impact on the whole economy, therefore, the Board had to commit itself to monetary overkill. Moreover, when in 1951 it asserted its independence of the Treasury and established itself as manager of the money system, the Board found itself in a guessing game at each turn of the business cycle. Because even monetary managers are human, each time the Board guessed wrong it raised the ante on its ability to call the next turn. The Board's actions during the 1950's and 1960's seemed to indicate that it had not studied the record of its predecessor management which, during the disastrous sequel to World War I, overinflated a postwar boom and then overdeflated a postwar bust. In 1957, it kicked a tired capital goods boom down from its peak, and kicked the economy down with it. In 1959, it knocked a tentative recovery on the head and committed the nation to three full years of "high-level stagnation."

Altogether, the timing of the Martin management of the Federal Reserve Board has been as amateurish as the integrity of its principles has been unquestioned. Presidents, however, have been willing to put up with the managerial minus because the political plus has offered them protection against the popular obsession with and fear of inflation. The White House has regularly gone along with the Martin Board in the teeth of Congressional criticism of the consequences of its actions. Each President, in turn, has found that the Chairman's pious slogans have more than outweighed his mistakes of judgment with the business and financial communities and with the press. Presidents, after all, are not expected to be financial pundits. When they find a pundit already installed in a position of power who can be counted on to say the right thing, they are unlikely to dismiss him merely for doing the wrong thing.

The short-lived money disturbance was as symptomatic as it was troublesome. It was made in Washington. When the Federal Reserve Board panicked, so did the President. The Federal Reserve Board had taken fright against the theoretical danger of major inflation in the private sector without assessing the real danger of a runaway in the public sector. Whatever Eisenhower may not have known or understood, he sensed the source of real danger—namely, the gathering momentum of government commitments for future spending unfunded in the present. He reacted against it in the only way he knew—by overreacting. Where the Federal Reserve Board had known too little about the workings of the governmental and private sectors,

Eisenhower knew too much. He knew, for example, that the Federal Government was accruing obligations to disburse cash in the future on a scale tens of billions of dollars in excess of funds approved by Congress in the budget or likely to be forthcoming from the taxpayers. Nevertheless, angry and afraid though he might be, no President had traditionally had the power to halt the process of new cash spending required by old contractual commitments. That is, until Eisenhower assumed it.

For once, Eisenhower lived up to the concept of military men as men of action. Cash disbursements by the armed services against current obligations, let alone future obligations, were simply cut off. In a remarkable document promulgated in the autumn of 1957, the Defense Department told its twenty-five leading contractors in so many words that, while the government freely acknowledged its contractual debts to them and wanted their products, it had run out of money and, therefore, it had no choice but to stop payment. Moreover, this same document volunteered the demoralizing information that the defense establishment had no plans for finding the money for payment. It set a new record for chaos among the government areas supposedly policed and coordinated by the National Security Council, in the sorry tradition of Louis Johnson's ill-timed decision to cut back on defense when Dean Acheson's hard-line diplomacy called for defense to be stepped up. The leading corporations of the country woke up to find their biggest bills uncollectible. Moreover, the Federal Reserve had chosen precisely this time to prevent them from borrowing at the banks against the government's debts.

A mature and responsible coordination between fiscal and monetary operations would have turned on the credit when the cash stopped flowing. In that case, the thrust of the governmental forces playing upon the economy would have been balanced. But the Federal Reserve Board ran the banks out of money as precipitously and as irresponsibly as the Federal Government ran the customers of the banks out of money. The result was panic—this time not a panic which Washington was asked to quell but, rather, one which it had made. At the height of the panic, in October, 1957, Russia put her first Sputnik into space.

Public psychology reacted to the Russian announcement that the space race was on with a parallel panic of its own. The echo of contraction from the economy, of panic from Washington, and of fear from the public broke the stock market. Demoralization was the order of the day—in government, in finance, in the economy and in the country. The growth of big government had confirmed the dependence of our entire society upon the Presidential nerve center. When it failed to function, panic was bound to spread.

With the Executive branch in a blue funk, the Congressional leaders of the opposition had a shot at policy-making, and they took it. Eisenhower was quick to recognize power when it came to bear against him. So long as he personified confidence at the summit of the public pyramid, the Congressional leaders had been his creatures, his conduits and his complacent fellow travelers. Nonetheless, they had their own independent bases of power throughout the country. When he set off a panic by freezing the money for disbursements they had authorized and then advertised the official adoption of this policy by the government, they split with him. And their split with him calmed him down. The Congressional leadership commanded no public charisma. Its principal figures were regional chiefs virtually unknown to the public at large and not given to operating in public outside the specialized areas of legislative power which their seniority and alliances had staked out. But the absence of popular public figures did not matter. As soon as an affirmative and authoritative leadership asserted itself in private upon the President, he followed it.

Although the panic had been monetary and financial in origin, the instrument of Congressional leadership which put the government back to work was the Defense Investigating Subcommittee of the Senate Armed Services Committee chaired by Lyndon Johnson. It integrated the monetary, fiscal, military and scientific aspects of the crisis. The Presidential mood of impatience with anything involving the expenditure of dollars had been aptly summed up by Sherman Adams, then still ensconced at the White House as Eisenhower's chief of staff, when he said that the Administration was not "intent on attaining a high score in any outer space basketball game." But, far more realistically, Chairman Russell of the Armed Services Committee asked Johnson to undertake a study of Russia's achievement and its implications for American policy and security. Edwin L. Weisl undertook the responsibility of guiding the investigation with Cyrus L. Vance (later McNamara's number-two man in the Defense Department) as his deputy. The Weisl study quickly recognized Sputnik as a serious challenge, but America's drift was identified as an even greater source of danger.

The Sputnik inquiry was a prod to Eisenhower. At the same time, it developed considerable reach into the interconnected strands of defense and scientific programming and the finance supporting these efforts. Congressional inquiries often leave encyclopaedic libraries as their monuments that more than likely prove to be studies in futility. Johnson's Sputnik inquiry produced such a report, but it also produced results. So effective was the opposition mounted by Russell and Johnson that Eisenhower quickly changed course and freed them for return to collaboration.

Johnson's brief but influential interlude of opposition to Eisenhower, and his subsequent assertion of leadership over the Eisenhower Administration, exerted a direct influence on the Martin management of the Federal Reserve Board; and this influence accented the Board's congenital disposition to volatility and encouraged its instinct for unfortunate timing. Having first injected too much fuel into the economy in 1955–6, the Board had then overcompensated by jamming on the brakes hard enough to shake up the passengers when it precipitated the squeeze of 1957. Now the Board reacted from the consequences of the money panic by adopting the most energetic recovery remedies just as the government began to open the valves again. Instead of "leaning into the wind" (as Chairman Martin had characterized its function), the Board manned the wind machines and accentuated the swing of the cycle instead of damping it down. Then, predictably, after the recovery of 1958 jetted upward, the Board developed a new case of inflation jitters. In 1959, the premature restraint it enforced neutralized the potential of full recovery. By 1960, the economy was sagging again, just when the Republican commitment to Nixon counted on it soar.

At the climax of the Kennedy–Nixon campaign, Barry Goldwater, then a rising star on the Republican horizon, won himself some spectacular headlines by warning at a Republican rally in Indiana that Nixon would lose the election by default unless he faced up to the issues and gave the country a choice between Republicanism and the New Deal–Fair Deal tradition. That night I participated in a TV round-table with Goldwater in Chicago. During an intermission, I remarked that Nixon, whose lead in the polls was rapidly melting, would be likely to lose the election if he failed to persuade Chairman Martin to ease up on money. "He won't try to do that, and he will lose," replied Goldwater, who was more clear-headed about Nixon's candidacy than he was about his own four years later. Given the razor-thin closeness of the outcome in 1960, the Fed-induced slowdown in the economy certainly slowed down Nixon's campaign enough to make the difference. The Eisenhower Administration had won eight years' worth of opportunities at home by steering clear of shooting involvements abroad. But the opportunities which international strategic "nonmanagement" provided were offset by its domestic economic mismanagement. In 1960, it paid the price.

Korea had demonstrated that a small war on a distant frontier could burden the American economy with runaway costs. Our only defense was a rate of economic expansion sufficient to keep the burden of the war relatively small even though its absolute costs mounted. Economic expansion had also offered America her one hope of retaining her economic flexibility and her political initiatives in the world's less remote power centers (while she fought out her local wars). In fact, when the atomic stalemate allowed the Cold War to develop into a series of limited hot wars on remote local fronts, America found herself on the defensive in her own economy. During the interval between the Korean stalemate and the Vietnam escalation, Russia attempted to provoke America into accepting the challenge of local wars. In Korea, she had managed to involve America in an Asian land war against a satellite. Eisenhower retrieved the position by withdrawing America from the Russian trap. Once free of it, he refused to take the bait again. But he fell into a trap of his own making within the American economy.

Commitments to send troops to remote and dubious outposts have constituted America's main weakness. Her main source of strategic strength was her economy. Eisenhower's failure to exploit the strategic opportunities offered him by American economic strength when his escape from Korea allowed him to do so was an error of omission. But the dissipation of American economic strength over which he presided represented a historic error of commission.

During Eisenhower's tenure in office, Washington's influence over the economy reached a new level and followed a new channel. Even while, after Korea, the defense budget was becoming neutralized as an engine of expansion, the mere size of big government made it a consumer and dispenser of money on an unprecedented scale. At the same time, the Federal Reserve involved itself in monetary management to an extent hitherto unknown. During the 1950's, the compulsion sloganized in the demand to keep the budget in balance at whatever cost in terms of imbalance for the economy (and in future imbalances for the budget) still prevailed: The Federal budget was not yet a flexible tool of economic management. But the dislocative impact of the tools of economic management which government was sanctioned by orthodox opinion to use—debt management and money management—was devastating. During the 1960 campaign, Kennedy taxed Nixon with the responsibility for Martin's mismanagement; and then, once elected, he exposed his Administration to the consequences of renewed mismanagement on Martin's part in order to take protective cover behind Martin's mystique.

Eisenhower's success in keeping the peace made it possible for his successor to begin with a clean slate internationally—at least in public relations terms. (Unfortunately, one of his successor's first acts in office was to involve himself needlessly in the Bay of Pigs fiasco.) But Eisenhower also made far more difficult the task of dealing with future breaches of the peace. Not only had the combat readiness of the American defense establishment seriously depreciated. The accompanying loss of economic dynamism and financial deterioration embodied an even more serious lag in strategic strength. Five years of catch-up in terms of military procurement and economic expansion were to elapse before the Vietnam escalation would again test America's capacity for local war, 1960's style. Those five years were barely enough.

20 : JOHNSON'S JUNGLES

LYNDON JOHNSON was the fifth Democrat to occupy the White House during the twentieth century. Woodrow Wilson had established the party's modern tradition, built its platform and set the tone and standard of performance for the Democrats who followed him: Roosevelt, Truman, Kennedy and Johnson. But Wilson had found himself thrust into the leadership of a coalition of the left and center which then still represented a minority force (and a preponderantly white minority at that). He himself had inherited a tradition formed by the money battles of the post-Civil-War era which molded the country's political evolution into the twentieth century. The Panic of 1907 had forced a consensus from both sides of the historic divide over money politics in favor of one or another kind of banking reform, and Wilson scored his greatest political and legislative achievement when he kept his campaign promise to provide it. When he did, he turned a badly timed Republican failure to deal with Congress into a decisive Democratic success. He gave the country's business interests a banking system that worked, and their customers a banking system that protected their money.

Thus Wilson, in the first phase of his Presidency—his Reform Presidency—was able to project liberalism as progress and progressivism as practicality. But when his War Presidency started, it blacked out immediate memories of the New Freedom. The war brought a more complete victory than any political fight can yield, but with it came demoralizing political frustration. Democratic crusading for domestic reform had paid political dividends when idealism demonstrated that it could be efficient. But where this crusade became international, it first ran afoul of harsh realities, and then suffered repudiation from a public opinion which expected reform to pay off.

Neither the superstitions of politicians nor the dogmas of historians nor even the dramatic improvisations of poets could have anticipated the fidelity with which Roosevelt's two-phase Presidency reproduced the rhythm and the form of Wilson's. Roosevelt's reform phase was dominated by his New Deal, which corresponded to Wilson's New Freedom and, in fact, was modeled after it. Roosevelt, like Wilson, made a success of his peacetime progressivism because he earned reform a reputation for practicality—both in the economy, as an antidote to panic, and in politics, as the sponsor of programs that Congress would buy and, therefore, could be sold to the voters. For Roosevelt, the change from Reform Presidency to War Presidency came quickly and completely, just as it had for Wilson. The parallel even extended to Roosevelt's reelection in 1940 on his promise to keep the country out of war. But for Roosevelt as for Wilson, a record of enduring accomplishment in the cause of practical idealism was offset by the sorry frustrations which idealistic absolutism ran into overseas.

Truman had won reelection by provoking Congress into rejecting his program. His crusade for the Fair Deal brought him victory in 1948 on the same bread-and-butter issues which had renewed Wilson's mandate to crusade for the New Freedom in 1916, and Roosevelt's to carry on the New Deal in 1940. But the dilemma which dominated Truman's War Presidency took over from the then unrealizable idealism which had inspired his Fair Deal Presidency. After he had parlayed his managerial failure with Congress into his coup of 1948, his retreat into military stalemate forced his political abdication in 1952. As with Wilson and Roosevelt before him, his inability to avoid the war of his time interrupted and diverted his domestic economic operation from its political goals; and his inability to win or even to end the war which had finished off his domestic experiment in reform cost him his political ascendancy.

When Kennedy's turn came, the new era of war-in-peace was well advanced. Kennedy's personality was tailored to fit the mood of the "soaring sixties." Stevenson's patient idealism had run its course concurrently with Eisenhower's pleasant quietism. The country was ready for a "can do" operator of the younger generation who could be trusted to make up for time lost with Ike and to act on Stevenson's ideas. But, by Kennedy's time, the country had outgrown the simple transitions from war to peace and from reform to emergency which had marked the Wilson, Roosevelt and Truman periods. The luxury of concentrating upon reform in a domestic vacuum was gone forever. Reciprocally, the priorities of war could no longer demand exclusive attention even in an emergency situation.

The mandate given Kennedy to get the country moving again was complicated by the concurrent challenge, to which he responded with flair, of the Cold War. He could afford no retreat from the lines already laid down, yet he was expected to make advances toward the contradictory goals of easing tensions and achieving propaganda victories over the Soviets that would look well in the headlines. The Kennedy Administration made a show of marching on toward a New Frontier. But the Bay of Pigs fiasco, the Berlin Wall and the deteriorating situation in Southeast Asia all demonstrated how difficult it is to operate in the real world with mere slogans. As fast as the Kennedy Administration moved to meet emergencies in the domestic area of political controversy and economic progress, old pressures combined with new ones from seething war fronts abroad to neutralize its purposes. The America which made Kennedy President had outgrown the historic division of labor between the problems of war and the problems of peace, as well as the historic distinction between the politics of reform and the politics of emergency.

History, when it assesses Kennedy's career, is likely to give him the benefit of the doubt on the grounds that the sorry frustration of his performance was more than offset by his inspired expressions of promise. Shakespeare was no more generous to Henry V than legend has been to JFK. Nevertheless, the literature which looks back on the Kennedy Administration gives Johnson credit for what he did to complete its unfinished business. Johnson accommodated himself to the carryover in psychology as well as to the changeover in politics. The circumstances of his succession qualified him as the trustee empowered to redeem Kennedy's failure to move Congress forward, to consolidate Kennedy's successes and to succeed where Kennedy had failed. Johnson was not under pressure to undertake any bold new program of his own. To get the country moving again in response to Kennedy's call, it was enough for Johnson to get Congress moving.

In a speech before the Detroit Economic Club ten days after the assassination, while the country was still reeling from shock and uncertain how far to trust the unknown quantity in the White House, I stated that Johnson would fulfill Kennedy's promise to get the country moving again; and that he would do so by getting the Congress moving again. I expressed the judgment that Johnson would play the stock market as his instrument for transforming political progress into economic momentum. And so it happened.

The assassination occurred on the Friday before Thanksgiving day. On the night of Kennedy's death, while the country sat up mesmerized by TV and mourning, only the margin clerks in the banks and the brokerage houses stayed at work. By Saturday morning, the mails were flooded with margin calls assuring a new collapse the following week. But the margin calls were never delivered. By Monday morning, all the operations of government and business were suspended in honor of Kennedy's memory. Mail deliveries stopped, and the banks and exchanges closed. The holiday gave Johnson the chance to make time his ally in preventing panic.

The ceremonial of mourning, the welling up of grief and the dramatic ritual which fastened all eyes first on the Capitol

and then on Arlington, functioned as a tragic reenactment of the
theatrics which had caught the imagination and raised the hopes
of the country during the crisis which greeted Roosevelt's entrance into the White House. Johnson scheduled his bank holiday for the first day of Thanksgiving week, and the public
involvement in the funeral indicated an extension into the second
day. Meanwhile, the White House was burning up the wires to
Wall Street; and, in response, Johnson's friends in Wall Street
were burning up the trans-Atlantic wires with the word that
Johnson was going to be good for business. On the first day of
mourning in America, the European exchanges marked up the
prices of the barometric American blue chips traded in their
stock markets. By the second day of the bank holiday, a new
American bull market had come to life in Europe while Wall
Street was still shut down. By Thanksgiving eve, the long holiday
weekend was on, and the bank holiday had run into Thanksgiving.

When the margin calls which had been mailed out on the
night of the assassination were finally received—not on the Monday preceding Thanksgiving but on the Monday following it—the
new Johnson confidence boom, which had bulled the quotations
of American stocks on European exchanges, sent the outdated
margin calls pouring unopened into wastebaskets. The Johnson
bull market had begun. Everything in the domestic political
economy was working for Johnson, and he made the most of it.

By Johnson's time, the frame of historical reference within
which political opinion judged Presidential exercises in economic management had changed. Reform was no longer on trial
to prove its practicality. Instead, the progress of prosperity had
come to mean social progress—prosperity was now the measure
and the guarantor of reform. But by Johnson's time, too, the
traditional political cycle of domestic reform and war emergency,
which had first worked to the advantage of Democratic Presidents and then to their disadvantage, had given way to the new
era of war-in-peace.

While the country had fought two-front wars before Johnson's term of office, it was still conditioned to an Administration
that attacked on one front at a time, whether the front was the

economy at home or a battlefield overseas. The Kennedy years were over before the new pattern became clear. Even so, it was evident that Kennedy's New Frontier had run along two fronts. On the foreign front, actual fighting had nearly erupted: when the 1954 settlement threatened to break down in Laos, when the Wall went up in Berlin, and again when the clouds of Armageddon hung over Cuba. Like Eisenhower before him, Kennedy had managed to avoid any large-scale public commitment of American troops to overseas wars. But, again like Eisenhower, he had been unable to take advantage of the opportunity which relative quiescence in international politics allowed him for domestic reform. Under Kennedy, the economy settled down to a state of siege where a breakthrough had been promised. Johnson became the first President caught in a desperate struggle to cope with emergencies abroad and at home as well.

This time, war did not wait to start until a Reform Presidency had run its course. The war was already there, and only public recognition of the volcanic escalation to come was delayed. Before the country fully realized that Vietnam was not a skirmish but a major second front coexisting with the Johnson confidence boom and the reforms projected for the Great Society, the demands of this perilous adventure had moved to first place and claimed priority over both prosperity and reform.

Thus, unlike the Wilson, Roosevelt and Truman Administrations, the Johnson Administration found its first war front ready and waiting. Then, in 1967, a new second front opened up in the ghettoes lying at the heart of every American city. Johnson's problem was to decide which front claimed priority. Before his first full term was three-quarters over, the course of history after Detroit's cataclysmic riot in July of 1967 showed that Johnson had given top priority to the wrong engagement. When the Detroit jungle exploded, he was caught overcommitted in the other jungle overseas.

As Vice President, Johnson had enjoyed a continuing ex officio opportunity to observe the design and construction of the straitjacket that was later to confine him in Vietnam. He was privy to the deliberations which resulted in the decision to have

President Ngo Dinh Diem removed from the scene. In the last months of the Kennedy Administration, the plan to drop Johnson in 1964 was nearly as far advanced as the military decision with respect to Diem. In this crisis, Johnson did venture to demur against the order to supersede Diem, for he saw the danger which loomed ahead once the American government assumed the responsibility for administering law in the Saigon jungle. This was Johnson's tragedy, the blight of his career. In his lieutenancy, served under Eisenhower and Kennedy, he warned of dangers to which he exposed himself in his own Presidency.

Thanks to Kennedy's decision to eliminate Diem, Johnson took over from Kennedy under the same kind of pressure to weigh and judge unknowns which Kennedy faced in Cuba when he succeeded Eisenhower, and which had confronted Truman when he learned of the existence of the atom bomb. Eisenhower, it will be recalled, had advised Kennedy that cancellation of the Bay of Pigs project would be preferable to failure. Johnson, however, needed no warning, for he had been in a better position than anyone else to observe how risks can outweigh benefits. America's blundering venture in welfare-imperialism had involved it in accepting political and military responsibility for another country which was unable and unwilling to fight for itself and which lacked the social base for effective mobilization. We had then undertaken to fight a protective war on a scale less total than our acceptance of political responsibility. This blueprint of Kennedy's design, which Johnson followed, invited political disaster without seeking military victory.

With his smashing victory over Goldwater in November, 1964, Johnson took over in his own right. As soon as he did, the clear pattern blurred. Although his performance continued to dazzle the eye for the better part of another year, a new uncertainty dominated his calculations, and the mystery which shrouded his strategy satisfied even his own passion for secrecy. The simple, objective resolve which had guided him through Kennedy's unfinished term seemed to break down into irresolution, unintelligible in a leader so apparently dominant and so plainly creative. His original guideline had kept him moving to finish Kennedy's unfinished business (which, as the legislative log-jam on Capitol Hill suggested even before November, 1963, was unfinishable by Kennedy). Once on his own, however, his path took him in opposite directions. Fear for his immediate political future compelled him to supplement his demonstration of devotion to Kennedy ideals with a personal appeasement of the Kennedy clan. At the same time, his native drives and long-standing ambition drove him to emulate and outdo his political sire, FDR. It was in response to the latter that Johnson made his sincere, if ineffective, moves toward waging war on poverty and discrimination. But it was the former—his envy of the Kennedy past and his fear of the Kennedy future—which came to dominate him and entrap him in Vietnam.

Johnson's crisis of confidence vis-à-vis the Kennedys went back twenty years to the jockeying for future political position at the high point of the Roosevelt era. Roosevelt himself had been clear that the next generation of liberal leadership would open up opportunities previously denied to candidates who emerged as the favorite sons of minority groups, whether ethnic or regional. No one had any better firsthand evidence than he of the potential appeal of an Irish candidacy. But he also recognized the political claim on the future of a Texas candidacy. Sam Rayburn had been the Texas entry for the Vice Presidency in 1944, when as every insider knew, victory meant sure succession to the White House. He had been eliminated by the factional divisions which neutralized Texas as a political factor in those days. But soon after Rayburn's protégé, Johnson, turned up in Washington, the young Congressman had been among the recipients of Roosevelt's confidential recipe for cooking up a Presidential candidacy.

Johnson never argued with Roosevelt or, for that matter, with any President, least of all when their political small-talk dovetailed with his own large ambitions. In the first term of the Eisenhower Presidency, Johnson had progressed further in his pursuit of power than he had in his pursuit of popularity. Post-1952 practicalities demanded acceptance of the fact that Eisenhower's personality dominated politics, and that Stevenson's appeal was as limited as it was intense. Johnson's interest lay in playing for the succession after Eisenhower had served his time, without committing his support to the rival challenge of Adlai Stevenson. Even if Stevenson had been able to inspire the enthusiasm and devotion within Congress which he commanded in the intellectual establishment, it is doubtful that he could have developed a breadth of national appeal comparable to Eisenhower's. And unless he won the firmest and closest of allegiances from the Johnson leadership of Congress, Stevenson had no chance of developing a real political challenge to Eisenhower.

In 1956, Johnson had had a rare opportunity to win by losing. A sacrificial campaign for the Presidency against Eisenhower would have established his leadership of the Democratic power with the mass of outsiders who did not know him, as well as with the few insiders who did. It would also have provided him with a base for making news and with the national audience which an active Presidential candidacy requires. The lack of such a reach haunted his last years in the Senate, diverting his attention as Majority Leader in 1959 and 1960 from the challenges of national leadership to those befitting a refugee from Texas. His failure to move left of center and to rise above complacency by using Eisenhower as a foil had locked him into a narrow regional stance and reduced his political appeal to that of a cloakroom chieftain. Even a successful fight for the Vice Presidential nomination, as a gesture of unity behind Stevenson in a year of Democratic disaster, would have been better than what happened—for Johnson, for the Democratic ticket and for the country after the election. (After all, as FDR liked to recall, that was how he had gained entry onto the national political scene—as the junior member of the ticket headed by the forgotten Cox which Harding swamped in 1920.)

In fact, the political unknown who made himself a national figure overnight by his unsuccessful fight for the Vice Presidential nomination at the second Stevenson convention was John F. Kennedy. Johnson's last-minute efforts to gain some backing for the number-two spot on Stevenson's ticket were ignored and forgotten. Consequently, in the four-year run-up to what loomed as a Democratic year in 1960, Johnson was frozen into his "responsible" position of cooperation with Eisenhower; Kennedy meanwhile was freed to use the Senate as the launching pad for the candidacy which he not only admitted but advertised. Eisenhower gained the short-term advantage of the alliance into which Johnson locked himself, but Kennedy gained the longer-term advantage by being free to run for President while Johnson was "minding the store."

Johnson's nemesis, indecision, showed up in his miscalculation of the risks and benefits offered by a challenge to either Eisenhower or Stevenson. He won no gratitude either from them or from Kennedy for the hesitation which led him to default on the political opportunities which could be exploited by losing on the issue of opposition in 1956. Nor, after a brave beginning, did he play out the challenge which he made to Eisenhower in 1958. Johnson's brief but incisive move into opposition during the Sputnik-and-dollar panic of 1957–8 ended by exerting a large influence over the politics of 1960, as well as over the economics of the incomplete 1959–60 recovery. Johnson challenged Eisenhower, and he did it successfully, as no one else had done. He chose Eisenhower's accepted area of expertise as the field of battle, and he took advantage of a moment when budget deficits had already shattered Eisenhower's complacent exterior. Moreover, his realistic study of Russia's scientific breakthrough came as a pincer movement against Eisenhower, catching him in a dilemma between financial maxims and national security. For once, the Majority Leader stared the President down. Briefly, a Johnson candidacy trembled on the verge of plausibility.

Then, at the height of his influence and with national opportunities open to him, Johnson turned defensive. Soon a permanent cleavage developed with the liberal elements in the Democratic Senate caucus who pressed him to broaden his challenge to Eisenhower and continue it along party lines. In turn, Johnson's breach with the Senate liberals drove him into the insecurity which cost him the Presidential nomination in 1960. It frightened him out of going after the nomination while Kennedy was still on the make (and, therefore, on the defensive).

The Kennedy legend has blandly alleged that his nomination expressed a universal mandate from the public and politicians alike. In fact, it was an exercise in bandwagon-building. Kennedy gambled on his ability to pyramid a string of decisive primary victories into a public-relations simulacrum of an invincible mandate. If Johnson had had the will and fortitude to enter the Indiana primary in early May, 1960, he might have defused the rocket that Kennedy subsequently sent flaring into the political skies in Wisconsin and West Virginia. Instead, smarting and sulking under the criticism of the liberals, Johnson retreated into legislatively effective but politically unintelligible power combinations with the Republicans—a pattern prophetic of his operation as President.

The background of public frustration and behind-the-scenes accomplishment (plus the equally mixed motivations which it bred) accounted for Johnson's concurrence in the grand design of the Kennedy Administration and his enactment of it in office. In his 1964 campaign, when his fear of the Kennedys served as protective armor against his own insecurity, Johnson knew how to play the Vietnam issue shrewdly enough: the moment he identified Goldwater as the war candidate, it was all over. Superficially, the drama, as it unfolded after the election, seemed to cast Johnson as the successor not only to Kennedy but to Wilson, Truman and Roosevelt as well. In fact, there was a difference. Neither Wilson, Roosevelt nor Truman had planned their wars. Johnson's decision, in his ex officio capacity as trustee for the Kennedy Administration, to go all the way in Vietnam was an act of political choice. It followed directly on the decision, which he himself had questioned while he was still Vice President, to eliminate Diem. It took the form of a military commitment to use troops and bombs to offset the continuing social, political, economic and military collapse of the society for which America had taken responsibility.

Why did LBJ go all the way for his subordinates in the holdover Kennedy Administration, whose members he mistrusted and with whom he dealt at arm's length? He began with the calculation that wrapping himself in the slogans of the Kennedy Administration would endow him with the protective aura of the Kennedy myth. Fear of Kennedy power and insecurity in the face of the Kennedy reputation for intellect were companion inducements. So perhaps was the temptation that a little war won might mean a large lift from popular patriotism. But the compelling incentive was the one which seemed to offer the most reliable shelter for insecurity. When Johnson went along with the recommendation of his Kennedy Administration to escalate in Vietnam, he assumed that his acceptance of its leadership would produce a mutual assistance pact: McNamara, Rusk and his former Attorney General would gain immunity-by-continuity from any past errors and lapses, and he would gain immunity from their hosility. Johnson fought his way through the Vietnam War by blaming his Kennedy heritage for its escalation. At the same time, as fast as he went along with pressures on him to escalate, the Kennedy position, as voiced by Senator Robert Kennedy as well as by writers sympathetic to him, blamed Johnson for having failed to keep Vietnam under control as President Kennedy seemed to have done in his day.

When Robert Kennedy decided to retain his independence by resigning the Attorney Generalship, Johnson's fears were sharpened and his appetite for appeasement whetted (especially as Kennedy retained de facto control over the apparatus of power with the Justice Department). Johnson first made his admitted and declared enemy a free gift of a Senate seat from New York, which, though surpassed in population by California, was still the Empire State, especially as a source of influence upon opinion. This monumentally amateurish calculation on Johnson's part was rationalized at the time on the dubious grounds that all freshman Senators, like all disposable Vice Presidents, are supposed to be seen but not heard. Johnson's loss of official control over Kennedy, as a result of Kennedy's renunciation of veto power over Johnson, intensified Johnson's dependence on McNamara, who had been Robert Kennedy's closest collaborator both before and after the assassination. Johnson calculated that, if he took sanctuary in McNamara's recommendations, Kennedy would never subject him to the attack which, both as practicing

politician and as legatee, he feared more than he feared anything else.

This calculation of Johnson's turned into a miscalculation
so complete that only sorcery or an excess of shrewdness could
have accounted for it. As if bewitched, Johnson went all the
way with McNamara. McNamara remained closer to Kennedy
than ever. Kennedy nonetheless blasted Johnson and dissociated
himself in public from the record which Johnson used against
him in private and to which Johnson had made himself a
prisoner in public. In the second act, of course, Kennedy in turn
miscalculated and burdened himself with a double liability—
first by attacking the War President who had been loyal to his
brother, and then by failing to follow through on the attack. In
form, it was a comedy of errors. In substance, it was a tragedy.

Within a year of his election, Johnson's Washington had
broken down into five separate and distinct power centers. The
most obvious were Congress and the press, ever present and self-
perpetuating. But the cumbersome and semi-autonomous Administration Johnson inherited from the Kennedys, and whose
continuity he was intent on maintaining, developed into another
power center operating at arm's length from the President.
Kennedy power constituted a fourth separate power center.
Finally, there was the Presidency—not only independent of the
four other power centers and increasingly isolated from them but
(and here was the startling new development) increasingly
hostile toward the branches of its own Administration. When
Senator Kennedy invoked the authority of Johnson's State Department against the President in their famous 1967 confrontation
over the bombing of North Vietnam, the President bewildered
the country but silenced the Senator when he shot back in fury,
"It's *your* State Department, not mine."

Johnson had in fact ceded control over the key posts in his
Administration to Kennedy holdovers, men not in his confidence
and not primarily loyal to him. Although he was playing the
Presidential game quite differently from the way Roosevelt had,
he had stumbled into Rooseveltian errors. For FDR, in his time,
had also fallen afoul of the two fundamental rules of Presidential
politics. The first axiom states that the Justice Department is the

most vital power center within the government and therefore puts the President on notice to have as his Attorney General a man who will keep him out of political trouble. But the worst of Roosevelt's inadequate appointees to this political nerve center, Homer Cummings, involved him in the most disastrous blunder of his entire Presidency, the provocative and self-defeating plan to pack the Supreme Court. The second rule identifies the Treasury as the counterpart in policy terms of the Justice Department as a power center, and there FDR had installed the incompetent Henry Morgenthau.

No President can hope to succeed without an Attorney General whom he can trust to keep him out of trouble, and without a Secretary of the Treasury whom he can trust to keep his policies out of trouble. American history is rich in positive as well as negative examples of both maxims. The cases which offer the most meaningful commentaries on the political trouble Roosevelt brought on himself at the Justice Department, and on the policy trouble he brought on himself at the Treasury, are those of the three Democratic Administrations which followed his. The strategy employed by the Truman, Kennedy and Johnson Administrations left no doubt that his successors were motivated in each case by vivid, firsthand memories of the risks Roosevelt had run, and the frustrations he had suffered, as the direct result of breaking these rules. (In the case of Kennedy, the firsthand experience had been noted by the Ambassador, his father, and the moral he had drawn from it was transmitted to his sons.)

Truman took no chances whatever. He ran scared and put his men in charge of both departments, making them adjuncts of the White House. Thus, he insured their loyalty to him. At the same time, he took the additional precaution (as Roosevelt had not felt obliged to do) of ascertaining that they enjoyed the most intimate of ties with the Congressional establishment he left behind him, so that they could and would keep his lines open with the other power centers in government, as the Justice Department and the Treasury had overtly and provocatively failed to do for Roosevelt.

When the time came for Cabinet-making by the Kennedys,

the patriarch was particularly and, indeed, articulately motivated by his determination to save his sons from the troubles which his shrewd eye had watched Roosevelt bring on himself: hence the twin decisions which kept the Attorney Generalship within the family and conceded the Treasury to a Republican as a matter of policy. Once control over the power center in the Justice Department had been secured in the family interest, family policy accorded an overriding priority to a display of bipartisanship in the Roosevelt tradition: so much so that, despite the Kennedy family's reputation for hard trading, Robert McNamara was given his choice of the Secretaryship of the Treasury or Defense. When he opted for Defense, he influenced the course of American history. McNamara's choice freed the Kennedy Administration to give the Treasury to Douglas Dillon who, as Eisenhower's Undersecretary of State, had established a proven record of Congressional acceptance. If McNamara had decided to enlist his energies on the dollar front instead of on the war front, the history of America and her role in the world would undoubtedly have taken a radically different turn.

The approach which Johnson, in his turn, developed to both problems revealed the complexities of his emotional makeup, and showed him at both his worst and his best. Exactly because he was so certain that the Justice Department is the motor center of the political power apparatus, he let it remain under the control of his hated rival, Bobby Kennedy. And because he was just as certain that the Treasury is the strategic center for the coordination, clearance and financing—or strangulation—of all government policies, he assured his brilliant start-up success by co-opting as his confidential Secretary-in-fact Donald Cook, by that time President of the prestigious American Electric Power Service Corporation, and, therefore, qualified by the standards of the world as well as his background of private association for the post. Cook, while still in government service, had been Truman's last Chairman of the SEC. But for years before, as a young SEC official, as counsel to Johnson's Investigation Subcommittee of the House Naval Affairs Committee during World War II, and again, as counsel to the Preparedness Investigating

Subcommittee of the Senate Armed Services Committee, Cook had assisted him up the Washington ladder on the policy side as closely as Abe Fortas had in the more personal area of lawyer–client relationships normally reserved for a prospective Attorney General. If Johnson had approached the Presidency in the manner of Truman, he would have cleared the Kennedy apparatus out of the Justice Department and installed Fortas as Attorney General. But this would have been entirely out of character for Johnson. Moreover, Fortas would have jeopardized his claim on elevation to the Supreme Court by running the risk of becoming a battle casualty on the political firing line.

It was typical of Johnson's wary, devious pragmatism that he kept Kennedy's acceptable and cooperative Republican in public view at the Treasury until the cooling-off period after his 1965 inauguration, while relying on Cook for the operational initiatives which made the caretaker phase of Johnson's Presidency such a sensational success. In fairness to Johnson, his plans for reorganizing his Administration after he had become President in his own right turned on his project for moving Cook into the Secretaryship of the Treasury. The surprise which knocked these plans awry on April Fool's Day, 1965, stands as the turning point in Johnson's Presidency: Cook refused the Secretaryship for personal reasons. With Dillon leaving, and Cook not coming, pique blacked out prudence and prompted him to appoint Henry Fowler, who had been an excellent number-two man to Dillon as Undersecretary and who, as Secretary, remained a competent number-two man, deferring to Federal Reserve Board Chairman Martin in lieu of a policy superior to guide him at the Treasury. Given to temper tantrums though Johnson was when denied his wishes, he was nevertheless not so impetuous as to overlook the need for personal loyalty at the Treasury even if he could not have competence. With the Fowler appointment, he settled for the personal devotion Roosevelt had found in Morgenthau. He received a comparable measure of competence. Both he and the economy were to pay for it.

The money squeeze of 1966 reached near–panic proportions as the direct result of the failure of the Treasury to require the Defense Department to keep it continuously informed of the rate of increase in war spending. At the height of the 1966 financial crisis, both the Federal Reserve Board and the President's Council of Economic Advisers complained that they found themselves obliged to perform their functions in an analytical vacuum because of the failure of the Treasury to function as their conduit with the Pentagon. The fear of military domination over the civilian authorities has a long and lurid history within the apparatus of government, as well as in the historic debate over the making of national policy and the manning of the national security apparatus; so does the fact. Johnson's characteristic decision to rely on the combination of a strong Secretary of Defense not in his confidence, and a weak Secretary of the Treasury very much in his confidence but unable to hold his own against the Secretary of Defense, added a sorry chapter to this history. It turned the clock back to the days before Forrestal had conceived of the mission Congress delegated to the National Security Council, as if he had not won his fight to rely on the Secretary of the Treasury to coordinate national policy with the money policy needed to support it.

The decision to escalate in Vietnam exposed the American economy to a double jeopardy—on the home front and on its exposed European flank. The exposure on the home front reflected the fact that Vietnam was too small a war to require direct controls over production, construction and consumption. Moreover, the economy which was called upon to support it was too big to require the restraint of rationing by direct controls. Vietnam, despite its escalation, remained a small war militarily. But it was a very expensive war. It taxed the country's financial resources more severely than it strained its physical resources: it left slack in the economy, while it created a shortage of finance. And it was here, in the financing of the war, that the weak link in the chain on the operating side was to be found. Official underestimation of the cost of the war loaded the money markets with more demand than they could meet and precipitated the money squeeze of 1966 that all but brought on a panic and did produce the unprecedented phenomenon of wartime stagnation in the economy.

The exposure on the economy's European flank was financial, too. European reconstruction had long since been refinanced. In fact, Europe had accumulated large reserves of foreign exchange, and America had developed a balance-of-payments problem. During the Korean War, America had still been strong enough, and Europe dependent enough, for American capital outflows to Europe to be welcomed and for Europe's excess liquidity to come to New York as a testimonial to the strength of the dollar. By the time of the Vietnam escalation, however, Europe no longer felt dependent on America. On the contrary, she had become worried about the stability of her dollar holdings. Moreover, the growing suspicion that America had become overinvolved militarily at the other end of the world was increasing the fear that she might end up overextended financially. When foreigners took fright for their dollar holdings and liquidated them into gold, their retreat into a sanctuary of presumed liquidity had the paradoxical effect of shrinking the liquidity they were trying to protect. Not only did foreigners hurt their immediate liquidity when they converted dollars into gold, but their own economies had become dependent on America's long-term foreign investment flow into plant and equipment abroad. When Europe's pressure on the dollar resulted in a slump over there, surprise and fear spread in Europe; and its pressure on the dollar increased. Thus, as the 1960's wore on, America found herself once more isolated, but this time not by choice. She was going it alone in the face of international suspicion, and under financial strain.

During the first two years of the Vietnam escalation, the international strain on the dollar was still minimal. For one thing, long lead times were involved in carrying out decisions for military spending. Secondly, the real measure of international confidence in the dollar was the domestic performance of the American economy and not the marginal statistics involved in the American payments balance. Certainly, no net dollar outflow of $2 billion or less a year was likely to bother Europe so long as the American economy remained strong and balanced, and therefore, so long as the dollars flowing out to Europe seemed likely to maintain their value. For, psychologically, confidence in the dollar rises and falls abroad not with the deficit in the payments account, but with the relative size of the domestic budget deficit, which is the real measure of balance and productivity within the American economy. Despite the near universal acceptance of the Keynesian proposition that deficits prime the pump for recovery, by 1966 deficits were once again being seen by many as threats to stability—even in wartime.

One of Johnson's standard techniques for justifying any position or action of his was to find a precedent either in the record of Eisenhower to the right of him or of Kennedy to the left of him. There he would take cover. But the technique can work in reverse. Both Eisenhower and Kennedy had stumbled into $12 billion deficits during their years of market reversals, as Johnson liked to recall during his salad days. He found that he had laughed too soon when, at the outset of the 1968 fiscal year, he found himself confronted with a prospective budget deficit at least twice that size. During World War I and World War II, the size of the domestic budget deficit had not been a source of exposure to foreign pressure. But Vietnam invited every other country in the world to sit in judgment, not on America's motives, but on her prudence in husbanding her resources. As the domestic budget deficit began to rise in the wake of war costs, so did foreign fears.

The position of the dollar during the Vietnam War provides an ironic contrast with its position during the Civil War and World War I—a contrast which is a study in the deterioration that too often sets in with strength. Johnson was conscious, of course, that heavy expenditures in Southeast Asia exposed him to criticism at home. His nervousness over keeping the Senate informed about outgos was evidence enough of this concern. But inexperience, a bias toward isolation, or a combination of both had prevented the realization that involvement in Asia raised doubts not only at home, but in Europe. For by that time the dollar had become the world's only international currency.

Military escalation in Vietnam shook the props under the dollar in Europe and necessitated financial improvisations which did nothing to strengthen confidence abroad. Still the war planners plunged on as if their actions were totally isolated from the rest of the American political economy, and as if that economy had no ties with the rest of the world. The need to end the military frustration in Vietnam became an obsession, subordinating all other issues. The dollar's exposure was ignored—until the small war off in the jungle ran the world's one big currency into deep trouble at home and in Europe. America had come full circle since the days when she renounced European militarism and dedicated herself to peace and prosperity in the isolation of her own continent. Now her military adventure in Asia was threatening a Europe newly dedicated to the American recipe for continental prosperity—peace.

Back in the 1860's, the dollar was a small currency and merely a local one. Then, trouble for the dollar did not automatically spell trouble for everyone. On the contrary, even with the dollar at a discount, America was still riding a rising tide of money-good exports to the more financially mature markets of Europe. By the time of Vietnam, however, the dollar was to all intents and purposes the world's reserve currency (sterling, the alternative, having become dependent on it as the result of England's decline). Consequently, any pressure on the dollar was bound to be reflected in a recessionary trend in money-good export markets; and, by 1967, it was. In fact, by the time of Vietnam, the American economy had grown so big that any weakening of the dollar had no chance of being offset by a strengthening of export earnings, as happened during the Civil War. The world economy had come to be dependent on a dollar presumed to be strong and, nevertheless, counted on to run at a substantial annual payments deficit; for the dollar payments deficit had come to furnish working capital for the rest of the world. Vietnam disrupted this flow and awakened fears where there had been confidence. Both the fears and the shortages reacted against America, adding to the wartime drag on the economy and stepping up the squeeze on the dollar.

A look at the contrast between our financial position in World War I and during the Vietnam crisis leaves no doubt that America's rise to world leadership had increased its vulnerability along with its power. The stresses suffered during World War I had been serious, but the dislocations they caused while the war lasted were purely domestic; although the moment Europe's markets reopened for business, the dislocation exported from New York disrupted them. This experience, its recurrence during World War II, and even the special case of the Korean War (fought while America was still financing Europe's reconstruction after World War II), could and should have alerted America to the hazards of a change in the expected norms of wartime finance. For any new crisis which turned the tables on America, involving her but leaving Europe free to enjoy the benefits of neutrality, was bound to raise the need for money controls and fiscal restraints—war surtaxes and credit rationing—even more urgently than World War II and the Korean War had.

Instead, however, the Johnson Administration marched blindly into a major blunder. It repeated the Wilson Administration's error of relying on free-market wartime financing; but, worse still, it made no provision to protect the dollar from the international exposure it faced for the first time. The Wilson Administration's sin against the first principle of wartime finance—ignoring the need for controls and surtaxes—had proven fatal, even though other circumstances had been favorable. The Johnson Administration's repeat performance of the Wilson fiasco occurred when circumstances had turned unfavorable, when America was subject to Europe's power to invoke dollar sanctions. During World War I, money had no place else to go. During World War II, money also had no place else to go. During the Korean War, American policy and European dependence made America's wartime dollar outflows to Europe a cause of confidence. But during the Vietnam crisis, money did have other places to go. And it went.

There were many "whys" for Vietnam. But, as escalation became a fact, the "how" became more important. The simplest answer to the question of "how" is provided by geography: Vietnam is a long way away. Our commitment there built up so

gradually that it did not obtrude upon, or distract from, preoccupations closer to home. During the months of gradual escalation, I published an interview with Ferdinand Eberstadt, who had
formulated the Controlled Materials Plan which had geared the
economy for victory in World War II, and who had collaborated
with Forrestal in the formulation of the National Security Act.
Eberstadt likened our adventure in Vietnam to "climbing up the
side of a fog bank." Politically and strategically, it was to prove
just as dangerous an attempt at brinkmanship as plunging off
a cliff.

The gradualness of the Vietnam adventure appealed to
Johnson just as strongly as did the continuity with the Kennedy
years of its sponsorship. For it encouraged the illusion that he
could handle the war without having to abandon his dedication
to the vision of the Great Society. Wilson, Roosevelt and Truman
had begun their tenures of office by concentrating on the blight
of poverty and the need for social reform. Each had been distracted by war. Each had failed to use the potential of America's
resources to reach his early peacetime goals. Moreover, all had
been forced to impose controls on the economy after war had
set it booming to full employment and to accept the inflationary
dislocations which war had brought. Though Johnson knew his
relevant modern history—better than anyone else—this very
knowledge, his trust in his own expertise and, above all, his
pride, combined to delude him into the gamble that he could be a
War President who was also a Prosperity President and a Reform
President at the same time. He bet that guns could coexist
not only with butter, but also with freedom from controls, with
progress in the war against poverty, and with the enjoyment of
stability. This feat would assure his place in history while it
earned his War Presidency a continuing popular mandate. Notwithstanding his self-imposed isolation from the four other
sources of power—the Congress, the press, the Kennedy power
center and his own Administration—Johnson assumed that his
popularity would be sustained and sheltered by prosperity as he
operated his two-front Presidency at war both in Asia and at
home.

In America's history, wartime expansion has again and

again brought military victory and then gone on to provide the indispensable drives toward social unity and economic advance which enabled her to benefit from victory. But when blind repetitive escalation turned involvement in Vietnam into a lethal danger to America, it first sapped the vitality of the economy. The promise of progress through prosperity fell victim to a credibility gap of its own. Uncontrolled, the American economy staggered under the burden of a wartime buildup that, for the first time in American history, cramped and pinched the economy instead of spurring its expansion. The hope of progress began to lose its ability to work as a cohesive force in the social jungle of the undeveloped areas within American cities. The high point of Johnson's career in the White House was reached on the day in August, 1965, when, displaying a degree of mastery unsurpassed and until then unimagined over Congress, he got the Voting Rights Bill through the House and the Medicare Bill through the Senate. (The previous summer he had made history by passing both the tax cut and his first Civil Rights Bill.) Just two years later, the bell tolled for Johnson's hope of enduring achievement when the ghettoes of America's cities exploded in riots born of frustrated hope, and proved that the legislative triumphs of Johnson's Reform Presidency were incapable of providing the base of social stability which his War Presidency required. The tax increase which he requested that summer, in turn, was earmarked for war, not for America's unfinished business at home. The advances of 1965 had turned into the retreats of 1967.

21: MC NAMARA'S MIRAGE

JOHNSON ENTERED the White House endowed with that rarest of Presidential opportunities—a second chance to redeem an error of national policy. The strategic situation confronting him in November, 1963, invited review and offered him an opportunity to reaffirm the vote he had cast against Secretary Dulles's initial commitment of "advisers" to Vietnam in 1954. Johnson had learned enough in the Senate and seen enough in the Vice Presidency to know that a new look at old commitments was overdue.

Kennedy had inherited a more awkward problem in 1961. The moment he took over from Eisenhower, the youthful President found himself hemmed in by the elderly hero's reputation for expertise in military matters. Dulles had traded on this acclaim; Majority Leader Johnson had catered to it; and Kennedy was too prudent to present an opposing profile in courage. Eisenhower's scorecard credited him with bringing no less than three wars to an end—the unavoidable big war of 1940–5, the unpopular small war of 1950–2 and the ambiguous Suez war of 1956. For Kennedy, continuing Eisenhower's policy in Vietnam seemed to offer no jeopardy. It was only in Cuba that

Eisenhower had warned him of heightening risk. Kennedy's decision to disregard Eisenhower's warning over Cuba argued for accepting his commitments in Vietnam.

When Johnson's turn came, he had the benefit of Kennedy's experience. He had seen at first hand how Kennedy had begun by accepting Eisenhower's commitments in Vietnam, how he had then found himself extending them, and how he had ended by losing control. Nevertheless, despite his ingrown resistance to activism, Johnson plunged ahead. He decided that to follow where both Eisenhower and Kennedy had led would guarantee him double indemnity against partisan attacks from conservatives and liberals alike. To retain his political flexibility of maneuver between right and left, Johnson emphasized that his policy continued that which was set under Eisenhower and Kennedy, and was thus above politics. Moving forward on the advice of Kennedy's Cabinet, Johnson at first carried the Eisenhower Republicans with him. Just as the evidence of continuity with Eisenhower and Kennedy gave him cover against flank attacks, so the fact of Goldwater's opposition protected his position in the center.

During his first two years in the White House, Johnson gradually established his freedom to escalate without exciting fears that he might go to war. With the example of Eisenhower and Kennedy behind him, with Goldwater against him, with Kennedy's team leading him and with Eisenhower's team calling for more, Johnson commanded a start-up consensus for his resolve to be a War President and a Reform President at one and the same time. The allure of this formidable alliance overrode any forebodings and fortified his claim to political achievement by an appeal to patriotism. Playing prosperity as reform and war as peace, Johnson draped a flag around his Santa Claus costume.

It was an approach that Marshall McLuhan would have approved: the medium was the message and public relations was politics. But mere success did not satisfy Johnson. He wanted acceptance and affection as well, and he operated under a compulsion to win them from the intellectuals who had given their allegiance to Kennedy while Johnson was the laughingstock of the New Frontier. Politicians are habitually suspicious of intellectuals, and Johnson was notoriously suspicious of everyone. If any combination of intellectuals or politicians in his circle had tried to sell him the blueprint for Vietnam which he bought from McNamara, Johnson would have ridiculed them and accused them of trying to ruin him. But once he developed his dependence on McNamara as his public answer to the Kennedys and his private link to them, Johnson elevated this dual-purpose confidant into his intellectual-in-charge. As he set out to administer McNamara's plan, he developed a new sense of security which fed on his old sense of insecurity.

From the outset, Johnson gambled on his ability to turn Vietnam into a clever exercise in coexistence between a war that seemed unreal enough to be tolerated and a peace that had become untrustworthy enough to call for insurance. McNamara had taken refuge behind Johnson's skill at selling other people's programs. Johnson had reciprocated by taking refuge behind McNamara's skill at packaging pretentious programs for politicians to sell. Thus, the President who had pyramided a career on his reputation for being the shrewdest dealer gambled on joint account with the technocrat who had come to Washington acclaimed as "Mr. Best Brains."

The political marriage of convenience between the master of the head-count and the master of the computer calculation seemed to have been made in public-relations heaven. The combination promised to be irresistible—not least because of the double-play Johnson thought he was making against Robert Kennedy by playing with McNamara. Johnson counted on his combination with McNamara to lock Kennedy out of contact with power, and at the same time to give himself contact with McNamara—who, during Johnson's Presidency, operated as the double agent between LBJ and RFK. This triangle was a textbook example of Johnson's fatal flaw—his compulsion to please those whom he had outgrown the need to appease.

Johnson's arrangement with McNamara remained a winning bet on public relations so long as it remained only public

relations. Escalation turned it into a losing bet on war and on
the prosperity needed to finance war. Throughout 1964 and
1965, so long as the pre-escalation boom lasted and until the
burden of financing it overtook the money markets, Johnson's
successful manipulation of the processes of political normalcy
provided plausible cover for McNamara's unsuccessful manipulation of the machinery of military mobilization. But Johnson's
political technique could work magic and command a consensus only so long as it could declare dividends on prosperity.

This effort to maintain coexistence between the war in
Vietnam and the prosperity of welfare in the Great Society was
unprecedentedly ambitious. In a simpler day, the classic Republicanism of Mark Hanna had merchandised the modest
achievement of the "full dinner pail." "Trickle down" prosperity
had been the Republican formula for success at the polls ever
since. Its repeated failures to meet the needs of wide segments
of America had, just as repeatedly, opened the door for Democratic reformers. From Cleveland through Truman, the Democrats who had preceded Kennedy had been reformers who were
not expected to produce prosperity; and, in fact, they had succeeded politically without producing it. Kennedy had failed to
harness business confidence to finance the dynamic expansion of
the economy he promised. Johnson determined to do this and
much more: to persuade business to finance the welfare state as
well. For Johnson, as for Wilson and the two Roosevelts before
him, as for Bismarck, who created the welfare state, and Lloyd
George, who adapted it for assimilation into Anglo–Saxon society, the welfare state evolved as a compound of militarism and
reform. In the case of Bismarck and Johnson, the modern pattern was established by design; in the case of its other architects,
it developed by force of circumstances.

Until the money squeeze of 1966 demonstrated that the
war was becoming bigger while the economy was not keeping
pace, the Johnson–McNamara formula for dealing with brush-
fire wars seemed to suggest a repeat performance by America
of the imperialistic power of Victorian England in all its
bourgeois majesty but with none of its overextended vulner-

ability. The first phase of the adventure in Vietnam promised to respect and repeat the pattern of Britain's colonial wars on the Indian frontier: never ending but always small; always clarified by a power objective and never complicated by the domestic politics of sentimentality or face; fought by professionals who volunteered for the military way of life beyond the fringe of civilization; insulated from the mainstream of life at home; and supported by the strength of sterling (for Britain never allowed her colonial skirmishing in India to take on the proportions of a financial burden).

The British, in their day of ascendancy, had been frank to proclaim their imperialist purpose, and they deceived neither the world nor themselves with idealistic cant about remaking the Indian village into a new Jerusalem. If Disraeli's England had had a TVA, it would not have dreamed of creating another for India. Indeed, when Palmerston and Gladstone were faced with national movements of liberation closer to home in Europe, each was careful to give just one cheer for democracy and to back it up with neither troops nor money. England was absorbed in manipulating the balance of power to guarantee her own security and to relieve her of the burden of war. For better or worse, her consistent refusal to back movements of liberation with more than talk and gestures helped to make the century of economic change between France's bid for European hegemony and Germany's a century of political peace.

Modern England has needed no Gibbon to reconstruct the pattern of her decline and fall. She had gone the way of Rome before her: the over-extension of empire had stretched her thin, and the inescapable wars growing out of her imperial commitments had drained her dry. America's drift down the classic road to ruin trod by Rome and Britain before her has been enshrouded in mystery—but not because the failure in Vietnam or the danger in China or the spread of race war from Saigon to Detroit has been novel. The mystery is that classic danger signals have been so clear, and have been so utterly ignored.

Carl Becker once remarked that H. G. Wells knew more about what had happened since 1900, and less about what had happened before, than anyone else in the world. The same comment applies to Lyndon Johnson. His absorption in the "solipsism of the present" after his arrival in Washington in 1937 exposed him to the familiar experience of those who ignore the lessons of history and are therefore condemned to repeat its errors.

The universe of discourse which Johnson inhabited was entirely aural: so complete was his mastery of the secret history of his generation, and so minute his power of total recall, that he felt no need of books. Neither did McNamara, whose intellectual orientation in any case was toward the abstract model-building of the games-theorists. Johnson was the practitioner of the hunch in the old political style. McNamara was the theoretician of planning in the new mathematical style. But though these approaches appeared to cover the field, with each offering a hedge against the limitations of the other, in practice each compounded weaknesses of the other. Feel and flair were wanted, and neither hedging nor programming could substitute.

If Johnson was ignorant of formal history before his time, he had been an intimate participant in the making of history during World War II. Roosevelt exasperated his critics and his advisers by his stubborn, wily and, as it turned out, practical refusal to trust blueprints or blueprint-makers for the mobilization of the home front. As my *Struggle for Survival* noted, he relied on nothing but the momentum of the economy to insure his leadership against the pretensions and ambitions of advisers. Johnson's refusal to profit by the history he witnessed under Roosevelt was more surprising than McNamara's arrogance in disregarding the same lessons. Together these insensitivities led the Johnson Administration to violate the first rule of national survival: that the way to strengthen the sources of military power is to expand the economy.

The standard college text on modern European history for the generation that grew up with Johnson was *Europe Since 1815*, written by Charles Downer Hazen in 1910. It drilled successive classes of literate Americans to respect this simple rule which England had followed in the days of her greatness, when she defeated Napoleon and won the Napoleonic Wars despite her earlier acceptance of defeat in the American wilderness. "Great Britain appeared in 1815, to the superficial observer, in a brilliant light . . .," wrote Hazen. "Her debt, it is true, had increased with appalling rapidity. Over a billion dollars in 1792, it was over four billion in 1815. The annual interest charge amounted to over 150,000,000 dollars. Her expenditures during those years exceeded seven billion dollars. But while her debt and the yearly expenditures grew at an unprecedented rate, the wealth of the country grew more rapidly, and the burden of the state was more easily borne than ever."

America, in each of her wars before the Korean expedition of 1950–3, had followed Britain's formula for victory in the Napoleonic Wars—though not by plan. Until Korea, the natural dynamic of America's expansion made her wars the catalyst of postwar success on the economic front after the enemy had been defeated on the field of battle. The Korean War produced America's first planned experiment in reproducing Britain's classic achievement in the Napoleonic Wars—economic expansion sufficient to reduce the *relative* burden of a vast increase in war expenditure—and the experiment was an unqualified success. Because America won the Korean War on the economic front, her failure to win it on the military and political fronts was not decisive and did not compromise her options on world leadership during the decade that followed. The Eisenhower years were inconclusive, Eisenhower's success in avoiding a massive military undertaking on the periphery of the world economy was offset by a failure at home: the inability of his Administration to engineer a rate of economic expansion projected to reduce the relative burden of the country's military overhead costs.

When Johnson, directed by McNamara and running political interference for him, repeated Britain's latter-day error of imperialistic overextension, he at the same time compounded the blunder as he, like Eisenhower, failed to follow Britain's earlier achievement of wartime economic expansion at a rate calculated to reduce the relative burden of war costs. Where the Roosevelt

War Administration had been able to rely on the impetus of a
no-longer-stagnant economy, and where the Truman Administration had planned for victory on the economic front during the
Korean War and during its aftermath of inevitable political reappraisal, the Johnson Administration's secret plan of war
escalation in Vietnam insured defeat in the economy just because
it was secret. Johnson's failure to develop a scheme of war
finance followed inescapably from his refusal to make timely and
continuous disclosure of his war plans to Congress.

When James Polk provoked his breach with Congress over
his claim to an undivided Presidential prerogative to make war,
no plan of war finance was needed, and the rudimentary economy of the day, spurred by the war, was well able to grow on
its own—although Polk did demand and win a declaration of
war from Congress. When Harry Truman provoked his breach
with Congress by failing to ask it to vote a declaration of war,
he nevertheless took the precaution of asking for the power to
tax and control which is indispensable to any modern war
economy; and, although Congress had not voted a declaration
of war, it was prompt to vote the power to finance it, which the
Truman Administration put to good use.

The game of "now you see it, now you don't" which Johnson played during the Vietnam escalation was calculated to
merge the economic habits and the financial incentives of
normalcy into the claims of emergency. It ended by confusing
his own Administration along with everybody else and frustrating
its hope that the economy, benefiting from the best of both war
and peace, would furnish the government with the sinews of war
without a forced draft of money as well as of men. The economy
was still big enough and the war, despite its escalation, was still
small enough to permit production, consumption and, indeed,
recession as usual. While escalation had turned the war into a
major financial undertaking, it remained a minor military operation. Only money and labor, not physical resources, had become short enough to raise the question of rationing.

The official calculation assumed a normal emergency-time
prosperity in an economy big enough to provide both guns and

butter. The official calculators expected the escalation of 1965 to stabilize the boom of 1964. They were astounded when, instead, it brought crisis to the money markets in 1966 and crisis to earning power in 1967. Surprise gave way to shock when the failure of earning power in 1967 threatened the Treasury with a crisis of war finance such as the government of the United States had not faced since the days of the Continental Congress; when it threatened the money markets with a rise in rates such as had not been seen since the mismanagement of World War I; and when it threatened the stock market with a drop in prices such as had not been possible since 1929.

As the country reacted to the consequences not only of war, but also of the Johnson Administration's failure to develop a plan for financing the war, it discovered that, far from enjoying the best of war and peace, it was suffering the worst of both. Johnson's hope of pulling off his coup had rested on his resolution to keep the war small, or, alternatively, on his skill in encouraging the economy to expand enough to pay for it. As the war grew larger, the economy continued to stagnate and, consequently, its generation of earnings grew smaller. When the emergency burden of financing the cost of government grew relatively larger, and when the Johnson Administration's money-raising requirements accelerated the dangerous process by which the burdens of government eroded the earning power needed to support the governmental apparatus, the fate of the great post-war bull market in Wall Street was sealed. Thanks to the Vietnam crisis, the first market crash since the coming of the welfare state to America became a clear and present danger.

One of the advantages of secretiveness about the planned scope of the war had been presumed to be avoidance of inflationary speculation, crippling controls and market crisis. But when the anticipated benefits of a small war and a big boom turned into the actual burdens of a big war and a costly squeeze, the economy was whipsawed between the inflation of costs and the deflation of earnings. The stock market was exposed to the shock which recognition of a war crisis always brings. Not until the Vietnam crisis had taken its toll of the money market,

of the earning power within the economy and of the stock
market, did either opinion or the government awaken to a
realization of how far out of control the financing of the war
was or how dislocative its economic consequences had become.
By that time, America had reverted to the old European practice
of making war at the expense of the economy.

For America, Vietnam was a sideshow in the Cold War,
just as for Britain, America had been a sideshow in the
struggle for empire at the end of the eighteenth century. Pitt's
Britain had recovered a sense of proportion and imposed the
discipline of strategic priorities on herself in time to disengage
on the periphery in the wilderness so that she could concentrate
on winning the fight for Europe that counted. McNamara committed America to exactly the opposite course. McNamara had
provoked a great deal of criticism by his unashamed insistence
on managing the news. But his technique for manufacturing
"reality" was even more pernicious, for it led him to deceive
himself as well as the President, instead of merely his intended
dupes.

As Vice President, Johnson had been privileged to observe McNamara's obtuseness on the political side of the
power struggle: in 1962, McNamara's recommendation had
been to ignore the discovery that Russia had put missiles into
Cuba on the supposedly realistic grounds that she could blow up
the world from her home bases without bothering with Cuba
and, therefore, that it was impractical for us to bother with Cuba
either. Nevertheless, instead of being forewarned against Mc-
Namara's lack of strategic sense or political sensitivity, Johnson
based his war plan on a highly speculative assumption conjured
up by his Secretary of Defense. McNamara felt sure that Russia's
fear of China was a quantifiable element which could be calculated to predict her alignment on our side when the chips
were down. Indeed, our reluctant and overextended British associates in Asia appeared to back up this judgment. For
Khrushchev had told Harold Macmillan, while he was still
Prime Minister, that in a showdown Russia "would line up with
the whites against China." Later, Prime Minister Harold Wilson,

as professional a Kremlinologist as there was in the West, con-
tended that a deal could be made by which American-financed
exports would be traded for a Russian-negotiated cease-fire in
Vietnam. McNamara was convinced that Russia's need to preserve the balance of power in Asia against the Chinese would
lead her to help us find a way to get out of the war at a con-
venient time without getting out of Asia. It was as if Lord
North had refuted Pitt by promising their demented monarch
that the French would join England in pacifying the American
colonies!

Russia helped us into Vietnam, but not out. Once we got in
over our heads, she saw to it that we stayed there. McNamara's
calculation that a common Russian–American interest against
China supplied the rationale for our escalation in Vietnam gave
the Kremlin an unexpected opportunity to renew the Cold War
and to exploit America's military entrapment and financial
difficulty.

During Russia's evolution under Stalin as under Lenin, the
prime requisite of Russian policy was a Plan—with a capital
"P." In the beginning, the Plan was directed toward domestic
development; but, after the Russian people and the American
economy saved Stalin from Hitler, it was redirected into the
export of aggression, into atomic power politics and into arms
for hungry satellites. America's World War II role as arsenal
has served Russia as her Cold War model for retaliation, incon-
clusively in Korea and unsatisfactorily in Cuba but successfully
in Vietnam; and the success of this tactic in tying America down
in Vietnam suggested its extension to a second front in the
Middle East. But McNamara's mirage of a common interest
between America and the Kremlin in Vietnam invited Russia
once more to change both Plan and course. America's sustained demonstration of economic strength had persuaded Stalin's
successors to face up to the economic failure of the Soviet system,
and to work toward an arrangement with Washington aimed at
swapping political accommodation for economic assistance. But
when America baited her own trap in Vietnam, and then dislocated her economy as she locked herself into that trap, Russia

turned away from her new plan for doing business with America
to the old design of fomenting wars of entrapment against her
on the fringes of the world economy.

It is an arresting fact that every major swing in the balance of
power during the twentieth century has been somehow connected
with a change in Russia's position. In 1905, her defeat announced
Japan's coming of age as a power and brought the Far East into
the arena of world politics. In 1914, her mobilization made
world war inevitable. And in 1917, her collapse into revolution
seemed to turn the tide of battle in Germany's favor—although,
in fact, its real effect was to change the terms of political competition everywhere for every country in the world.

In World War II, Russia again functioned as the pivot, or
"swing," factor in twentieth-century power politics. In 1939,
Stalin's alliance with Hitler determined the time and the place
for the outbreak of World War II and set the opening odds against
the West. In 1941, the about-face forced on her by Hitler's
attack prepared the way for the two-front offensive which would
crush Nazism in 1944–5.

In the late 1940's, Stalin's declaration of cold war and his
resolve to arm the satellites against the West put America on
notice to develop a system which could set a limit to war short
of all-out atomic attack. Her plan worked in Korea, and its
success involved American military power against a Russian
satellite at the very time when Russia was developing her own
nuclear capability. The outcome added a new dimension of
conventional warfare and economic gamesmanship to the running duel for initiative and position in the atomic stalemate
between Moscow and Washington.

During the years of Johnson's ascendancy on the American
scene, 1964 and 1965, Russia wavered in her determination to
reapply her Korean formula in the face of America's renewed
demonstration of economic vigor. In 1966, when America
showed signs of economic strain, Russia weighed the alternative
attractions of economic accommodation and military confrontation. And, in 1967, when the American economy faltered, she
subjected the equilibrium of world power to a new change of

course back to an old and all-too-familiar stance. In the sophomoric era of Bolshevism, Lenin had sounded the call to arms for a new epoch of wars and revolutions which he proclaimed and predicted would attack the weak links of the capitalist system. By 1967, Russia had long since outgrown what Lenin had criticized as "infantile Communism," although the Russian economy had by no means outgrown its infantilism. The generation of his successors embodied the managerial revolution—their political habitat was not the barracks but the committee room. Nevertheless, their changed course—from the economics of coexistence back to the military politics of the Cold War—announced still another era of wars and revolutions. In 1967, Russia's changed course took America by surprise and produced erratic gyrations in the balance of power, which threatened to explode the small war in Vietnam, advertised as controllable, into a big war which was uncontrollable.

The Vietnam War coincided with China's development of her nuclear capability. As America began to discover that Russia was not her ally against China, she also began to suspect that McNamara's escalation had invited America to fight Russia's war against China. By that time, military stalemate had come to seem an acceptable war aim, even an optimistic one, and the American economy had become a conspicuous war casualty.

Forty years earlier, in November, 1927, Stalin—fresh from victory over his rival Leon Trotsky—had sneered publicly at the aspirations of capitalism, and the way "the whole world bowed low before the dollar." Such illusions, he declared, were already collapsing. The leaders of Communism, of course, have always had partisan reasons for predicting the imminent downfall of capitalism, but this bias in their judgment does not necessarily discredit their observation. Stalin was right in descrying the obeisances of other world currencies and peoples to the dollar, and the situation he described has continued and deepened.

Again, we can question the judgment which led Stalin to declare in May of 1929, "I think the moment is not far off when a revolutionary crisis will develop in America." A crisis indeed developed, but revolution did not follow. In the 1960's, however, when we faced a graver social crisis at home than we had for a generation—one compounded by the drain of a seemingly insoluble foreign conflict, now hot, now cold, now both—we read Stalin's words less easily than we had in the prosperous postwar 1950's. And however troubled we may have been by the renewed timeliness of Stalin's point, we had to admit the universal truth of the Soviet leader's observation that "when a revolutionary crisis develops in America, that will be the beginning of the end of world capitalism as a whole." These words of Stalin ring truer as they become further removed in time from the day he uttered them.

During World War II, concern for the dollar and all it symbolizes impeded the mobilization of the economic resources by which America eventually beat back the military challenge of the dictators. During the Korean War, the strength of the dollar enabled America to offset her military frustration with an unparalleled assertion of economic primacy. By the time of the Vietnam crisis, the dollar had become a strategic asset in the Cold War. But the war America found herself fighting in Vietnam began to threaten disaster for the dollar and all it symbolizes, and this omen of financial disaster developed into a more potent cause of the contraction of American influence in the world than the expansive thrust of Soviet power.

Meanwhile, America's inability to win her war against Communism in Vietnam was isolating her, throwing her on the defensive and turning her greatest source of strength—the American economy—into a decisive source of weakness. The economic front on which America had won each and every one of her previous wars threatened to be where America would lose the Vietnam War to her Communist enemies who, by a perverse turn of the dialectic, were divided among themselves, hampered by economic weaknesses and plagued by congenital failures to maximize productivity. Johnson's obsession with the military side of the war stemmed from a grim and increasingly feverish determination to see it through—although, as it dragged on, he time and again sought comfort in the belief that "the American people always back up a President in time of war." (Truman might have advised him not to put that conviction to too sharp a test.) But this very drive to put military victory ahead of economic expansion and social progress held the seeds of its own defeat. It seemed that Johnson had forgotten—or had never learned—that the only effective way to make war against Communism is to outperform it in time of peace. Just because no belligerent can win a modern war, Communism cannot lose one.

McNamara's mirage was, in fact, the lineal descendant of the great illusion which Norman Angell exposed at the height of the imperialist fever before World War I. No developed modern society can expect military victory, much less unconditional surrender, against a coequal: the atomic deterrent has wiped out this illusion. But our escalation in Vietnam was encouraged by the firm and fond belief that an advanced power could easily pacify an underdeveloped society. Now this speculation too has been proved an illusion. The absence of a deterrent in the hands of our colonial quarry has thrown us back into dependence upon our wisdom and our prudence, and in these we have been lacking.

In the past, America has repeatedly proved her mastery over the economics of crisis. In each of her wars, her economy expanded faster than the cost of combat rose—until Vietnam. Until Vietnam, history knew no phenomenon comparable to the new American economy as it emerged triumphant and reinvigorated from successive crises. America has made its mark and asserted its primacy in the world by means of its economic vigor, not its political wisdom. No power has or can have the political wisdom to anticipate or to control events without the ability to dominate the world (which England commanded under Victoria and as America does not) or the willingness to fight challengers to a pax Americana (which the nuclear deterrent now prevents). For America to aspire to the role of world policeman, or of self-appointed surrogate for a world peace-keeping authority, is to fall into the old Greek sin of *hubris*— of overweening pride which challenges the gods and tempts fate to strike it down.

When politicians and their technocrats claim a degree of omniscience which no mere makers of policy in any country can have, and when they reach for more power than leaders can hold, they too are apt to catch the attention of Nemesis. Other countries lack the wherewithal to confront America with a direct economic challenge or to use their economic power to exert decisive leverage on the political balance in the world. Only America has the capacity to use its economic power to swing the world political balance. The strategy of strength calls for America to rely on the economic power which even her enemies admit she has. Instead, some fatal failure of imagination has led Johnson and McNamara to rely on military power of a kind not native to America, nor congenial to Americans, nor even effective as used in Vietnam. It was not only the use of such power that shocked the modern standards of world morality which have evolved in revulsion from the potential for destructiveness of modern military technology; it was also the inability of the Johnson Administration to rethink its commitment to military might; to seek alternative responses to the Soviet challenge; and to give priority to America's unfinished business at home.

America's stake in mastering once again the economics of crisis is as simple as it is overwhelming. For on that mastery depends her ability to come to grips with every problem of public concern from Detroit to Vietnam. Money, and what money can mobilize, will not alone solve these problems; but only the strength of an expanding economy can give America the opportunity to do so—without defaulting on her international obligations, and certainly without abandoning Asia to Soviet imperialism of whichever brand. Mastering the economics of crisis is the necessary condition of a future in which we can once more enjoy the luxury of the politics of peace.

BIBLIOGRAPHY

ACHESON, DEAN, *The Pattern of Responsibility,* edited by McGeorge Bundy, Houghton Mifflin (Boston, 1952).

———, *Power and Diplomacy,* Harvard University Press (Cambridge, Mass., 1958).

ADAMS, HENRY, *The Education of Henry Adams: An Autobiography,* Houghton Mifflin (Boston, 1918).

ALLEN, FREDERICK LEWIS, *The Great Pierpont Morgan,* Harper & Row (New York, 1949).

ANGELL, NORMAN, *The Great Illusion: A Study of the Relation of Military Power to National Advantage,* Heinemann (London, 1914).

ARNOLD, THURMAN W., *The Folklore of Capitalism,* Yale University Press (New Haven, Conn., 1937).

BAGEHOT, WALTER, *Lombard Street: A Description of the Money Market,* Scribner, Armstrong and Company (New York, 1873).

BARRIGER, JOHN W., "Railroads in the Civil War," *The Bulletin: National Railway Historical Society,* Vol. 31, No. 6 (1966), pp. 6–33.

BARUCH, BERNARD M., *American Industry in the War: A Report of the War Industries Board (March 1921),* Prentice-Hall (New York, 1941).

BEARD, CHARLES A., and MARY R. BEARD, *America in Midpassage,* Macmillan (New York, 1939).

———, *The Rise of American Civilization,* 2 volumes, Macmillan (New York, 1927).

BEAVERBROOK, LORD, *The Decline and Fall of Lloyd George,* Duell, Sloan & Pearce (New York, 1963).

BECKER, CARL L., *The Declaration of Independence: A Study in the History of Political Ideas,* Knopf (New York, 1942).

BECKER, CARL L., *The Heavenly City of the Eighteenth-Century Philosophers*, Yale University Press (New Haven, Conn., 1932).

——, *Modern History: The Rise of a Democratic, Scientific, and Industrial Civilization*, Silver, Burdett (Morristown, N. J., 1931).

BEER, SAMUEL, *Modern British Politics*, Faber (London, 1965).

BERLE, ADOLPH A. JR., and GARDINER C. MEANS, *The Modern Corporation and Private Property*, Commerce Clearing House (New York, 1932).

BLAKE, ROBERT, *Disraeli*, St Martin's (New York, 1967).

BLUM, JOHN MORTON, *From The Morgenthau Diaries*, 2 volumes, Houghton Mifflin (Boston, 1959).

BOLLES, ALBERT S., *The Financial History of the United States*, 3 volumes, Appleton (New York, 1879–86).

CHAMBERLAIN, JOSEPH, *Mr. Chamberlain's Speeches*, edited by Charles W. Boyd, Houghton Mifflin (Boston, 1914).

CHANDLER, LESTER V., *Benjamin Strong: Central Banker*, The Brookings Institution (Washington D.C., 1958).

CHILDS, MARQUIS W., *Sweden: The Middle Way*, Yale University Press (New Haven, Conn., 1936).

CLAPHAM, J. H., *An Economic History of Modern Britain*, 3 volumes, Cambridge University Press (Cambridge, 1930–38).

COIT, MARGARET L., *John C. Calhoun: American Portrait*, Houghton Mifflin (Boston, 1950).

——, *Mr. Baruch*, Houghton Mifflin (Boston, 1957).

CONNERY, ROBERT H., *The Navy and the Industrial Mobilization in World War II*, Princeton University Press (Princeton, N. J., 1951).

CRUM, WILLIAM L., ET AL., *Fiscal Planning for Total War*, National Bureau of Economic Research (New York, 1942).

CURRIE, LAUCHLIN, *The Supply and Control of Money in the United States*, Harvard University Press (Cambridge, Mass., 1934).

DALLIN, DAVID J., *The Changing World of Soviet Russia*, Yale University Press (New Haven, Conn., 1956).

DEWEY, DAVIS RICH, *Financial History of the United States*, Longmans (New York, 1903).

DOBB, MAURICE H., *Capitalist Enterprise and Social Progress*, Routledge (London, 1925).

DUBERMAN, MARTIN B., *Charles Francis Adams, 1807–1886*, Houghton Mifflin (Boston, 1961).

DUBERMAN, MARTIN B., editor, *The Antislavery Vanguard: New Essays on the Abolitionists*, Princeton University Press (Princeton, N. J., 1965).

DUNNE, F. P., *Mr. Dooley In Peace and In War*, Small, Maynard and Company (Boston, 1898).

ECCLES, MARRINER S., *Beckoning Frontiers: Public and Personal Recollections*, Knopf (New York, 1951).

EDWARDS, GEORGE W., *The Evolution of Finance Capitalism*, Longmans (New York, 1938).

EDWARDS, R. DUDLEY, and T. DESMOND WILLIAMS, editors, *The Great Famine: Studies in Irish History, 1845–52*, New York University Press (New York, 1957).

EVANS, ROWLAND, and ROBERT NOVAK, *Lyndon B. Johnson: The Exercise of Power,* New American Library (New York, 1966).

EYCK, ERICH, *Bismarck and The German Empire,* Allen & Unwin (London, 1950).

FALL, BERNARD B., *Street Without Joy: Indochina at War, 1946–54,* Stackpole Company (Harrisburg, Pa., 1961).

———, *The Two Vietnams: A Political and Military Analysis,* Praeger (New York, 1963).

———, *Vietnam Witness: 1953–66,* Praeger (New York, 1966).

FARLEY, JAMES A., *Behind the Ballots: The Personal History of a Politician,* Harcourt (New York, 1938).

———, *Jim Farley's Story: The Roosevelt Years,* McGraw-Hill (New York, 1948).

FEIS, HERBERT, *The Road to Pearl Harbor: The Coming of War Between the United States and Japan,* Princeton University Press (Princeton, N. J., 1950).

FISH, CARL R., "Notes and Suggestions: Back to Peace in 1865," *The American Historical Review,* Vol. XXIV, No. 3 (April, 1919), 435–43.

———, *The Path of Empire: A Chronicle of the United States As a World Power,* Yale University Press (New Haven, Conn., 1921).

FISHER, IRVING, *Booms and Depressions: Some First Principles,* Adelphi Company (New York, 1932).

———, *The Purchasing Power of Money: Its Determination and Relation to Credit, Interest, and Crises,* Macmillan (New York, 1922).

FLYNN, EDWARD J., *You're The Boss,* Viking (New York, 1947).

FORRESTAL, JAMES, *The Forrestal Diaries,* edited by Walter Millis, Viking (New York, 1951).

FRANK, JEROME, *If Men Were Angels: Some Aspects of Government in a Democracy,* Harper & Row (New York, 1930).

———, *Save America First: How to Make Our Democracy Work,* Harper & Row (New York, 1938).

FREIDEL, FRANK B., *Franklin Delano Roosevelt,* 3 volumes, Little, Brown (Boston, 1952–56).

FRIEDMAN, MILTON, and ANNA JACOBSON SCHWARTZ, *A Monetary History of the United States, 1867–1960,* Princeton University Press (Princeton, N. J., 1963).

GLASS, CARTER, *An Adventure in Constructive Finance,* Doubleday (Garden City, N. Y., 1927).

GURLEY, JOHN G., and EDWARD S. SHAW, *Money In A Theory of Finance,* The Brookings Institution (Washington D.C., 1960).

HAMLIN, CHARLES S., *Diary, 1887–1937* (Hamlin Papers, Manuscript Division, Library of Congress).

HAMMOND, BRAY, *Banks and Politics in America: From the Revolution to the Civil War,* Princeton University Press (Princeton, N. J., 1957).

HARRIS, SEYMOUR E., *Prices and Related Controls in the United States,* McGraw-Hill (New York, 1945).

HARROD, R. F., *The Life of John Maynard Keynes*, Harcourt, Brace (New York, 1951).

HAWTREY, R. G., *Currency and Credit*, Longmans (London, 1923).

HAYEK, FRIEDRICH A., *Prices and Production*, Routledge (London, 1935).

HAZEN, CHARLES DOWNER, *Europe Since 1815*, Holt (New York, 1910).

HENDRICK, BURTON J., *The Age of Big Business*, Yale University Press (New Haven, Conn., 1921).

————, *Lincoln's War Cabinet*, Little, Brown (Boston, 1946).

HERNDON, WILLIAM H., and JESSE W. WEIK, *Herndon's Life of Lincoln: The History and Personal Recollections of Abraham Lincoln as Originally Written by William H. Herndon and Jesse W. Weik*, World Publishing (Cleveland, 1942).

HITCH, CHARLES J., *America's Economic Strength*, Oxford University Press (Fair Lawn, N. J., 1941).

HOBSON, JOHN A., *The Evolution of Modern Capitalism: A Study of Machine Production*, Scribner (New York, 1894).

————, *Imperialism: A Study*, University of Michigan Press (Ann Arbor, Mich., 1965).

HOVEY, CARL, *The Life Story of J. Pierpont Morgan*, Heinemann (London, 1912).

HOWLAND, HAROLD, *Theodore Roosevelt and His Times: A Chronicle of the Progressive Movement*, Yale University Press (New Haven, Conn., 1921).

ICKES, HAROLD L., *The Autobiography of a Curmudgeon*, Reynal & Hitchcock (New York, 1943).

————, *The Secret Diary of Harold L. Ickes*, 3 volumes, Simon and Schuster (New York, 1953–54).

"ISRAEL," *Atlantic Monthly* (March 1967), pp. 14–22.

JAMES, MARQUIS, *The Life of Andrew Jackson*, Bobbs-Merrill (Indianapolis, Ind., 1938).

JAMESON, J. FRANKLIN, *The American Revolution Considered As a Social Movement*, Princeton University Press (Princeton, N. J., 1940).

JANEWAY, ELIOT, "The Drive and Direction of Mobilization," *Harvard Business Review*, Vol. XXIX (September 1951), pp. 99–109.

————, "Mobilizing The Economy: Old Errors in a New Crisis," *The Yale Review* (December 1950), pp. 201–19.

————, *The Struggle for Survival: A Chronicle of Economic Mobilization in World War II*, Yale University Press (New Haven, Conn., 1951).

JANEWAY, MICHAEL C., "Lyndon Johnson and the Rise of Conservatism in Texas" (Unpublished thesis, Harvard University, 1962).

KAHN, R. F., "The Relation of Home Investment to Employment," *Economic Journal*, Vol. 41, No. 162 (1931).

KAPLAN, A. D. H., *The Liquidation of War Production: Cancellation of War Contracts and Disposal of Government-owned Plants and Surpluses*, McGraw-Hill (New York, 1944).

KENNAN, GEORGE F., *American Diplomacy, 1900–1950*, University of Chicago Press (Chicago, 1951).

————, *On Dealing With the Communist World,* Harper & Row (New York, 1964).

————, *Russia and the West Under Lenin and Stalin,* Little, Brown (Boston, 1961).

————, *Russia, The Atom and the West,* Oxford (London, 1958).

KEYNES, JOHN MAYNARD, *The Economic Consequences of the Peace,* Harcourt, Brace (New York, 1920).

————, *Essays in Biography,* edited by Geoffrey Keynes, Horizon (New York, 1951).

————, *Essays in Persuasion,* Rupert Hart-Davis (London, 1951).

————, *The General Theory of Employment Interest and Money,* Harcourt, Brace (New York, 1935).

————, *How to Pay for the War: A Radical Plan for the Chancellor of of the Exchequer,* Harcourt, Brace (New York, 1940).

————, *A Tract on Monetary Reform,* Macmillan (London, 1923).

————, *A Treatise on Money,* 2 volumes, Harcourt, Brace (New York, 1930).

KEYNES, JOHN MAYNARD, and H. D. HENDERSON, *Can Lloyd George Do It? An Examination of the Liberal Pledge,* The Nation and Athenaeum (London, 1929).

KROUT, JOHN ALLEN, and DIXON RYAN FOX, *The Completion of Independence, 1790–1830,* Macmillan (New York, 1944).

LACOUTURE, JEAN, *Vietnam: Between Two Truces,* Random House (New York, 1966).

LANGER, WILLIAM L., *The Diplomacy of Imperialism: 1890–1902,* 2 volumes, Knopf (New York, 1935).

LENIN, V. I., *Imperialism,* International Publishers (New York, 1933).

————, *The Imperialist War: The Struggle Against Social-Chauvinism and Social Pacifism, 1914–1915,* International Publishers (New York, 1930).

————, *The Iskra Period: 1900–1902,* 2 volumes, International Publishers (New York, 1929).

————, *Left-wing Communism: An Infantile Disorder,* International Publishers (New York, 1934).

————, *The State and Revolution,* International Publishers (New York, 1932).

————, *Toward the Seizure of Power, the Revolution of 1917: From the July Days to the October Revolution,* 2 volumes, International Publishers (New York, 1932).

LEUCHTENBURG, WILLIAM E., *Franklin D. Roosevelt and the New Deal: 1932–1940,* Harper & Row (New York, 1963).

LONG, JOHN D., *The New American Navy,* 2 volumes, The Outlook Company (New York, 1903).

LOWE, CHARLES, *Prince Bismarck: An Historical Biography,* 2 volumes, Cassell and Company (New York, 1886).

LYON, LEVERETT S., and VICTOR ABRAMSON, *Government and Economic Life,* The Brookings Institution (Washington D.C., 1940).

MACHLUP, FRITZ, *International Payments, Debts, and Gold: Collected Essays,* Scribner (New York, 1964).

——, "Involuntary Foreign Lending," *Wicksell Lectures, 1965,* Almqvist and Wiksell (Stockholm).

MC KITRICK, ERIC L., *Andrew Johnson and Reconstruction,* The University of Chicago Press (Chicago, 1960).

MACMILLAN, HAROLD, *Winds of Change, 1914–1939,* Harper & Row (New York, 1966).

MALTHUS, THOMAS R., *An Essay on the Principle of Population.*

——, *Principles of Political Economy Considered With a View to Their Practical Application.*

MARSHALL, ALFRED, *Principles of Economics: An Introductory Volume,* Macmillan (New York, 1948).

MARSHALL, JOHN, *The Life of George Washington,* 2 volumes, Crissy and Markley (Philadelphia, 1850).

MARX, KARL, *Capital: A Critique of Political Economy.*

——, *Communist Manifesto.*

——, *The Eighteenth Brumaire of Louis Bonaparte,* International Publishers (New York, 1926).

MARX, KARL, and FREDERICK ENGELS, *The Civil War in the United States,* International Publishers (New York, 1937).

MASON, ALPHEUS THOMAS, *Brandeis: A Free Man's Life,* Viking (New York, 1946).

MILL, JOHN STUART, *Principles of Political Economy: With Some of Their Applications to Social Philosophy.*

MITGANG, HERBERT, "The Mexican War Dove," *The New Republic* (February 11, 1967), pp. 23–24.

MOLEY, RAYMOND, *After Seven Years,* Harper & Row (New York, 1939).

——, *The First New Deal,* Harcourt, Brace (New York, 1966).

MOODY, JOHN, *The Railroad Builders: A Chronicle of the Welding of the States,* Yale University Press (New Haven, Conn., 1919).

MYERS, GUSTAVUS, *History of the Great American Fortunes,* 3 volumes, Charles H. Kerr and Company (Chicago, 1909–10).

NELSON, DONALD M., *Arsenal of Democracy: The Story of American War Production,* Harcourt, Brace (New York, 1946).

NEVINS, ALLAN, *The Emergence of Modern America 1865–1878,* Macmillan (New York, 1927).

NEWCOMB, SIMON, *A Critical Examination of our Financial Policy During the Southern Rebellion,* Appleton (New York, 1865).

O'BRIAN, JOHN LORD, and MANLY FLEISCHMANN, "The War Production Board: Administrative Policies and Procedures," *The George Washington Law Review* (December 1944).

OWEN, FRANK, *Tempestuous Journey: Lloyd George, His Life and Times,* McGraw-Hill (New York, 1955).

PARETO, VILFREDO, *The Mind and Society: Trattato di Sociologia Generale by Vilfredo Pareto,* 4 volumes, edited by Arthur Livingston, Harcourt, Brace (New York, 1935).

PARTON, JAMES, *Life of Andrew Jackson,* 3 volumes, Mason Brothers (New York, 1861).

PERKINS, FRANCES, *The Roosevelt I Knew,* Viking (New York, 1946).

PIGOU, A. C., *The Economics of Welfare,* Macmillan (London, 1920).

POTTER, DAVID M., *People of Plenty: Economic Abundance and the American Character,* The University of Chicago Press (Chicago, 1954).

PRINGLE, HENRY F., *Theodore Roosevelt: A Biography,* Harcourt, Brace (New York, 1931).

RANDALL, J. G., *Lincoln the President,* 4 volumes, Dodd, Mead (New York, 1945–55).

RANDALL, J. G., and DAVID DONALD, *The Civil War and Reconstruction,* Heath (Boston, 1961).

RICARDO, DAVID, *On the Principles of Political Economy, and Taxation.*

RIST, CHARLES, *History of Monetary and Credit Theory: From John Law to the Present Day,* Macmillan (New York, 1940).

ROBINSON, JOAN, *Economics: An Awkward Corner,* Allen and Unwin (London, 1966).

ROLL, ERIC, *History of Economic Thought,* Prentice-Hall (New York, 1956).

ROOSEVELT, ELEANOR, *This I Remember,* Harper & Row (New York, 1949).

SALANT, WALTER, *Capital Markets and the Balance of Payments of a Financial Center,* The Brookings Institution, Reprint 123 (Washington D.C., 1966).

SALANT, WALTER, ET AL., *The United States Balance of Payments in 1968,* The Brookings Institution (Washington D.C., 1963).

SANDBURG, CARL, *Abraham Lincoln: The Prairie Years,* Harcourt, Brace (New York, 1925).

SCHLESINGER, ARTHUR M. JR., *The Age of Jackson,* Book Find Club (New York, 1945).

———, *The Age of Roosevelt,* 3 volumes, Houghton Mifflin (Boston, 1957–60).

SCHONFIELD, ANDREW, *Modern Capitalism,* Oxford (London, 1966).

SCHUMPETER, JOSEPH A., *Business Cycles: A Theoretical, Historical, and Statistical Analysis of the Capitalist Process,* 2 volumes, McGraw-Hill (New York, 1939).

———, *History of Economic Analysis,* edited by Elizabeth Boody Schumpeter, Oxford University Press (Fair Lawn, N. J., 1954).

———, *Imperialism and Social Classes,* edited by Paul M. Sweezy, Augustus M. Kelley (New York, 1951).

———, *The Theory of Economic Development: An Inquiry Into Profits, Capital, Credit, Interest, and the Business Cycle,* Harvard University Press (Cambridge, Mass., 1936).

SCHURZ, CARL, *Henry Clay,* 2 volumes, Houghton Mifflin (Boston, 1915).

SHERWOOD, ROBERT E., *Roosevelt and Hopkins: An Intimate History,* Harper & Row (New York, 1948).

SMITH, ADAM, *An Inquiry Into the Nature and Causes of the Wealth of Nations.*

SNOW, C. P., *Variety of Men,* Scribner (New York, 1966).

SOMERS, HERMAN MILES, *Presidential Agency: OWMR, The Office of War Mobilization and Reconversion,* Harvard University Press (Cambridge, Mass., 1950).

STALIN, JOSEPH, *Leninism,* International Publishers (New York, 1928).

STAMPP, KENNETH M., *The Era of Reconstruction: 1865–1877,* Knopf (New York, 1965).

STERN, PHILIP VAN DOREN, editor, *The Life and Writings of Abraham Lincoln,* Random House (New York, 1940).

STIMSON, HENRY L., and MC GEORGE BUNDY, *On Active Service in Peace and War,* Harper & Row (New York, 1948).

STRACHEY, JOHN, *The Coming Struggle for Power,* Covici, Friede (New York, 1933).

SUMNER, WILLIAM GRAHAM, *Folkways: A Study of the Sociological Importance of Usages, Manners, Customs, Mores, and Morals,* Ginn (Boston, 1906).

SWEEZY, PAUL M., *The Theory of Capitalist Development: Principles of Marxian Political Economy,* Oxford University Press (Fair Lawn, N. J., 1942).

TAYLOR, A. J. P., *Bismarck: The Man and the Statesman,* Hamish Hamilton (London, 1955).

THOMPSON, ROBERT, *Defeating Communist Insurgency: Experiences from Malaya and Vietnam,* Chatto & Windus (London, 1966).

TOULMIN, HARRY AUBREY, *Diary of Democracy: The Senate War Investigating Committee,* R. R. Smith (New York, 1947).

TRIFFIN, ROBERT, *The Evolution of the International Monetary System: Historical Reappraisal and Future Perspectives,* Princeton Studies in International Finance No. 12 (Princeton, N. J., 1964).

———, *Gold and the Dollar Crisis: The Future of Convertibility,* Yale University Press (New Haven, Conn., 1960).

———, *The World Money Maze: National Currencies in International Payments,* Yale University Press (New Haven, Conn., 1966).

TURNER, FREDERICK JACKSON, *The Frontier in American History,* Holt (New York, 1920).

U.S. BUREAU OF THE BUDGET, *The United States at War: Development and Administration of the War Program by the Federal Government,* U.S. Government Printing Office (Washington D.C., 1946).

U.S. BUREAU OF THE CENSUS, *Historical Statistics of the United States, 1789–1957,* U.S. Government Printing Office (Washington D.C., 1960).

U.S. CONGRESS, *Investigation of Concentration of Economic Power,* Hearings before the Temporary National Economic Committee, Congress of the United States, 76th Congress, First, Second and Third Sessions, U.S. Government Printing Office (Washington D.C., 1939–41).

U.S. SENATE, *Inquiry into Satellite and Missile Programs,* Hearings before the Preparedness Investigating Subcommittee of the Committee on Armed Services, United States Senate, 85th Congress, First and Second Sessions, U.S. Government Printing Office (Washington D.C., 1958).

——, *Investigation of the National Defense Program,* Hearings before a Special Committee Investigating the National Defense Program, United States Senate, 80th Congress, First Session, U.S. Government Printing Office (Washington D.C., 1947).

VARGA, EUGENE, *The Great Crisis and Its Political Consequences: Economics and Politics, 1928–1934,* International Publishers (New York, 1934).

VEBLEN, THORSTEIN, *The Engineers and the Price System,* Viking (New York, 1933).

——, *Imperial Germany and the Industrial Revolution,* Macmillan (New York, 1915).

——, *The Theory of the Leisure Class: An Economic Study of Institutions,* B. W. Huebsch (New York, 1919).

WARBURG, PAUL M., *The Federal Reserve System: Its Origin and Growth, Reflections and Recollections,* 2 volumes, Macmillan (New York, 1930).

WARREN, CHARLES, *The Supreme Court in United States History,* 2 volumes, Little, Brown (Boston, 1928).

WERNER, M. R., editor, *Stalin's Kampf: Joseph Stalin's Credo, Written by Himself,* Howell, Soskin and Company (New York, 1940).

WHALEN, RICHARD J., *The Founding Father: The Story of Joseph P. Kennedy,* New American Library (New York, 1964).

WHEELER-BENNETT, JOHN W., *Wooden Titan: Hindenburg in Twenty Years of German History, 1914–1934,* Morrow (New York, 1936).

——, *The Wreck of Reparations: Being the Political Background of the Lausanne Agreement 1932,* Morrow (New York, 1933).

WILLIAMS, WAYNE C., *William Jennings Bryan,* Putnam (New York, 1936).

WOODHAM SMITH, CECIL B., *The Great Hunger: Ireland, 1845–1849,* Hamish Hamilton (London, 1962).

WOODWARD, C. VANN, *Reunion and Reaction: The Compromise of 1877 and the End of Reconstruction,* Little, Brown (Boston, 1951).

——, *The Strange Career of Jim Crow,* Oxford University Press (Fair Lawn, N. J., 1955).

INDEX OF NAMES